WILD RUINS

The explorer's guide to Britain's lost castles, follies, relics and remains

Dave Hamilton

Carreg Cennen p150

WILD RUINS

Racton Folly p72

CONTENTS

INTRODUCTIONS

BEST FORS

THE RUINS

THE RUINS
— MAP —
N
S
W
E
25 The Scottish Isles
24 Northern Scottish Highlands
27 Southern Scottish Highlands
20 Aberdeenshire & Cairngorms
23 South East Scotland
28 South West Scotland & Arran
21 Northumberland & The North East
22 Cumbria & The Pennines
20 Bronte Country
19 North York Moors & Middlesbrough
North Wales 18
13 Lincolnshire
14 Peak District & North West Midlands
15 Welsh Borders
10 North Norfolk
South Wales 16
17 Mid Wales
12 South Midlands
11 Suffolk & South Norfolk
London & Surrounds 9
Wye Valley & Bristol Area 5
7 Sussex & the High Weald
8 Kent & Essex
2 Devon
1 Cornwall
3 Exmoor, Somerset & West Dorset
4 Dorset, Wiltshire & the New Forest
6 Hampshire & Isle of Wight

SOUTH WEST

SOUTH & EAST

MIDLANDS

WALES

NORTH

SCOTLAND

Baron Hill estate in Beaumaris, Anglesey, unlisted

FOREWORD
by Tony Robinson

Few experiences are more inspiring than exploring Britain's history through its lost ruins. You can discover long-abandoned villages, the weathered defences of Victorian coastal forts, derelict mills, crumbling towers, deserted houses and ancient quays, all in a variety of shapes and sizes. These intriguing signposts to another time pepper the British landscape and are just waiting to be explored.

Many of them are now weathered and decayed, but they remain frozen moments of history. They allow us to marvel at how our country and its people's lives have changed. They are some of the most beautiful and intriguing destinations in Britain – if you know how to find them!

Corfe Castle, p56

This book provides the perfect guide. It's a treasure map of Britain's most exciting ruins, and a collection of some of its greatest stories. It's impossible for me to pick just one favourite, but here are a few that are particularly special to me:

ROCHE ROCK p32

No one knows precisely why the chapel at Roche Rock was built. Some say it was a beacon to guide travellers across the wild moor. Others that it was a stop-off point for travellers en route to the number one medieval tourist destination, St Michael's Mount. It's one of the most dramatic sites in South West England, and somewhere I always visit when heading to St Austell and beyond. Did you know?

- Roche is French for "Rock", so Roche Rock means Rock Rock!
- There's a myth that the rugged, granite rock was originally completely covered by earth, until Noah's flood scoured it clean.

CORFE CASTLE p56

My childhood holidays were spent in Swanage, and a trip to Corfe Castle was always a high point. I'd march round the battlements wielding my imaginary sword, acting out my knightly adventures. And to be honest, when I go there now I do pretty much the same thing! Corfe is a breath-taking ruin and a truly awesome sight. It's a must visit for anyone with children. Did you know...

- In Saxon times 15-year-old King Edward the Martyr was murdered here. His step-mother Queen Elfrida swore she was innocent, but her own ghastly son Ethelred the Unready became the next king!
- "Corfe" is Anglo-Saxon for gap, because it overlooks a strategic cutting in the Purbeck Hills.

LEWES PRIORY p80

Lewes was one of the most magnificent priories in the country and dates back to the reign of William the Conqueror. It's jam-packed with history, and survived for 450 years until it was pulled down on the orders of Thomas Cromwell (of Wolf Hall fame), who characteristically turned the Priory House into a swanky home for his son, Gregory. But Thomas couldn't destroy the sense of grandeur that emanates from the Priory, and though nowadays it's a peaceful and relaxing place to visit, it's still awe-inspiring. Did you know...

- The priory was dedicated to St Pancras.
- The stone used for its construction came from Normandy and the Isle of Wight.
- A specialist demolition team pulled it down in 1537, under an Italian engineer Giovanni Portinari, who recorded its destruction meticulously.

TOP WITHENS p183

I only discovered this wonderful ruin recently when I was shooting a documentary about the Brontës. It's a must-see for fans of those extraordinary sisters, because it's said to be the inspiration for Healthcliff's home, Wuthering Heights. The majesty of the windswept moors rolling out in front of you makes for an unforgettable trek up to these lonely ruins. The perfect place to dream that you are Heathcliff or Cathy! Did you know?

- Top Withens doesn't look anything like Emily Bronte's description of Wuthering Heights, but its moorland setting may have been a big inspiration for her.
- It was originally an Elizabethan farmhouse, became a chicken farm, and didn't fall into disuse until the mid 1920's.

ORONSAY p223

Just getting to Oronsay is an adventure. The ruins of its remote priory stand on a tidal causeway off the coast of the sparsely habited Isle of Colonsay in the Inner Hebrides. On the island's white sandy beaches, your only company is likely to be the odd basking seal or passing seabird. Did you know?

- It's thought the Priory dates back to the 6th century, and was established by St Columba before he headed off to set up his famous Abbey at Iona.
- It has two magnificent carved crosses. The Great Cross was probably created in the 14th Century for Malcolm MacDuffie, chief of Clan Duffie.

These are just a few of my favourite places, but this book opens a Pandora's box of mysteries, exploration and investigation. I hope you'll enjoy discovering your very own special wild ruins too!

Sir Tony Robinson
March 2015

WILD RUINS

The stark beauty of a ruin can inspire intrigue in a way no renovated building ever can. They have a haunting presence, always begging one overriding question, 'Why?'

Britain has had a unique, rich and varied history over the last 1000 years. War, disease, the rise and fall of industry, the evolution of transport and shifts in rural land management are amongst the many forces that have shaped this island's unique architecture. Many of our buildings remain in use and stand complete as tourist attractions or working buildings. However, hidden away in the wilds of this island, often just out of sight, there is an alternative history, the story of the buildings that have fallen into disrepair. Our multitude of abandoned buildings chronicles the ephemeral nature of our time on the planet in an incredibly vivid and real way. They tell the story of our mistakes, failures, gambles that didn't pay off, as well as our successes and achievements. They link us with the generations that came before us, and visiting them allows us to literally walk their paths and imagine their lives.

Racton Folly p72

Early on in my journey across Britain, I walked across Dartmoor in Devon to the 13th century village at Hound Tor. This incredible place is now nothing more than a number of stone works marking out the perimeter of what was once a collection of farmsteads set high on Dartmoor's rugged terrain. Walking through the old doorways, I climbed on what remained of the walls and stopped to pick whortleberries growing out of the cottage walls. With the taste of ancient food in my mouth I couldn't help but picture the wrench these hill-farmers would have felt when a worsening climate forced them to leave their homes.

Books, films and museums can all give us a sense of what life must have been like in these castles, cottages, villages and industrial fortresses. But there is nothing quite like walking the routes our forebears took, sitting by their hearths, walking through their doorways and looking out of their windows, to really feel what they felt and see what they see.

In exploring ruins, we can make up our own stories, play in imaginary worlds and act like archaeologists uncovering the past. The historic facts and figures only enhance our imagination. Ruined forts, mines, mills, quays, castles, monasteries, grand houses and village churches are amongst the incredible wild playgrounds just waiting to be discovered. Imagine walking an ancient footpath picturing families and friends making their way to a loved one's

St Mary's Somerton p104

Author at Darren Quarry p159

wedding in a now-overgrown, tumbling-down church. Or walk the well-worn stone steps that a Victorian steelworker took on his way home after a day working in the blistering heat of a furnace. Sit by his hearth, close your eyes, and feel the heat of fires long since burned warming your face on a cold winter's day. Discovering our wealth of wild ruins can change the way we experience the past and open up a world of adventure.

I did not set out to write a guidebook to ruined buildings. My interest always lay in wild plants more than the wild places they grow. However, I kept chancing on them in search of good foraging sites. I would find houses left in woodlands whilst hunting ceps in the autumn or stumble on coastal forts while searching for rock samphire and sea beet. After a while, I could no longer ignore the presence of these forgotten relics. Nature was slowly reclaiming these buildings, taking back what was once part of the earth, covering the signs of man's influence on the landscape. In stone, ivy, moss, lichen, weeds and trees the circle of life was there in front of me, a testament to the ephemeral nature of our human existence. I began to see these ruins in awe, to wonder about their past and after a little time I began to fall inexplicably and deeply in love with them.

Wild ruins are truly special places and my hope is this book will stir something in all who read it, providing hundreds of unique days out for everyone, at every age.

Dave Hamilton
March 2015

Pont CeunantFrongoch *p159*

FINDING THE RUINS

CO-ORDINATES AND POSTCODES

To help you find the ruins, latitude and longitude co-ordinates (Lat-Long) and postcodes have been provided (for example 52.2384, -0.9218, NN5 5FJ). Both can be fed into an ordinary Sat Nav to aid with directions. The postcode will give the rough location but, especially in rural areas, this can be some distance from the ruins themselves. The Lat-Long provides a more accurate location useful for hand-held GPS devices and online mapping services. With a car Sat Nav the Lat-Long often only directs you to the nearest road. In some cases there will be a river, lake/loch or railway track between you and the ruin and you will have to use the appropriate map to navigate the remainder of the journey.

MAPS

The Landranger and Explorer (purple and orange) Ordnance Survey maps are very useful tools for navigation. They can provide the location of parking places and footpaths and mark out the general site of more well-known ruins in italics next to an outline of the ruin itself. For smaller ruins only the outline of the building might be depicted. Non-ruined buildings are also depicted by their outline so it will help to cross-reference with an online map or handheld device with mapping software (feeding in the Lat-Long). Mapping software such as MemoryMap, EveryTrail or ViewRanger can be accessed on phones or tablets but do note that some tablets won't have built-in GPS making them less useful in the field.

It will be best to access online maps before you head off exploring as it can be hard, if not impossible, to pick up a 3G or 4G signal in remote locations. Bing.com, Streetmap.co.uk, ordnancesurveyleisure.co.uk are all useful sites and print outs can be made before you leave home.

Some Sat Nav have an off road feature – these are a useful back up but as the battery-life, along with the terrain and footpath information, are all limited they are by no means an ideal means of navigation.

ACCESS AND THE LAW

MANAGED RUINS

A managed ruin is an abandoned building which is actively looked after. It may have been cleared of vegetation, had its masonry secured and it may even have new stairs or walkways fitted. Typically these will be (although not exclusively) old castles, churches, monasteries or priories managed by large organisations such as English Heritage, Historic Scotland, Cadw or the National Trust.

STAFFED – Staffed ruins do have their risks but they are amongst the safest of ruins to visit if you follow the guidance on site.

UNSTAFFED – Unstaffed but managed properties pose more of a risk but they will be regularly visited to ensure they are safe and in no immediate risk of collapse.

In both unstaffed and staffed buildings, unless there are signs on the contrary, it should be fine to explore cellars, climb stairs etc with caution. However, staircases may be narrow with uneven stairs and floors may be uneven so take care not to slip or fall.

Never climb on walls – it is dangerous and can damage what remains of the building.

UNMANAGED BUILDINGS

Many ruins are not managed and do not encourage visitors. Careful judgment is required before entering. There is no certainty these buildings are not in risk of collapse. There may be high risks of falling masonry or unfenced drop-offs. If in doubt, do not enter.

FENCED-OFF RUINS OR THOSE ON PRIVATE LAND

This book does not recommend you enter private property. I have usually stated if a ruin is on private land or only to be viewed from the footpath. However I am not infallible, and buildings can change ownership. If in doubt then, do not enter the building or trespass.

Trespass is a civil offence, not a criminal offence. This means it is never a matter for the police (unless you refuse to leave when asked to) and you cannot be arrested. However you can be sued for damages if you cause damage to a building and, if you refuse to leave when asked, force can be used to evict you (though 'no more than is reasonably necessary').

MINING AND INDUSTRIAL BUILDINGS

Although the majority of mineshafts have been capped or covered by metal gratings there may be one or two mining and quarrying sites with open mineshafts. Some shafts can be explored with the help of a potholing expert such as Go Cave in Cumbria 01768 489125 or Dolomite Training in Derbyshire 01629 735691.

EX-MILITARY OR MILITARY OWNED SITES

There is a risk of unexploded military debris on old or active military sites. To stay safe, keep within in the designated areas.

GOING WILD

SAFETY

Climbing a tree and rolling down a hill can be dangerous activities yet I would not deny anyone the joy of either by overstating the dangers. Likewise exploring a derelict or ruined building can be a really fun thing to do and staying safe whilst exploring should not detract from its enjoyment Take great care when entering any old buildings, and if in doubt stay out.

SUPPLIES AND EQUIPMENT

Some ruins are very remote and will take some effort to find. This is part of the fun. It will help to have a map of the area, a compass and/or a GPS device. Do not visit remote or mountainous sites alone. Ensure you have brought enough food and water and have the correct clothing and footwear for the time of year. A torch can also come in handy when exploring.

Longtown Castle

FRUIT

Apple, plum, cherry and pear trees left to go wild are not uncommon sights in the gardens of derelict cottages, grand houses and farmhouses. No different than domestic fruit they can be eaten and prepared in the normal way.

Typically sloes and cherries are added to gin and brandy respectively but these aren't the only liqueurs you can make. Cherry plum gin, sloe whisky, mulberry vodka are all excellent fruit-in-alcohol combinations.

Bilberries or whortleberries grow on moorland from Cornwall up to the tip of Scotland. They are related to the blueberry and have just as much the antioxidant-rich superfood as their cultivated cousins. Kids seem to love them too!

The fruit of the hawthorn is an often-forgotten edible and can make great ketchup (just follow a tomato ketchup recipe).

WILD LEAVES

Wild salad leaves can pep up the blandest cheese sandwich or stronger-tasting leaves can be gathered to make a pesto.

Sorrel, ground elder and wild garlic are all instantly recognisable weeds. Pick a large handful of one or a mix of the leaves and place in a bowl. Add olive oil, a sprinkle of ground pine nuts (or cashews), grated parmesan cheese and use a handheld blender to turn into a paste. If the flavour is overpowering you can add a blander leaf such as chickweed or nettle (blanched in hot water to remove the sting) to mellow the flavour.

Lime leaves and hawthorn leaves are edible when they first emerge. Neither has a strong flavour so they are best used in a mixed salad.

WILD FLOWERS

When the elder is in full blossom it is the true mark that summer is well on the way. The elder flower, along with primroses, clover, evening primrose, wild violets, gorse flowers and hawthorn blossom can all help to make a summer salad or cocktail a little more interesting.

GUIDE TO FORAGING

Whether it is a wayside nibble or a part of a breakfast on the beach, foraging for wild food is a delicious way to connect with a landscape.

Staying safe

- The golden rule of foraging is never to eat something unless you are 100% certain you have identified it correctly. A good foraging course will help you ID with some certainty as will a good field guide, cross-referenced with an internet image search or a phone app.
- In old graveyards lead-lined coffins can present a risk of soil contamination as can the heavy metals and waste materials present in ex-industrial sites. Salad leaves and mushrooms are amongst the worst offenders to soak up these contaminants.
- Be sure not to over-pick, wild food can be a treat for us but it is an important part of the food chain for many species of wildlife.

Ensure you have enough petrol if driving and that you have brought enough food and water. The British weather can be somewhat unpredictable, so ensure you have the correct clothing and footwear for the time of year. A torch can also come in handy when exploring.

Best for Foraging & Wildlife

Most Dramatic or Romantic Ruins

Castle Stalker p239

Best for Picnics and Summer Days

Best for Beautiful Walks

St Mary's Saxlingham p112

Best for Ghost Stories

Most Wild and Secluded

Ardvreck Castle p216

Best for Children and Families

Best for Camping

St Dogmael

Weirdest and Strangest Ruins

Best for Pubs and Days Out

Rhosydd Quarry p170

CHAPTER 1

CORNWALL

Cornwall is a wild, rugged county with a coastline exposed to strong Atlantic winds. The varied landscape reflects the rich mineral deposits which have been exploited since Neolithic times. Early written records show that the Greeks referred to Britain as one of their 'tin islands' and they, along with the Romans and the Phoenicians, may have traded with Cornwall for the mineral that was an essential raw ingredient in the production of bronze. Cornwall's Bronze Age inhabitants were not just miners; they would have farmed and traded throughout the area. The remains of two early communities stand remarkably intact at Carn Euny and Chysauster, offering us a window into the far and distant past.

More recently, in 2006 UNESCO granted the mining regions of Devon and Cornwall World Heritage status. Ten areas within these counties have been seen as places of historical significance in terms of their contribution to the international mining industry. Some of my favourites are featured here including the area of St Just, a few miles north of Land's End. Here you can see the mining remains at Cape Cornwall and the engine houses at Botallack Mine perched on a rocky outcrop surrounded by the deep blue of the Atlantic.

Due to foreign competition at the end of the 19th and beginning of the 20th century, mines all over Cornwall closed, one by one. The skills of the workforce would be redundant in their home towns and, at the risk of starvation, they would have been forced to move to places where they were more needed. Often these were as far away as America, South Africa and Australia .

Further up the county the blue of the ocean gives way to the lush greens of two more UNESCO sites: Kennall Vale and its ruined gunpowder works, and Luxulyan with its numerous industrial ruins (including clay works, a corn mill, a mineral railway and a quarry and mining works). Once industrial strongholds, Kennall Vale and Luxulyan have slowly over the years become re-inhabited by the natural world. Nowadays the machines have been silenced, the workers gone and visiting these rich areas of fauna and flora feels likes a return to a much older wilder England.

1 BOTALLACK MINE
BOTALLACK, ST JUST

On this westerly tip of Cornwall, framed by the large expanse of the Atlantic Ocean, are the twin engine houses at Botallack Head, set just above the crashing waves. Along with these two ruins there are numerous mining remains running right across the coastline. From the engine house a large shaft descends diagonally beneath the ocean to a depth of 240 metres. For the workers this would have been a precarious way to earn a living, extracting tin from beneath the surface of the sea. Considering the perilous conditions it might seem shocking that this dangerous mine shaft became a tourist attraction. In the 1865 this proved so popular that even the Prince and Princess of Wales came to visit. It seems they were not put off by an accident, just two years before, when a tourist party of eight men and one child fell hurtling to their deaths.

Follow B3306 N out of St Just. After Tregeseal, at Botallack village take L fork. Pass Queen's Arms (TR19 7QG) and turn L at the corner (limited parking), past farm and Botallack Manor. You will see a mine chimney straight ahead, on the coast, and the road becomes a dirt track. There are mining remains to explore all over here but the iconic engine houses stand below the cliffs 15 minutes, easy walk away. There are mainline trains to Penzance and a 10 bus will take you from there to Botallack village (also bus 300 in the summer).

50.1388, -5.6868, TR19 7QQ

2 ST HELEN'S ORATORY
AND CAPE CORNWALL TIN MINE

When the Ordnance Survey mapped the area 200 years ago, Cape Cornwall relinquished the honour of most westerly point in Britain. For me Cape Cornwall is still the real end of England, a magical place where sky, land and sea meet. All that remains of the tin mine is the ornate chimney at the end of a bracing walk at the peak of the Cape. The most interesting ruin however is St Helen's Oratory. Tufts of grass and wild flowers sprout from the lichen-covered grey walls of this beautiful and ancient roofless ruin. Its position overlooking the expanse of the ocean only adds to its innate beauty. There has been a place of worship on the site since the 5th century. St Helen's Oratory is just off the South West Coast Path.

From St Just head N on Market Square and turn L at clock to follow the Cape Cornwall road out of St Just. Turn L at large white Boswedden House B&B (TR19 7NJ, 01736 788733). Continue to coast where there is a National Trust car park to L of the ruin or a café with car parking for customers further up the hill.

50.1275, -5.7058, TR19 7NN

3 CARN EUNY
ANCIENT VILLAGE

There have been stone structures on this site for the last 2,100 years, with wooden structures pre-dating these by at least a hundred more. It is one of the best-preserved Iron Age villages in the country. The highlight is a 20-metre-long, partly underground passageway know as a fogou. This is a man-made cave made up of large stone slabs over underground stone walls. It is of historical importance, and also a great place in which to shelter. Nearby is Sancreed Clootie Well, 50.1074, -5.6127. Clootie wells were healing places where strips of cloth are tied to a tree, with a prayer. Take a short, often muddy walk W along a footpath opposite Sancreed Church.

Take the western road towards St Just for about a mile and a half from Sancreed and follow English Heritage signs. Parking is 600 metres away in Brane 50.1004,-5.6343.

50.1027, -5.6339, TR20 8RB

4 SOUTH WHEAL FRANCES

Often referred to as the Cathedral of Cornish Mining, South Wheal Frances is a must visit. The site is extensive and many of the buildings are incredibly intact giving a good impression of what life must have been like on the site. Although mining began in the early 18th century on the site, it wasn't until the mid-19th that the mine really saw its heyday. The mine ceased operation towards the end of the First World War when the price of tin plummeted.

From Camborne Station take the Trevu Rd SE away from the rail crossing. Continue onto Fore St then L past Methodist Church onto Condurrow Rd. At end of road turn L (Wheal Grenville mine is R), then 1st right. Continue to crossroads, take L then 1st R. Head past Wheal Frances then take R and 1st R to car park.

50.2087, -5.2520, TR16 6JX

5 KENNALL VALE
GUNPOWDER WORKS

The peaceful Kennall Vale shows little sign of its destructive past. The buildings, nestled among trees, are now home to ferns, ivy and mosses. Things were very different in the early 19th century when this was the home of a large complex responsible for the manufacture of the explosives necessary for mining. In May 1838 a huge accident at the plant saw five mills explode, one after another. Unfortunately, this was not an isolated incident, for there were at least three further reports of explosions throughout the mill's history, making it a very dangerous place to work. Near Kennall Vale is the mining district of Gwennap, once called the richest square mile in the old world. Of particular interest there are remains at Poldice Mine and Wheal Busy.

Kennall Vale reserve is W of the village of Ponsanooth off the A393. Turn down Park Road at the village shop/post office at the N end of the village. Follow lane for 500m before following the rough track R, at entrance to Kennall House. Parking is limited so consider finding somewhere in the village to park, a 20 minute, moderate walk away.

50.1933, -5.1551, TR3 7HW

6 ROCHE ROCK
ROCHE VILLAGE

The imposing ruin of Roche Chapel overlooks Roche village from 20 metres up on its granite outcrop. You can reach the chapel by means of carved stone steps in the side of the rock, via a field filled with bilberries in late summer. Story has it that Jan Tregeagle, a sort of Cornish Faustian figure, while trying to escape demon guards got caught with his head inside the chapel's window but the rest of his body stuck outside. His head was in the sanctuary of the holy building but the rest of him was at the mercy of the demons. After he had suffered days of torment, a local priest was forced to remove him with the help of two saints. Although a fascinating fable it does beg the question why he came in through the window when the door is a much easier form of entry? The site features in many climbing guides and is suitable for all levels of climber from beginner to expert.

From Cornwall Services on the A30 take the B3274 heading W to Roche, Victoria and the station. After 1¼ miles turn left to stay on the B3274 towards Roche and St Austell. 2nd exit at the roundabout in Roche past the Temperance Hall. Continue over second roundabout, 2nd exit and pull in to the lay-by 200m on the L near the sports ground. Walk through car park, along football pitch then follow paths into the field where Roche Rock is situated. If a match is on, walk via the road, to the footpath off the Bugle road (L at the roundabout).

50.4020, -4.8312, PL26 8HB

7 WHEAL COATES
ST AGNES

The iconic cliff-top engine houses and processing buildings at Wheal Coates tin mine are some of the most dramatically located and best preserved mining buildings in Cornwall. There has been mining at the site since prehistoric times but modern mining began here in 1802 and at its peak it employed 138 men and boys. At low tide it is possible to explore the old mine shaft beneath the engine house via the large sea cave on Chapel Porth beach. To the north west of the ruins, on Tubby's Head headland, a blow hole in the cliffs forces sea water to spray out, like a surfacing whale. Don't be tempted to peer down the hole as the water can spray out at speeds approaching 100mph!

6

Head N from St Agnes on the Trevaunance Rd, drive past the white cottage of the Beacon Cottage Farm touring park and pull into the unmarked car park on right. The ruins are 5 minutes walk toward the sea. Or park at Chapel Porth beach and walk N on the coast path 10 minutes.

50.3059, -5.2327, TR5 0NT

8 DING DONG MINE
BOSILIACK

Ding Dong mine is reputedly one of the oldest in Cornwall having been worked since Roman times. Greenburrow engine house is the most prominent part of the mine and stands tall amongst the wild desolate Cornish landscape. The mine shaft is grated over but you can look down it and get a sense of its depth. The engine house seems a little unloved in this remote and out of the way location. To the south you will find the ancient stones of Lanyon Quoit.

Ding Dong is a difficult drive down a labyrinth of windy Cornish lanes. From the A30 in Penzance take the turning onto the B3312 towards Madron and Heamoor. Just over a mile from Madron take the R fork off main road to Bosiliack. Head up until road runs out and park on the L. Pull in at 50.1510,-5.5883. Here follow track until a footpath to the engine house branches off to the left.

50.1543, -5.5929, TR20 8XY

9 CHYSAUSTER
ANCIENT VILLAGE

Set on a hill, Chysauster is one of the best preserved Iron Age settlements in Britain, with superb views across the countryside and the coast. It is believed that people settled here around 100BC and would have remained in this area through a good proportion of the Roman Occupation. Around ten of the site's distinctive stone-walled buildings known as courtyard houses remain, eight of which would have made two 'streets' running alongside each other. Visitors can enter the man-made underground cave or fogou at the site.

Chysauster is an easy drive from Penzance and signposted off the B3311.

50.1587, -5.5439, TR20 8XA

10 LUXULYAN VALLEY
BLAZEY

In its 1920s guide to the area, the Great Western Railway described the Luxulyan Valley as "one of the most glorious walks in all Cornwall". Not much has changed since then, and walks around this ancient wooded valley are still enchanting. A hundred years before the GWR guide was published, Joseph Treffry inherited the site and began to develop it, exploiting much of its mineral wealth. Among other things he developed the harbour at Par, had a canal created, built the large dual-purpose viaduct and aqueduct, developed the existing granite quarries, built leats, or artificial streams, to power large water wheels and set to work on a mineral railway. The aqueduct still bears his name.

The Treffry Viaduct is just under a mile from Luxulyan station by road or footpath. It is just off National Cycle Route 3. 3 miles NW of St Blazey, off A390. Heading N on A390, turn L to Ponts Mill and car park. Or for a short walk to the aqueduct, stay on A390 for a further ½ mile turning L just before row of cottages. Continue for a mile until to car park on the L just before junction.

50.3808, -4.7298, PL24 2SA

10

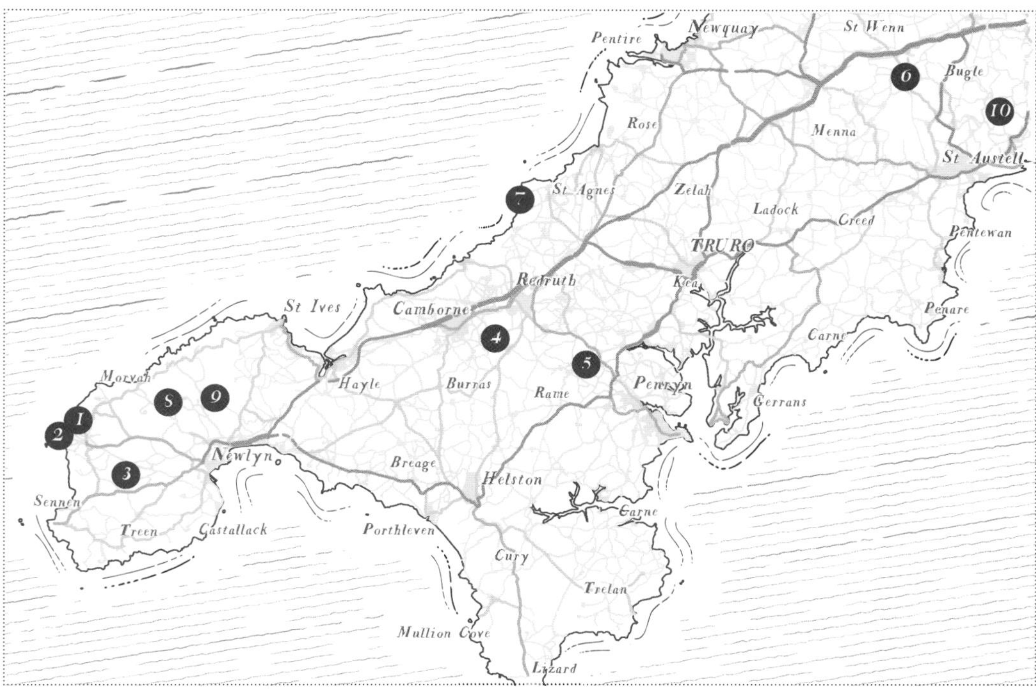
Pentire
Newquay
St Wenn
Bugle
6
10
Rose
Menna
St Austell
7
St Agnes
Zelah
Ladock
Creed
Pentewan
TRURO
Redruth
Kea
St Ives
Camborne
Penare
4
Carne
5
Morvah
8
9
Hayle
Burras
Rame
Penryn
Gerrans
1
2
Newlyn
3
Breage
Helston
Sennen
Carne
Treen
Castallack
Porthleven
Cury
Trelan
Mullion Cove
Lizard

CHAPTER 2

DEVON

In Norman times large parts of Devon were made into a royal forest and deer would wander freely across its fields and lanes. Farmers would have found the deer a nuisance so built up the banks and laid hedges to keep out these hungry herbivores. Over 33,000 miles of these still remain throughout this rural county, providing an essential home to wildlife. Among the wild flowers are primroses, the national flower of Devon, which brighten up the banks, along with many wayside nibbles such as pennywort. For the ruin-hunter the hedgerows can conceal surprises waiting to be discovered. The roofless church of South Huish reveals itself round the twists and turns of a coastal lane while the ruined priory of Cornworthy appears in a field after miles of high banked hedges.

The vast open space of Dartmoor stands in contrast to the lowland lanes, its windswept desolate plain proving many examples of an ancient life based on mining and farming, such as Hound Tor. Indeed some of the oldest settlements in Britain are here, dating from prehistoric times. They include the mining settlement of Grimspound, a late Bronze Age settlement, probably dating from about 450-750BC. Tin was very important in that period, as bronze is an alloy of copper with up to one third tin. In the medieval period, Dartmoor tin was so important that four stannary towns were established, where refined tin was assessed, coined and sold. They had the right to the jurisdiction of special local stannary courts that regulated the tin industry. On the large open plains, the remains of pre-Roman industry, medieval quarrying and Victorian mining can be discovered too. Foggintor and Wheal Betsy are amongst the best of these. With much of Foggintor collapsed from the winds and rain, the main ruin to see is the manager's house with its two windows looking out over the bleak beauty of the moors.

Devon's two coastlines are very different. The north coast is rugged and wild, battered by the swell of the Atlantic. Here the families of fishermen and sailors must have prayed for their safe return in the many churches, such as the one at Braunton, now a ghostly hilltop ruin set above the land. The south coast, in contrast, is characterised by sheltered estuaries and seaside towns, a much more sedate place than the towns and villages of its northern counterpart. When bad weather hits this region it hits it hard, a fact we saw all too clearly when the storms of 2014 hit the coast. Across the news we saw dramatic pictures of Devon with the train line at Dawlish all but falling to the ravages of the sea. Nearly a hundred years previously, on 26th January 1917, the 128 inhabitants of Hallsands were hit by a storm of equal ferocity. The storm raged through the night and four houses were lost to it by midnight; at dawn the next day just one house remained perched on the hillside.

1
3
2
4

1 HALLSANDS
START BAY

Clinging to the cliff-side, just off the South West Coast Path, the crumbling shells that once made up the houses of Hallsands act as a stark reminder of the potentially destructive power of our weather. It is not possible to walk among the buildings at Hallsands but the village can be seen from a viewing platform near Trouts Apartments at South Hallsands. Afterwards, head up the coast to the Rocket Café at the Seabreeze B&B (seabreezebreaks.com/cafe) at Torcross. It serves excellent coffee and pancakes.

Hallsands ruins are on the South West Coast path between Slapton and Start Point. Join the A379 at Dartmouth or Kingsbridge and make your way to Stokenham. At mini roundabout follow signs to Prawle and Beesands. Follow Cycle Route 2, branch off at signs to Start Point and Hallsands. Continue to Bickerton then turn right to follow signs to South Hallsands. Reasonably sized car park 50.2377,-3.6598. Follow coast path to viewing point.

50.2364, -3.6591, TQ7 2EY

2 NEWQUAY
MORWELLHAM

As you fight your way through dense thicket to reveal the deserted settlement of Newquay it feels as if you are unearthing a lost civilisation, forgotten in time among the wild jungle of Devon. Compared with the vibrant, active open air museum of Morwellham Quay, its ruinous neighbour feels forgotten and unloved. Newquay was once a thriving port, shipping raw material from the local mines. At its height in the mid-19th century it was a bustling village with an inn and a number of dwellings. The port was abandoned in the early 20th century but its last inhabitant didn't move out until the 1950s.

You can access the site by many routes. Take footpath from Gawton to the S or, for a longer walk, head to the Tamar Trails Centre which has a flyer of walks in the area (PL19 8JE, adjacent to Tavistock Sawmills 50.5325, -4.2035). From Morwellham (admission fee) walk down the railway line (talk to engine driver first to ensure safe route), continue to end of track and walk through the trees until you see the buildings. Please note the ruins are on private land so observe from footpath.

50.5062, -4.1819, PL19 8JJ

3 ST ANDREW'S CHURCH
SOUTH HUISH

The 13th-century church at South Huish is tucked away down a snaking mass of lanes, flanked by high banked Devon hedges. In spring the lanes are full of primroses, a delicate, edible flower and the floral symbol for Devon. Visit later in the year, from early summer onward, and you'll find the church sprouting flowering red valerian. The church is run by the 'Friends of Friendless Churches' who preserved it as the stable ruin you see today. Although the church began life in the 13th century much of it was built later, in the 15th. As the population of South Huish moved away to nearby Galmpton the church fell into ruin. By 1866 it was abandoned and a new church was built at Galmpton.

About 3 miles cycle from Salcombe or 1½ from Malborough village down the lanes. In peak season these lanes get busy and despite there being a small pull-in at the site, it is likely to be taken. The site is therefore best visited on foot or bicycle. From the coast path, head in at Woolman Point on the lanes, until a footpath cuts towards South Huish at Galmpton.

50.2555, -3.8318, TQ7 3EH

4 CORNWORTHY PRIORY
TUCKENHAY

From its position down a mass of high-hedged Devon lanes, the sleepy village of Cornworthy is almost completely hidden from the outside world. At the top of the village, at the end of a fairly unassuming field, is the large gateway arch of Cornworthy Priory. This was once the largest building in the parish and home to 13 Augustinian nuns. By the time of the Dissolution of the Monasteries in the 16th century there were only around seven in residence, well below the required amount, which may in part have been due to its isolated location.

If heading north on A381, about ½ mile S of Harbertonford take R towards Cornworthy and Washbourne. Cross river and turn L, signed Cornworthy. Continue about 1 mile, straight past turn to Tuckenhay. Stay on L fork until you see the priory in front of you. To park, continue on L fork, Abbey Rd, to pull-in at 50.3892, -3.6566. The priory is accessible via gate in hedge.

50.3884, -3.6587, TQ9 7ET

5 HOUND TOR VILLAGE
WIDECOMBE IN THE MOOR

High on the moors, the foot-high remains of this deserted medieval settlement are clearly visible among the ferns, foxgloves, bilberries and heather. The walk over the tor is invigorating, although not as challenging as many in the region. During the 1300s the climate in this part of the world gradually got wetter and wetter. The inhabitants of the village must have found life increasingly challenging. They would no longer be able to dry grain in the sun; instead they built large kilns to dry it in the heat of a fire. This would have added to their workload as the kilns needed constant monitoring and maintenance. The extra workload must have made life for the residents of Hound Tor feel like drudgery. The village was abandoned by the early 15th century, with the residents perhaps moving to better land that had become available after rural depopulation caused by the Black Death, which ravaged Devon in the 1300s, killing more than a third of the population.

Hound Tor is signed of the B3387 between Widecombe in the Moor and Haytor. Follow road past tor on your right to parking at 50.598901, -3.782270. From here head up and over Hound Tor. Follow path from the top to the village. It is part-signposted but for the other part you will have to follow your nose.

50.5951, -3.7728, TQ13 9XQ

6 GRIMSPOUND VILLAGE
POSTBRIDGE, YELVERTON

Grimspound is reportedly one of the oldest settlements on Dartmoor. Here are the remains of 24 dwellings. They are surrounded by a stone perimeter boundary which may have acted as a way of keeping livestock in and predators out. Little is known about the inhabitants but around the time of settlement in 1300BC the population would have almost certainly been a farming one. It is thought that the name 'Grim' is an Anglo-Saxon derivative of Odin or Woden, the god of war.

Take B3212 N of Two Bridges for about 7½ miles (through Postbridge), then R at Challacombe Cross. Pass Hookney Tor and park by road at 50.6131,-3.8429. Follow footpath to the site.

50.6131, -3.8377, PL20 6TB

7 FOGGINTOR QUARRY
PRINCETOWN

Even on a misty day Foggintor quarry has a stark beauty to it. The grey rock of the area seems to mimic descending clouds giving the area an otherworldly appearance. On a sunny day the rocks reflect the light and the area comes into its own. Buzzards will often circle overhead on thermals looking for mice and small animals to eat. On a hot day you may find lizards and adders warming themselves on the rocks in the sun. For walkers, the quarry it is on the route of the 90-mile circular Dartmoor Way. The 10-mile linear walk between Princetown and Tavistock, taking in both Foggintor and Sweltor quarries, makes a good outing (but if you want to get the bus back do check times first as they are infrequent). For a shorter walk to Foggintor, take the two-mile walk from the National Park visitor centre (Tavistock Road, Princetown, Yelverton, PL20 6QF).

Take B3357 W towards Tavistock from Two Bridges. Go past Princetown turning and park in small car park on L past boarded up house at 50.5568, -4.0238. Walk up track past Yellowmeade Farm to quarry.

50.5492, -4.0254, PL20 6SS

8 LEATHER TOR FARM
NEAR YELVERTON

The moss-covered ruins of Leather Tor Farm lie hidden amongst the trees a short walk away from Burrator Reservoir. An older building predated the ruin which was thought to have been built during the mid to late 19th century. The owner would have been forced to leave when Burrator Reservoir was created in the 1920's.

Just off footpath E of Leather Tor. Park in car park off B3212 and walk down or follow path N from top end of Burrator Reservoir.

50.5106, -4.0226, PL20 6PE

5

9 WHITEWORKS MINE
YELVERTON

The old tin mine of Whiteworks is in a very isolated site location, well worth the walk or drive down the single-lane track. There are numerous earthworks and stone remains around the site with many of the walls now covered in moss and wild plants. Whiteworks feels remote and off the beaten track making for a quiet, contemplative place to visit. Its mine shafts mean it isn't suitable for younger visitors.

Follow Tor Royal Lane out of Princetown to the E dropping S. The tin mine is at the end of lane about 2 ½ miles down.

50.5234, -3.9584, PL20 6SL

10 OKEHAMPTON CASTLE

The remains of the largest castle in Devon, Okehampton is worth the diversion off the A30. Its position on the banks of the river, surrounded by meadow and woodland walks make it the perfect spot for an afternoon stroll followed by a summer picnic. It is a steep climb up to the castle but once up there the views are stunning. It is home to one of the area's most notable ghost stories: that of Mary Howard who lost four husbands in suspicious circumstances. It is said she is cursed to ride a coach driven by a headless driver along the road to Tavistock.

12

Okehampton castle is well signed by English Heritage. It is ½ a mile W of town centre down Castle Rd by the post office. On-site parking is limited and it is only a short walk from the town.

50.7308, -4.0082, EX20 1JA

11 HOLY TRINITY
BUCKFASTLEIGH

It is said that Satan was kept away from this church by the building of the 196 steps to access it (presumably there is no gym in Hell). Holy Trinity is perhaps the most unlucky ruin I have come across; it was damaged by arson in 1849, then lightning in 1884, the stained glass windows were damaged by a nearby bomb in the Second World War and then finally in 1992 arsonists struck again and the church was gutted.

By far the best way to visit Buckfastleigh is to come via Totnes on the steam railway. It is about 20-30 minute walk to the church via the town centre. You'll find some pretty good chips in the town of Buckfastleigh and of course Buckfast Abbey, famed for its 'tonic' drink, is a short walk via road and footpath from the ruined church. The famous steep steps to the church are opposite Station Road car park, behind a one way sign. Once you are up the steps it leads to a path and through a kissing gate.

50.4854, -3.7748, TQ11 0EZ

12 WHEAL BETSY
TAVISTOCK

Depending on what angle you look at it, Wheal Betsy looks like any other engine house. However, as you walk towards it, you realise why it has been dubbed 'the leaning tower of Dartmoor'. This tell-tale lean was as a result of the building's exposed position on windswept Dartmoor. The National Trust now owns the site and has secured the structure to ensure the lean doesn't lean any more than it needs to!

Head N on A386 from Tavistock for 5 miles. 1 mile after Mary Tavy there is a layby at 50.6136, -4.1083. Park and walk down to the tower, visible from the road. 1-2 mins moderate walk.

50.6131, -4.1071, PL19 9QG

13 BLEAK HOUSE
LYDFORD

Despite its name Bleak House can be a pleasant hike across the moors on a sunny day. This was the old site manager's house for the Rattlebrook peat works. The site operated for around 30 years in the early part of the last century. An old railway once served the site, the path of which can be walked along today.

From the R of the car park of the Dartmoor Inn, on the A386 at Lydford (EX20 4AY), take a short track NE to a car park. Continue on this track to a footpath, cross the ford and stay on the path heading E to Dicks Well (look out for the boundary stone). Head E, then N on this path for about ½ mile, then cross the river to the ruined house. 2½ miles, 1-1½ hours strenuous walk.

50.6601, -4.0391, EX20 4HF

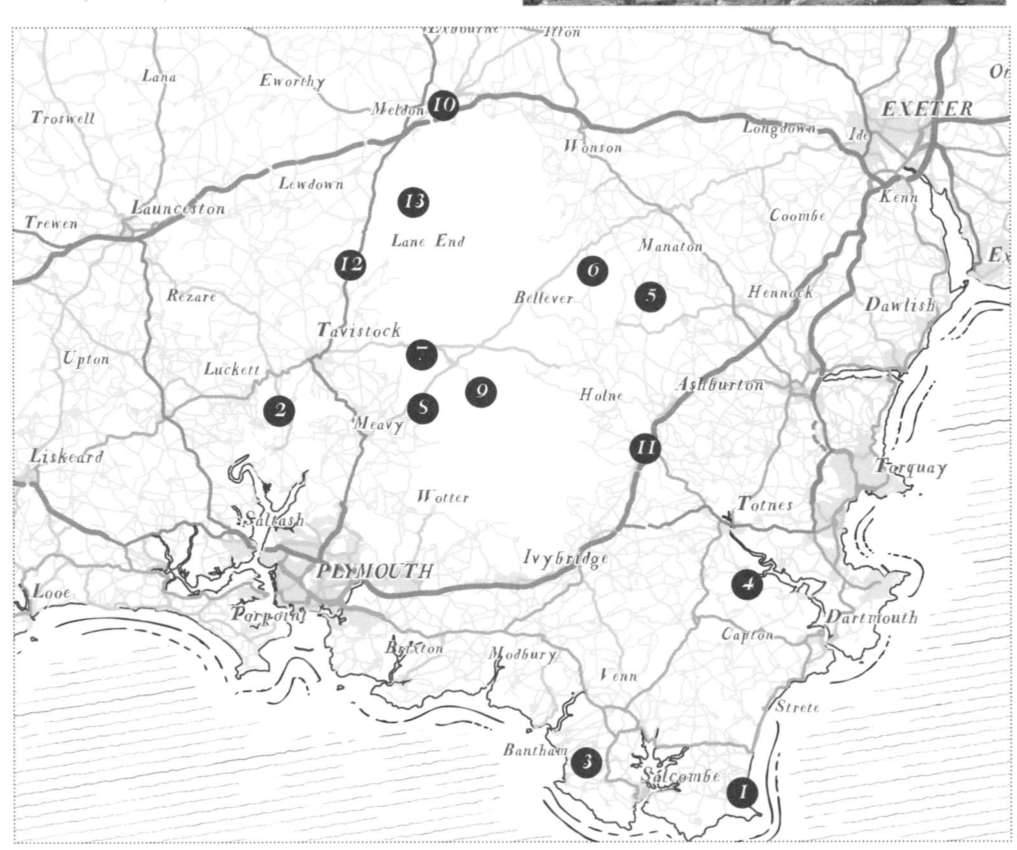

CHAPTER 3

EXMOOR, SOMERSET AND WEST DORSET

The West Country is an exceptionally beautiful part of the UK. None more so than this large corner containing the stunning unspoilt expanse of Exmoor and its National Park and the rolling Quantock hills rising above the low lying plains of the Somerset Levels. It has one of the largest concentrations of Areas of Outstanding Natural Beauty in the country; highlights include the Blackdown Hills on the Devon/Somerset border, the North Devon coast and Mendip Hills, East Devon and Dorset.

Within the Dorset Area of Outstanding Natural Beauty are the modest remains of St Gabriel's chapel. The chapel is a short but pleasant walk across a picturesque pastoral coastal landscape. The vivid blues of the sky and sea here still attract watercolour artists and photographers to the area. Despite its pleasant and modest beauty the chapel holds a chequered past, once being used as a warehouse for smugglers.

The hills of the West Country are not just a thing of beauty but, due to the presence of valuable minerals such as iron ore, copper and even gold, they have been important to the British economy. In order to move these precious raw materials an ambitious mineral railway was commissioned. The railway ran from Watchet in the north to the small hamlet of Comberow in the south (the line was later extended further west). Part of the railway had to head 800 feet uphill for a distance of half a mile, which would be an impressive engineering feat now, let alone more than 150 years ago. Remains of this railway can still be seen throughout the Brendon Hills, including the site of the winding house used to haul trucks laden with minerals up the incline.

1 DOWN HOUSE COTTAGES
SAUNTON SANDS

On a sunny day the view from Down House Cottages over Saunton Sands beach is quite unbeatable. From this vantage point, you get a bird's eye view of the shore and the dunes that helped this area to become one of the country's first designated Biosphere Reserve. From the entrance to Saunton Sands Hotel turn left and head up the path through the woods rather than the coast path. The ruined cottages are on the left as you emerge into the field. Afterwards, you can walk through the field and down to re-join the coastal path. The farm cottages, or Down House Cottages as they are known locally, were inhabited right up until the early 20th century. As they are unsecured ruins, take care when exploring. For a resort its size Saunton Sands has been host to a more than its fair share of newsworthy incidents including at least two large beached whales (one 50 feet long), an emergency plane landing and a number of shipwrecks. It was even home to a camel train during a 1930s film shoot. For a spot of luxury, pop into Saunton Sands Hotel for a tea or coffee on the patio overlooking the beach, or if you are feeling flush the evening menu always has plenty to offer; reservations recommended 01271 890212.

Saunton Sands is on the B3231, 3 miles W of Braunton. Park in public car park next to Saunton Sands Hotel.

51.1203, -4.2190, EX33 1LQ

2 WILLETT TOWER
ELWORTHY

The walk up to Willett Tower is still as beguiling as it would have been when it was built. During the month of May is the best time to visit as this 'ruin' stands tall from a bluebell wood surrounded by the blossoming hawthorn. Built in the late 18th century, it would have very much been inspired by fashion of the day for romantic ruins. It is not, as it seems to be, a ruined church tower. It is nothing more than an extravagant garden ornament built to look like a decaying structure on top of a hill.

Off the B3224, just E of Elworthy. From Elworthy, look for the Forestry Commission's Willett Hill car park shortly on the L. Park, and follow winding track, turn R when half way up and walk up footpath to crest of the hill.

51.0939, -3.2926, TA4 3QB

3 ST GABRIEL'S CHAPEL
NEAR CHIDEOCK

This is a picture postcard ruin with sweeping views of the Dorset Hills and coastline. On a sunny day the walk over Golden Cap hill is a pleasant amble. The church is said to have been built by a shipwrecked newly-wed who, after praying to St Gabriel during a two-day storm, landed on the coast here. Sadly his wife died shortly after they landed but the groom, Bertram, built the chapel in honour of the saint. During the mid-19th century the church was no longer used for religious purposes but as a warehouse for smuggled goods such as tobacco and French silk.

Turn off the A35 at Chideock (W of Bridport) follow road to the coast towards Seatown and park at coast car park 50.7166 -2.7838. From here follow the coast path W for approx. 1½ miles over Golden Cap before dipping down to the chapel (signposted). Alternatively there are footpaths and a map of the area from the National Trust car park at Langdon Hill 50.7343, -2.8339.

50.7282, -2.8485, DT6 6EP

4 BREAN DOWN FORT
BREAN

Brean Down Fort sits strategically on top of a rocky outcrop, offering views right down the Bristol Channel. It is often referred to as one of Palmerston's follies. These were not true follies, but a group of forts commissioned by prime minister Lord Palmerston in the 1860s. They were built at great expense, to protect Britain from the French fleet. However, by the time they were finished, not only were their weapons out of date but the threat from the French had largely passed. The fort was used again in the Second World War when lots of concrete was unsympathetically used to strengthen the fort's defences. A walk up the Down is an invigorating climb, and from the top you will be rewarded with views over the Bristol Channel towards south Wales and inland over the Somerset Levels.

Head north from Brean on Church/Warren Rd. A National Trust car park is at the end of the road. The fort is a mile from here at the end of the Down. The steps up to the Down are the hardest part, otherwise it is a reasonable walk. Brean is on the 21 bus route from Weston-super-Mare.

51.3256, -3.0290, TA8 2RS

5 FUSSELLS IRON WORKS
MELLS

Hidden in the woods near the picturesque village of Mells, the sprawling ruin of Fussells iron works stretches out across the banks of the river. There is an odd romance about the site. It is no place for an unaccompanied child but exploring the stairways leading nowhere, its abandoned machinery and moss-clad walls make it a place to rediscover the child within you. Iron was worked here since 1744 and prospered for a number of years making 'edge' tools such as spades and scythes along with other agricultural equipment. When English agriculture and the iron trade both went into decline in the late 19th century, the company went bankrupt and in 1894 the site was forced to close. In summer cherries and wild strawberries grow by the side of the path.

From the village shop in Mells walk E towards Great Elm on the middle of the three roads. The footpath is ¼ mile on the right. Room for one car or park in village.

51.2386, -2.3750, BA11 3PA

6 ST MICHAEL'S CHAPEL
BRAUNTON

The chapel, built in the 15th century, once served fishermen and sailors. Across the years many have spotted the same, white, clerical figure moving through the ruins of the chapel. Trying to cash in tales of this shadowy spectre a local photographer faked a series of photos and sold them to unsuspecting locals.

From the town centre, head E on East St, continuing into North Down Rd. 1st L to Sylvan Dr, 1st R to Hazel Ave. Park where you can. Follow path up hill at end of Havel Ave, a 10 min moderate-to-difficult walk. A sign rather ambiguously states "When gate is closed there is no entry to the Chapel", but there is no information on opening times.

51.1152, -4.1566, EX33 2EN

7 CONYGAR TOWER
DUNSTER

Conygar tower is a huge three-storey folly tower at the top of a wooded hill near the town of Dunster. The climb to the base of the tower is steep but pleasant and you'll pass two more folly ruins, those of a 'ruined' gatehouse, on the way. Landowner and MP Henry Fownes Luttrell of Dunster Castle had Conygar tower built in 1775. It was one of a series of improvements he made to the castle and the estate. The tower was designed as a decorative folly in order to improve the views from the castle. Park in Dunster National Park car park (51.1853, -3.4423). Walk to the information centre, following pavement for 30 metres, then cross to head up small path adjacent to St Thomas Street.

You will see the tower from the car park on a wooded mount opposite. Cross road and head up the path. You can walk straight to the tower 10 minutes moderate to strenuous or take an hour-long circular walk taking in the gatehouse arches to the west of the tower. Conygar is off the Macmillan Way West.

51.1870, -3.4441, TA24 6AS

8 BURROW FARM ENGINE HOUSE

Today in the Brandon Hills, all you will hear is the odd tractor, the distant baa of sheep or a gentle breeze rustling through the trees. There is little to indicate the bustle and noise of the iron ore industry that once took place here. Two of the most impressive ruins left are the winding house and Burrow Farm Engine House. The winding house would have housed the massive cables needed to haul the loaded carriages up the Incline railway. A short walk from the winding house, along the route of the old West Somerset mineral railway, you'll find the engine house. It was built in around 1860 to house a Cornish pumping engine.

Ralegh's Cross (Raleigh on some maps) is on the B3224 15 miles NW of Taunton. Heading W past Ralegh's Cross Inn, look for winding house on L; pull-in here on R just as road begins to get wooded again. For engine house; from the Incline, take path W across 3 fields, turn L back towards main road. Turn R then L along a minor road. Follow this to the footpath along the old railway to Burrow Farm 51.1013, -3.41723.

51.1010, -3.3963, TA23 0LL

5

2

9 ST MICHAELS
BURROW MUMP

Although it may look like an ancient earthwork, Burrow Mump is actually a natural hill. It has been in use since around 937 and there has been a church since the 12th century. However the current church was built later, in the 15th century. It is a reasonable effort to get to the church up the hill which may have been a factor in its decline. After it had become a ruin there was an effort to raise money to save it, and among those who contributed were the politician William Pitt the Younger. However not enough money was raised as the project didn't have much local support. It seems parishioners were growing tired of their church on the hill and didn't want to go to the effort of climbing to the top anymore. The nearby King Alfred Pub serves fresh local food and sometimes plays live music.

Follow the A361 between Taunton and Street. From Taunton head through the village, around the mound. Parking is immediately on R. From Street look out for a house on L with shutters just before the village; parking is immediately after this on L.

51.0704, -2.9161, TA7 0RB

10 ST LUKE'S CHAPEL
NEAR ABBOTSBURY

The 13th-century chapel at Long Bredy, near Abbotsbury, is simply enchanting. All that remains is a single arch, a number of gravestones (including one for Sir David Milne-Watson, a notable gas industrialist), a carved wooden cross and the old altar upon which candles are still placed. The chapel once served the medieval village of Sterte but was left to fall into ruin as far back as 1545.

Heading W from Abbotsbury on B3157, take first R signed 'Ashley Chase Only'. Private roads lead to St Luke's so you need to park outside the boundaries of the estate to access it. Park at the triangle at the top of the hill 50.6825, -2.6280. Take footpath/lane to R, continue to pedestrian gate on R, follow path through woods to the church. It is a 10-15 minutes moderate walk.

50.6894, -2.6272, DT3 4JZ

2

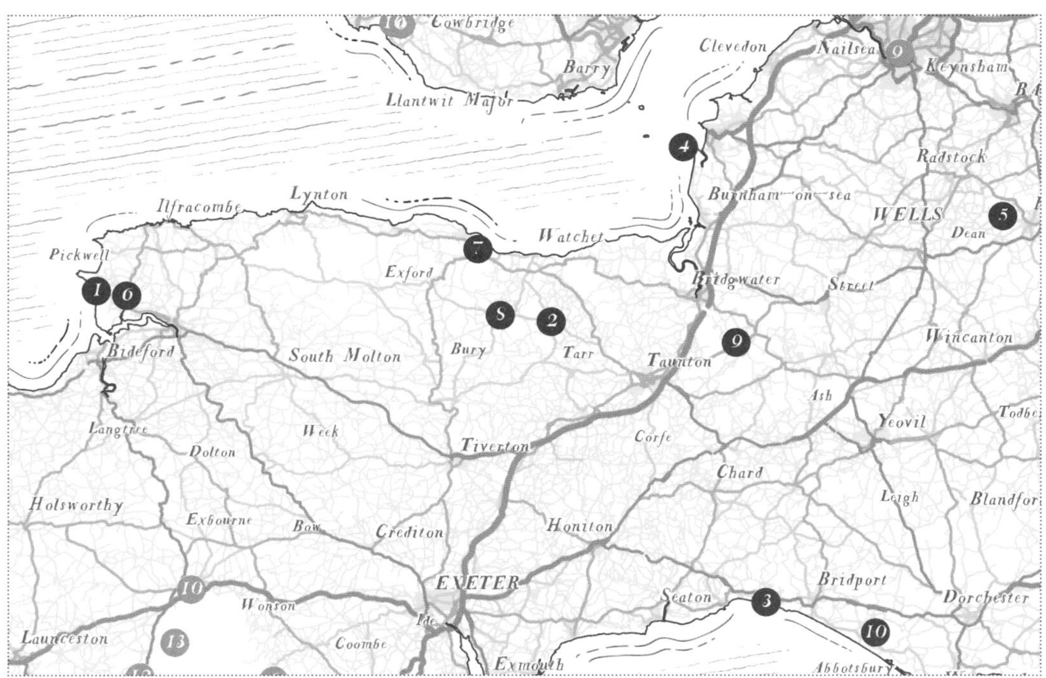
Cowbridge
Barry
Llantwit Major
Clevedon
Nailsea
Keynsham
Radstock
Burnham-on-sea
WELLS
Dean
Ilfracombe
Lynton
Watchet
Pickwell
Exford
Bridgwater
Street
Bideford
South Molton
Bury
Tarr
Taunton
Wincanton
Ash
Yeovil
Langtree
Week
Corfe
Tiverton
Dolton
Chard
Holsworthy
Leigh
Exbourne
Bow
Crediton
Honiton
EXETER
Bridport
Seaton
Dorchester
Wonson
Launceston
Coombe
Exmouth
Abbotsbury

CHAPTER 4

DORSET, WILTSHIRE & THE NEW FOREST

I

The large chalk plateau of Salisbury Plain is a place of contradictions. Since before the Second World War, the British Army has used the area, along with large parts of the Dorset countryside, for military exercises. On both the coast and the plain there are examples of ghost villages, abandoned by their communities. Two of these, Imber and Tyneham, were commandeered for use by the War Office (now MoD) as training grounds. In both cases the residents were forced out, given only a few weeks to leave. Tyneham is open to the public at certain times, and you are able to wander freely into houses where features such as fireplaces, and even an old built-in washing basin, are still visible. Imber is still on an active firing range and open less often. With the village only accessible on a few days a year, it seems shrouded in secrecy, a mysterious village amid the lonely expanse of Salisbury Plain.

It might be assumed the presence of the military would be a destructive one, yet since the public has been excluded from these training areas the wildlife has thrived. As undisturbed, unimproved chalk land, the area also supports many species of rare invertebrates that in turn go towards feeding the plain's bird population – more than 300 different species have been recorded there. Along with the fauna, there are thriving populations of flora: the wild flowers include orchids, vetches, campanulas and the rare early gentian.

Another ghost village is the medieval hamlet of Knowlton, depopulated as a result of the Black Death. All that remains is the roofless church, sat on top of a much earlier earthwork.

Around the town of Salisbury itself, many visitors flock to the well-known attractions such as Stonehenge and Salisbury cathedral, perhaps neglecting the lesser known old Salisbury or 'Old Sarum'. Legend has it that an arrow was fired into the air from here to mark the foundations of the new cathedral. It promptly hit a deer who ran in the direction of the new city and came to its end where the new cathedral now lies.

One of the most striking ruins in the area is that of Old Wardour Castle. By the 18th century it had become a romantic ruin incorporated into the gardens of the New Wardour House, but in 1643 the castle was still a stronghold. During that year its strength was put to the test as 1,300 Parliamentary troops laid siege to the formidable fortress. With her husband away, 61-year-old Lady Blanche Arundell was left to defend the castle with just 25 trained troops and 25 or so servants. Despite being massively outnumbered they held out for five days before surrendering. The following year her son, Henry 3rd Lord Arundell, blew half of the castle up during a siege to win it back. It was damaged beyond repair and has been in ruins ever since.

1 *OLD WARDOUR CASTLE*
TISBURY

Set by a lake and woods, in rolling downland, this out-of-the-way castle has substantial remains, large grounds and romantic gardens to explore. It was built in the 14th century as a luxury fortified house but was badly damaged during the Civil War. By the 18th century, the castle was admired as a romantic ruin and became a feature in a landscaped garden. For the garden grotto, built around this time, stone was used from the castle and from nearby Tisbury stone circle. Today you can climb a spiral staircase to the top of the turrets for superb views over the countryside. The Wessex Ridgeway long distance path passes alongside the castle, offering excellent short strolls or long hikes in the area.

Head S out of Tisbury past station. Take R fork and look for English Heritage sign 1½ miles on L. Car park is 70 metres from the castle.

51.0365, -2.0888, SP3 6RR

2 *LUDGERSHALL CASTLE*
LUDGERSHALL, WILTSHIRE

Crumbling outside the picturesque little town of Ludgershall lie the weathered flint remains of Ludgershall Castle. There are earthworks and banks to climb and views across the surrounding countryside. Built in the 11th century by Edward of Salisbury, the Sheriff of Wiltshire, it was later owned by Henry III who converted the castle into a fortified house in the 13th century. By the 15th century much of the stone had been appropriated for local buildings, and the castle fell into disuse. There is a pleasant 1½-mile walk to nearby Collingbourne Woods from here, where the forest floor glows with bluebells in spring: follow the footpath north from the site. A 13-mile cycle ride, Ludgershall Loop, starts not far from the castle. It runs alongside the A342 before taking a right down Reith Way in Charlton then snaking back to Ludgershall along country lanes.

7 miles NW of Andover on the A342. Once in Ludgershall follow the English Heritage signposts to car park. 2 mins walk from castle car park.

51.2597, -1.6230, SP11 9QT

3 *TYNEHAM VILLAGE*
KIMMERIDGE

The ghost village of Tyneham feels like it's caught in time, as if life has stood still since the residents hastily departed. You are free to pass in and out of the houses which, although completely gutted and roofless, still give an insight into how villagers would have lived in the 1930s. Residents were given just one month to evacuate during the Second World War as their homes were needed as a training ground for the D-Day landings. It is much more complete than Imber village, making it a very unusual but compelling tourist destination. The old school and church have been turned into museums giving the natural and social history of the area. Tyneham village, and its beautiful beach (Worbarrow Bay) is still on MOD land, but the area is open most weekends (check at dorsetforyou.com/lulworth-range-walks). Nearby is Grange Arch or Creech Folly, built in the form of a triple arch (50.6356, -2.1249). There is parking off Grange Hill (50.6348,-2.1362). From here a footpath leads to the site.

Heading SE on A351 towards Swanage and head past Corfe Castle then turn R signposted Church Knowle, Steeple and Kimmeridge. Continue toward Steeple, avoiding the Kimmeridge turn. At Steeple Leaze Farm follow road to R and up hill. Take L turn by gate with green portacabin. After 1/3 mile head L down into Tyneham valley.

50.6224 ,-2.1687, BH20 5DE

4 *CHRISTCHURCH CASTLE AND NORMAN HOUSE*

Christchurch Castle and Norman House are set in parkland in the middle of Christchurch. The stone keep was built in 1300 replacing an earlier wooden castle. The Norman House is more complete with one of the few remaining Norman chimneys still intact.

Christchurch Castle and Norman House are on Christchurch High Street. The nearest parking is in the Priory car park.

50.7339, -1.7765, BH23 1AS

5 HORTON TOWER
HORTON, WIMBORNE

Horton Tower was built in 1750, an imposing seven-storey gothic folly set on a small hill amid peaceful Dorset farmland. It once had the title of the tallest non-religious building in England. It was built by Humphrey Sturt, an MP and wealthy landowner. One story goes that he built it so he could watch the local hunt when he was too old and infirm to take part anymore. You can't enter the tower, but it's a wonderful surprise to see in the otherwise typically English countryside, a fantastically eerie remnant of the past.

From Horton village follow the road south to Chalbury Common and Wimbourne. There is a pull-in just before the Chalbury Common sign, opposite Chase View BH21 7ER. The path to the folly is behind you on the opposite side of the road.

50.8602, -1.9581, BH21 7EP

6 OLD SARUM
SALISBURY

This settlement, set on a semi-natural hilltop, has a long and varied past. Its visitors come for the wonderful views and the incredible sense of history that wandering around these ancient remains can bring. It seems that almost every civilization in the British Isles has, at one time, made a claim to Old Sarum and its surrounds. Arguably, the first settlers to the hilltop were Neolithic and there is evidence to suggest some Iron Age activity on the site too. Roman next settled in the area and Saxons settlers used it as a fort, defending themselves against Viking invaders. Later still the Norman town of Sarisberie, with its stone castle and royal palace, stood on this mound outside the present city of Salisbury. A cathedral was built here in the 11th century which was damaged by a storm just five days after being consecrated. The cathedral ruins we see today are a later construction dating back to the early 12th century.

Old Sarum is 2 miles N of Salisbury off the A345. It comes up quite quickly as you leave the city boundary, look L just past signs for the Harvester Pub.

51.0933, -1.8048, SP1 3SD

7 CORFE CASTLE
PURBECK HILLS

It is almost impossible not to gasp with wonder at the first sight of Corfe Castle, whose splendidly romantic ruins are set on a steep hill. This picturesque castle once dominated the landscape from its strategic position in a gap between the Purbeck Hills (the word Corfe derives its name from the Saxon word for gap) and from the top of the hill there are superb views. The castle was built by William the Conqueror in the 11th century but the stone castle that remains today took shape over the following 200 years. During the Civil War it was the last remaining Royalist stronghold in southern England. It was twice laid to siege before Parliamentarians won the castle and eventually destroyed it in 1645. There are games and activities for children of all ages including a dressing up box with costumes for mini-knights and micro-princesses and a Castle Quest activity booklet. The grounds of the castle are perfect for a picnic and the banks great for a mighty big roll down.

On A351, 4 miles SE of Wareham. National Trust car park a few hundred yards away.

50.6338,-2.0535, BH20 5EZ R

8 IMBER VILLAGE
WARMINSTER

As you travel across the wide open expanse of Salisbury Plain to Imber you get a very clear sense of how isolated this village once was. This intimate community would have been quite self-sufficient and protected from outside dangers such as plague. However isolation wasn't without its downsides. The road into Warminster was long and during bad weather the village would be cut off for days or weeks on end. Highwaymen took full advantage of this, regularly holding up farmers returning from market. The British Army first took up residence here in 1897, using the remote area as a training ground for large guns. Life for villagers became increasingly stressful and by 1943 Imber was fully surrounded by live firing ranges on all sides. Safety for its inhabitants could not be guaranteed so the War Office made the decision to evacuate and gave the remaining 135 villagers just 47 days to pack up their things and leave. Now the village is a haven for wildlife.

Hoverflies pollinating the lime trees outside the manor house are so numerous that they are almost deafening and rare wild flowers grow all over the village. Imber is a fascinating place to visit but is only open on a few days each year (see imberchurch.org.uk).

From Warminster Town Centre, continue on Market Place and head E past Nationwide bank, over mini-roundabout onto East St. Go past Esso garage and Rose and Crown pub. Turn L onto Imber Rd. Stay on this to entrance to firing range. You will be allowed to pass through if range is open to public. Continue for 4 miles to village, where there is parking. It is possible to cycle to the village, or book a seat on the special 23A bus service from Warminster.

51.2358, -2.0502, SN10 4NG

9 *CLARENDON PALACE*
SALISBURY

Although there isn't much left of this ruin it is set in particularly beautiful Wiltshire farmland, and where the views to Salisbury Cathedral are wonderful. A friendly family of alpacas shares the field with the ruin, making a visit here a somewhat surreal experience. Clarendon Palace was once a site of great importance. In the 12th and 13th centuries it was a royal residence. During the reign of Henry II it was the site of the Assize of Clarendon, a royal act that transformed medieval law away from trial by ordeal, towards trial by evidence and inquiry – and led to the trial by jury that we have today. The Clarendon Way is a long distance track which runs between Salisbury Cathedral via the Clarendon Palace to Winchester Cathedral. It has been reported to be anything from 24 to 27 miles in length. Perhaps the shorter length is to encourage people on the walk and the longer is what you boast about afterwards?

Head out of Salisbury on the A36 Southampton road and take L at the lights onto New Petersfinger Rd, just past park and ride. Keep on this road then take R at T-junction down Queen Manor Rd. Park before gates marking the private road (for cars) into the estate SP5 3BS, walk down the private road until it joins Clarendon Way, which leads across a field then up a track to the ruin.

51.0703, -1.7422, SP5 3ET

10 *KNOWLTON CHURCH*
KNOWLTON

This ruined 12th-century Norman church is a great spot for a picnic and kids will enjoy running around its grassy banks and ditches. Originally built in the centre of a Neolithic earth-built henge, it may be that the siting of the church was a deliberate way of encouraging the population to convert to Christianity. The village of Knowlton thrived for centuries before being wiped out by the Black Death in 1485. Despite the disappearance of the village, the church continued to be in use until 1747 when a new roof was fitted. It is said the roof promptly collapsed, marking the end of the church's use. Later the church bell vanished and legend has it that the Devil stole it and threw it the nearby River Allen, cursing it to never be retrieved. More than likely it was stolen by thieves who soon realised that carrying a giant bell might be beyond their capability and ditched it in the river before they were caught.

Head N on B3078 from Wimbourne Minster. After around 7 miles church will be signed L. There is a pull-in with limited parking.

50.8920, -1.9674, BH21 5AE

10

3
Ubley
Radstock
Westbury
Marden
Brunton
Upton
Enford
WELLS
Frome
Tilshead
Milston
Amport
Andover
Warminster
Shepton Mallet
Kentsboro
Wonston
Wylye
Mere
Wilton
Pitton
Wincanton
SALISBURY
Brook
Fovant
Shaftesbury
Nunton
Belbins
Tidpit
Yeovil
Haydon
Manston
Dean
Fordingbridge
Durley
Totton
SOUTHAMP
Leigh
Droop
Blandford Forum
Verwood
Ringwood
Bank
Hythe
Hilfield
Plush
Wimborne Minster
Avon
Sway
Lepe
Poole
Hordle
Dorchester
Yarmouth
Wareham
Newpo
Fleet
Weymouth
Swanage
Kingston
Brook
Pyle

CHAPTER 5

WYE VALLEY & BRISTOL AREA

Bristol has a friendly relaxed West Country feel yet the real buzz of a metropolis, making it unique and a gem of a city. Bristol was nominated European Green Capital 2015, and among its urban streets are little escape routes for its wildlife and human residents. The blitz-damaged churches of Temple Church and St Peter's are just two examples. Tucked away within the city centre, they make a perfect stop-off for a quick bite to eat or a more relaxed picnic. A little way from the city centre, another sign of the war can be seen in a little-known suburb. The large expanse of Purdown, with its high vantage point, was seen as a perfect spot for gun emplacements built to take down incoming German planes. The concrete blocks that marked their position can still be seen but nowadays you are more likely to find wild raspberries and blackberries than heavy artillery. In easy reach of the city is the rousing landscape of the Wye Valley. In the late 18th century artist and author William Gilpin wrote about the valley in the rather catchily titled 'Observations on the River Wye and Several Parts of South Wales'. At the time, the industrial revolution seemed to be coming at a breakneck speed; fearing what could be lost forever, the population sought the need to connect with a vanishing yet romanticised past. So, despite the name, Gilpin's book soon became a best seller and thousands flocked to the Wye Valley area. The abbey at Tintern became a hotspot, as tourists turned up with their sketch pads and canvases in much the same way as we do with cameras today.

It is not hard to see what they saw, for the accessible wilderness of the Wye Valley and Bristol Channel are still beautiful places to visit. It is an important area for wildlife, with birds of prey such as peregrines, goshawks and buzzards nesting in the area around Symonds Yat. At the right time of year you may see birds preying on salmon, on the last stage of their epic 6,000 mile journey from the Sub-Arctic Atlantic.

1
6
2
4

1 RAG MILL
SLAUGHTERFORD

Slaughterford is a peaceful and pleasant little village. The remains of the mill and a high pressure boiler are just a short walk from the village down a leafy lane. The site is maintained by local volunteers, who have a gardening project there and are campaigning for money to keep the mill from falling into further ruin. Rag Mill or Overshot Mill, started life as a weaving mill, possibly dating back to the Middle Ages. During the 19th century it became one of the first paper mills in the country. The high pressure boiler was designed by Richard Trevithick, a Cornish engineer and early pioneer of steam transport. (He was also chief engineer at Ding Dong mine – see Cornwall chapter).

Slaughterford is just S of the A420, 7 miles W of Chippenham. Park near church, walk past cottages on raised path, road bends to L and footpath is on the R, entrance signposted Rag Mill. The mill is on private property but it can be seen from the path.

51.4629, -2.2329, SN14 8RF

2 DARK HILL IRONWORKS
ELLWOOD

The sprawling remains of this Victorian ironworks peer out from among the trees, giving the appearance of a Mayan Temple in the middle of the Wye Valley. It is best viewed from the high vantage point on the main path but closer views can be gained on a lower path. From the low path you will find a picturesque, seldom visited millpond. On a late spring visit wispy, wind-dispersed seeds fill the air. Dark Hill Ironworks were home to the dark tale of Robert 'Forester' Mushet and the villainous Sir Henry Bessemer. History tells us that it was Bessemer we have to thank for inventing the 'Bessemer process', a way of metal working, whereby cheap and plentiful steel could be produced. However, it was thanks to the thousands of experiments by Mushet at Dark Hill that this process could produce impurity-free and therefore commercially viable steel. The site is just off one of the Wye Valley's best cycle tracks which runs from Coleford to Parkend where you can zoom through the trees under your own steam.

Park at Forestry Commission car park 51.7748, -2.5983 between Milkwall and Ellwood. Follow path at back of car park, take RH fork and follow to viewing platform.

51.7763, -2.5954, GL16 7LX

3 PARKEND FARMHOUSE
PARKEND

A ruined house not far from Dark Hill Ironworks, Ellwood. Possibly linked to the ironworks in the area.

From Fountains Inn, Parkend, go L down Fountain Way. Turn R at T-junction, then first L and park at pull-in. Follow track; ruin is covered in nettles on left.

51.7710, -2.5649, GL15 4JH

4 TINTERN ABBEY AND ST MARY'S

The Cistercian Abbey at Tintern has to be one of the most well-known ruins in the country. Part of its appeal is its stunning location in this picturesque valley. The large Gothic windows frame the wooded landscape perfectly and you can tell why it helped spur the craze for romantic ruins in the 18th century. During this time, artists would come to paint the ruins in much the same way photographers visit sites nowadays. Tintern is no doubt a beautiful romantic ruin but it is not the only one worth visiting in the area. Up on the wooded hill overlooking the abbey are the remains of St Mary's church, where a church has stood since medieval times. The present church was rebuilt in 1866 and destroyed by fire in 1977, when a young man died. Ruins are always a reminder of the transience of human life and St Mary's is no exception. Explore with caution as the ruin is not secure.

Tintern Abbey is off the A466 and well signposted. For St Mary's, from the Abbey Hotel car park turn L and walk a few yards until you see a post box and Wye Valley Walk sign. Follow this up, past a bungalow with solar panels, up the steps and along the cobbled path. 10 minutes strenuous walk. St Mary's 51.6965,-2.6811.

51.6968, -2.6770, NP16 6SE

5 WOODCHESTER MANSION

Despite its missing windows, missing rooms and half-finished interior, Woodchester isn't technically a ruin but a building that was never completed. Commissioned by William Leigh, a Roman Catholic convert, it championed the then-fashionable Gothic Revival movement. Unfortunately after his death in 1873 the work stopped.

Oddly, his family did not share his passion for living in a damp, draughty Gothic mansion and wanted to level Woodchester and start again. They commissioned another architect, but his plans for an elaborate Italianate style mansion proved too costly. Plans were shelved and the mansion remained unfinished and unloved. Benjamin Bucknall, William Leigh's original architect, was no doubt heartbroken as his work was never completed. He wrote to Leigh's son: "there is nothing more sad to the sight than an unfinished work and it is even more forlorn than a ruin of a building which has served its purpose". Today the building is open on certain days, with tea room, guided tours and a live video of the Woodchester bat colony.

Just off B4066 (Stroud to Dursley road) near Nympsfield. Check website for open days (woodchestermansion.org.uk). The mansion is set in Woodchester Park (National Trust). Minibus to mansion runs from car park 51.7110, -2.2978. Note for Sat Navs: there is no entrance from A46.

51.7106, -2.2775, GL10 3TS

6 ST JAMES'S
LANCAUT

The 12th-century church of St James is all that remains of the medieval village of Lancaut. It lies in a picturesque loop in the river Wye forming a beautiful little peninsula of around 200 acres. In Saxon times the church would have been central to a vibrant community that lived at Lancaut. In 1710 this had dwindled to four households and by 1750 just two. By the 19th century, with a declining population and congregation, services began to take place in nearby Tidenham and only seasonal services were held at St James's. St James Church is not far from the start of the Offa's Dyke long distance path near Chepstow. It is well worth the diversion which branches off along the banks of the Wye at Woodcroft. It is a pleasant, moderate, 2-mile walk from Chepstow Castle (and a slightly more strenuous one back).

From Chepstow head N towards Tutshill and take the B4228. After Woodcroft take L down no-through road. Park on Lancaut Lane 51.6671, -2.6670. The church is accessible via signposted footpath to right. 20 mins strenuous walk.

51.6651, -2.6709, NP16 7JB

7 PENYARD CASTLE
WESTON UNDER PENYARD

Penyard Park is a throwback to the times of old country estates, with wild boar running free. The castle is nothing more than a single-walled ruin, but behind this is the more substantial ruin of Penyard House. During my visit I met the present owner who was friendly but very firm in reminding me that visitors should keep to the footpath. This only allows a distant viewing of both the house and castle but enough to make the trip worthwhile. I visited on a misty morning and watched the mist slowly clear from the wooded valley below. The view was breathtaking and stays with me as a very special moment.

Head E from Ross-on-Wye on the A40. At Weston under Penyard cross the roundabout then take the R behind the church and park. Walk up the road and head past Lawns Farm and keep to the footpath. Path bends to R and castle and house are down in the field on the L. 30-40 mins moderate walk.

51.9005, -2.5563, HR9 5TH

5

8 CHURCH OF ST MARY
AVENBURY

The church of St Mary's Avenbury holds the title for being the most haunted church in Herefordshire. It is on private property but clearly visible from the footpath especially in the winter. Lanes nearby are narrow and parking limited so best to park in Bromyard and walk down. The much less wild but more accessible Brockhampton Estate is 1¾ miles north east and has a pretty little ruined chapel in the grounds.

From Bromyard take the A44 by-pass E, go over the river and turn R. Continue for 1 mile follow road as it curves round to a staggered crossroads, take the road in the direction of Munderfield to the R, park next to the orchard and cross the road to follow the footpath to the church. It is hidden in a clump of trees in the RH corner of the field.

52.1755, -2.4964, HR7 4LD

9 ST PETER'S CHURCH
BRISTOL

The two blitz-torn churches of St Peter's and Temple Church lie close to the city centre. The roofless St Peter's dominates Castle Park and makes for a great spot to munch on a wide range of food such as veggie samosas, goat meat curry or falafel from nearby St Nick's market. The graveyard of Temple Church is now a public garden, perfect for a romantic stroll away from the hustle and bustle of the city. Although the ruins are locked you can still peer into the impressive St Peter's Church. Park in the Galleries car park; Castle Park is opposite the Newgate St Exit or walk to the top of Union St, past the Galleries (BS1 3XD).

Walk towards the main road from the train station and turn R, cross the roundabout and take Victoria St (signposted City Centre and Broadmead). Cross the road and take a R at Church St.

51.4520, -2.5870, BS1 6DE

10 ALMONRY GATE HOUSE
STANDISH

The 14th-century gatehouse was built by the Abbot of Gloucester. It now stands at the top of a private driveway but is visible from public land.

There are some nice walks around the area but those up for more of an adventure could park at the National Trust car park (GL6 6PR) and head over the hill for 2 miles. For a closer view, take B4008 N of Stonehouse for approx. 2 miles, turn L onto Standish La and park where you can. The arch is on the other side of the green.

51.7737, -2.2911, GL10 3DW

11 GOODRICH CASTLE
NEAR ROSS-ON-WYE

Climb to the top of the keep of this ancient castle for stunning views of the surrounding landscape. It is a great place for a family day for young and grown up families alike. There are plenty of spiral staircases to climb, battlements to look out over and even spooky dungeons. The castle was established in 11th century with the stone keep added in the mid to late 12th century. Full facilities including a café, a shop and baby changing facilities.

Goodrich is 5 miles SW of Ross-on-Wye, just E of A40.

51.8767, -2.6158, HR9 6HY

9

11

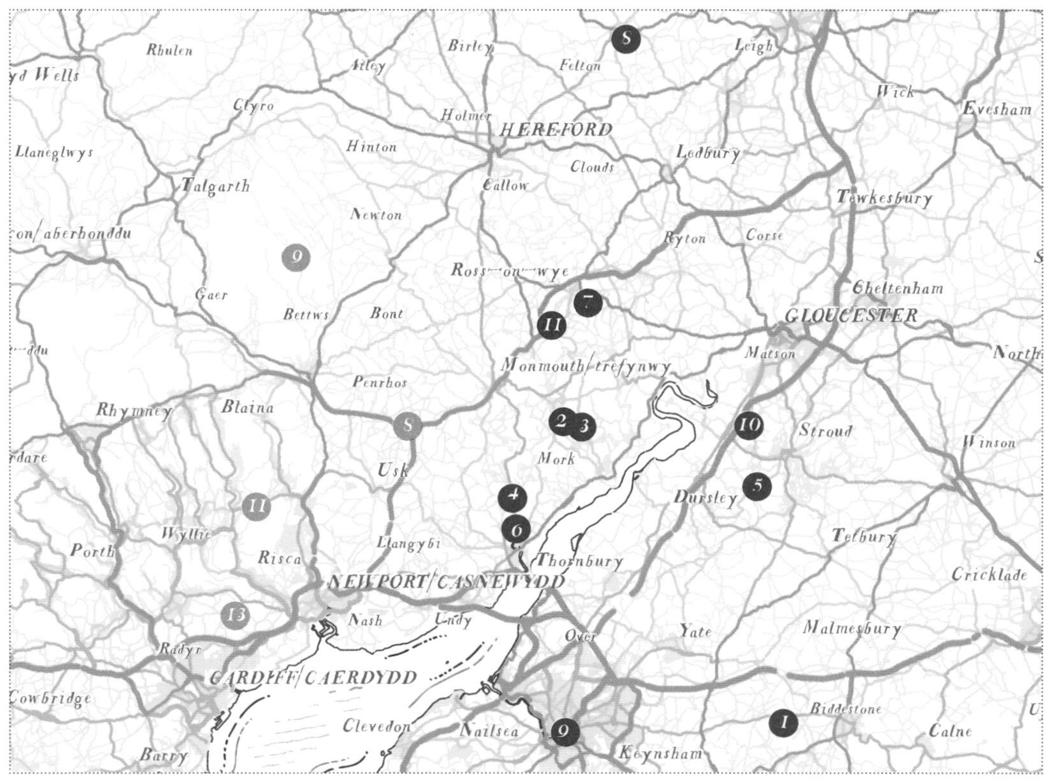
Rhulen
Birley
Felton
Leigh
Atley
Clyro
Wick
Evesham
Holmer
HEREFORD
Llaneglwys
Hinton
Clouds
Ledbury
Talgarth
Callow
Tewkesbury
Newton
Ryton
Corse
Ross-on-wye
Cheltenham
Gaer
Bettws
Bont
GLOUCESTER
Monmouth/trefynwy
Matson
Penrhos
Rhymney
Blaina
Stroud
Winson
Mork
Usk
Dursley
Wyllie
Llangybi
Tetbury
Porth
Risca
Thornbury
NEWPORT/CASNEWYDD
Cricklade
Nash
Undy
Yate
Malmesbury
Radyr
Over
CARDIFF/CAERDYDD
Cowbridge
Biddestone
Clevedon
Nailsea
Calne
Barry
Keynsham

CHAPTER 6

HAMPSHIRE AND ISLE OF WIGHT

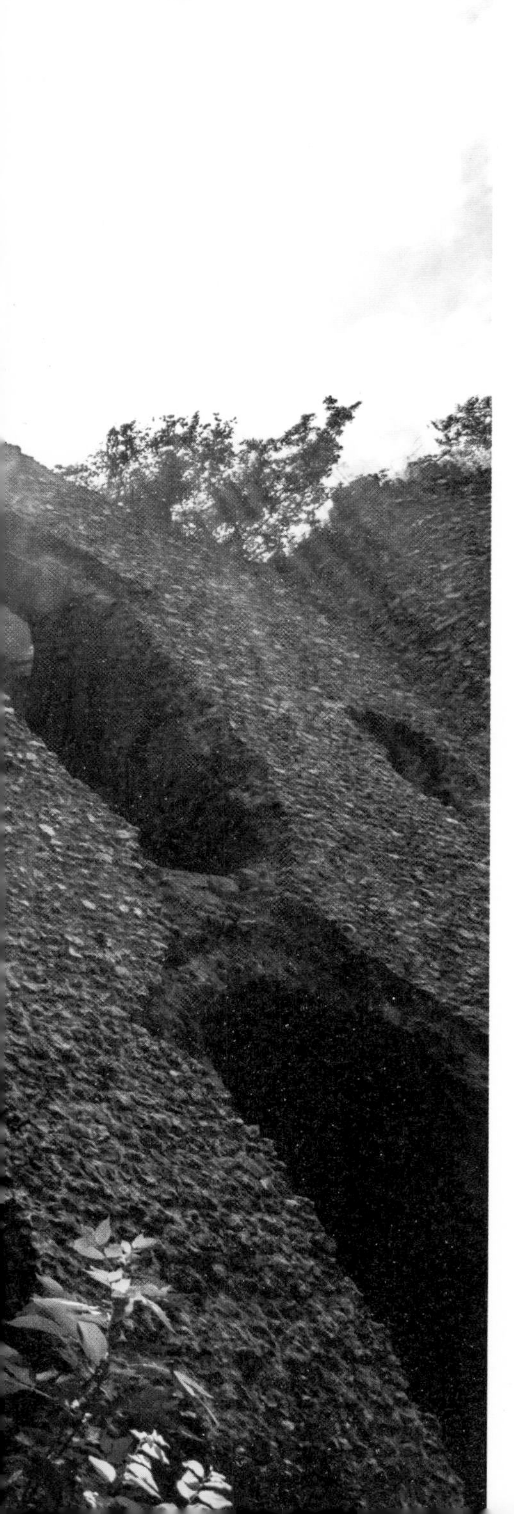

This large county was something of a surprise to me. How could anywhere 45 minutes from the huge sprawling metropolis of London be anything special? As I travelled through the expanse of the South Downs I was charmed by the open meadows, rolling hills, ancient woodland and near-perfect tiny villages. It may not be as wild as the Peak District or Cumbria but it has its own charm. From the late 18th to mid-19th century, artists, poets and writers came to the area to paint or walk around among the large romantic ruins. Amongst the famous visitors to Netley Abbey were the artists John Constable, Joseph Turner, Francis Towne and Samuel Prout. The romance of the abbey was not to be lost on Constable as he visited with his new wife during their honeymoon in 1816.

For centuries Hampshire has been a wealthy county, and even now it boast one of the highest standards of living in the UK. This has attracted wealthy landowners who have made their mark in the county's architecture. There are still the remains of many grand castles such as Cowdray, Donnington in Berkshire and Odiham. The strangest mark many of these landowners made was the building of large follies and they don't come any stranger or larger than Racton Folly near Petersfield.

Sitting within this chapter is one of the most personal ruins I came across during my journey and the only one that is within my living memory. The abandoned airbase at Greenham Common, Berkshire, was once home to the largest runway of any airbase in Europe and of course home to a large proportion of the country's nuclear arsenal. I was really too young know what was really happening but I remember the cold, stark feeling I felt as I realised the destructive power of the missiles housed at Greenham. The site has now been transformed into a nature reserve offering the surreal experience of watching bees pollinate wild flowers a stone's throw from a nuclear bunker.

1
2
3
4

1 ODIHAM CASTLE
NORTH WARNBOROUGH

Known locally as King John's Castle. In today's money it would have cost the equivalent of around £12 million to build. It took seven years and would have been a grand structure when work ceased in 1214. Only two years later the castle fell under siege from French forces and the tiny garrison, of just 13 people, was forced to surrender. All that is left today is part of the octagonal keep and surrounding earth works. The river and meadow leading up to the castle offer a pleasant stroll on a spring morning. Nearby, the Fox and Goose in Greywall, is an unspoilt country pub serving good food and real ales.

Come off the M3 motorway at Junction 5 and follow signs to Odiham and North Warnborough on the A287 then B3349. Head through Warnborough, past the garage, take the 2nd exit at roundabout (North Warnborough St) then the first R down Tunnel Lane. Park here at 51.2597, -0.9566. Cross the bridge, then follow riverside path to R to the castle.

51.2613, -0.9616, RG29 1HQ

2 NETLEY ABBEY
NEAR BURSLEDON

Built in a French-influenced Gothic style, the romance of Netley Abbey was not lost on artists and poets such as John Constable and William Sotheby. After a summer afternoon walk around its cloisters you too may feel inspired to pick up a brush or a pen – or simply to pick up a sandwich, to enjoy a picnic among the majesty of this 13th century ruin. Contemporary reports say there is an underground stream accessible, with a rope running through the abbey and out to the woods (where it is gated off). A local myth suggests the tunnel is guarded by a ghostly monk. The Cistercian monks who lived at Netley Abbey from the 13th century would have had an austere existence of contemplation and self sufficiency, with few personal possessions. The nearby Cottage Pub on the Woolston Road (SO31 5FN), has low beams, real ales, friendly staff and good food.

7 miles E of Southampton. From A3025 at Old Netley, take Grange Rd towards coast. Take R at T-junction. The abbey is on your R, off Victoria Rd. The abbey is free to enter, but only open at weekends.

50.8787, -1.3575, SO31 5HB

3 WOLVESEY CASTLE
WINCHESTER

Wolvesey Castle is a free-to-enter ruined grand house in the centre of Winchester. The city's bishops were amongst the most powerful in the country and a large residence was needed for the wealthy bishops of Winchester. Its thick walls would have protected the resident bishop in troubled times. There are lovely walks through water meadows to the palace along the river. The palace also marks the tail end of the Clarendon Way long distance path from Salisbury.

15 minutes ¾ mile from train station.

51.0591, -1.3099, SO23 9ND

4 DONNINGTON CASTLE
NEAR NEWBURY

The two great towers still have a commanding presence at the top of this steep hill overlooking the town of Newbury. Much of the gate-house remains along with a reconstructed outline of the curtain wall. When it was built in 1386, Donnington Castle would have overlooked two of the major roads in England, one heading north to south, the other east to west. In 1415 the castle was sold off and became the residence of Thomas Chaucer, son of the famous poet, Geoffrey Chaucer. During the Civil War, between 1644 and 1646 the castle fell under siege. Donnington eventually fell, and in April 1646 Colonel John Boys, along with his troops who were defending the castle, were granted permission to go free on account of their bravery during the siege. However, as punishment all but the gatehouse of the castle was destroyed. The vantage point of the castle means not only does it offer great views of Newbury, it is also a fantastic spot for sledging. A mile north of the site is Snelsmore Common Country Park, a beautiful spot for walkers and where it is said that you can hear the call of nightingales at dusk.

From the A4 at Donnington (between A34 and A339 north of Newbury) turn N onto Oxford Road, B4494 at the Waitrose roundabout. About ½ mile, L into Castle Lane, through gates until you reach the castle car park.

51.4196, -1.3381, RG14 2LA

5 GREENHAM COMMON
NEWBURY

Compared to its potentially destructive past this is now a thoroughly pleasant place to be, home to wild flowers, dog walkers and nesting populations of wild birds. Much of the old airbase building is now a business park but in the 1980s this was home to a large proportion of the UK's nuclear deterrent. Many of us are old enough to remember the news reports of the huge women's peace movement camping out at the site. At the height of these protests, 70,000 people formed a human chain from Greenham to the Atomic Weapon Research centre at Aldermaston. The main missile silos are fenced off but near these, to the west of the business park, there are various buildings and a memorial to the US troops who died in the Second World War (51.3754, -1.2936). On the other side of the park the control tower still stands.

Greenham is just off the A339 south of Newbury, heading to Basingstoke. Follow signs to the Greenham Common Business Park. You are able to park in the business park after hours. There is also parking at the eastern edge of the park off the Old Thornford Road 51.3781, -1.2528.

51.3773, -1.2903, RG19 6HX

6 RACTON FOLLY
NEAR WALDERTON

Racton Ruin isn't on any tourist map but it is well known among ghost hunters, Urban Explorers (Urbex), folly enthusiasts and even devil worshippers. It is over 80 feet tall, completely gutted and roofless, giving a spectacular view of the night sky from the central tower (that is if you dare go at night). Despite its spooky credentials and obvious neglect it is an intriguing place to visit. It has the feel of somewhere teenagers go with their friends, to tell ghost stories to try and scare each other witless. It was George Montagu-Dunk, the second Earl of Halifax who commissioned Racton Folly. There is no conclusive account to say why it was built; some say it was as a summerhouse, others a viewing point to watch ships come in from the Solent. It was constructed between 1766 and 1775 and designed by Theodosius Keene, the son of Henry Keene, the architect responsible for the Radcliffe Observatory in Oxford. Nearby Compton has a lovely shop.

From the A259 (off A27 between Chichester and Portsmouth) take the turning away from the coast to Southbourne station. Cross A27 take L to Westbourne, then R to Petersfield on B2147. Past church, park on R next to post box 50.8784, -0.8902 before B2146. Follow lane up to ruin.

50.8794, -0.8976, PO18 9DU

7 HURST CASTLE
NEAR KEYHAVEN

As you take the ferry ride to Hurst Castle you can imagine how 17th-century prisoners must have felt as they were shipped out to England's very own answer to Alcatraz Island. It was built by Henry VIII during a time when England was subjected to frequent French raids. It protected the passage to Southampton and to Henry's naval base at Portsmouth, home to his flagship the 'Mary Rose'. If you want a bit of exercise and don't want to take the ferry, the castle is connected to the mainland by a shingle spit and it is possible to walk the 1½ miles along the narrow coastal path to the castle.

Travel from Keyhaven, 4 miles SW of Lymington, off the A337. In Keyhaven, park in car park on the sea front. Take ferry (01590 642344) or walk to castle.

50.7072, -1.5514, SO41 0TP

8 TITCHFIELD ABBEY
FAREHAM

The magnificent turreted Tudor gatehouse dwarfs the nearby remains of Titchfield Abbey itself. Established in 1232 for Premonstratensian or White Canons, the abbey was later bought by Thomas Wriothesley, 1st Earl of Southampton, who built his grand gatehouse over the nave of the existing church. It is thought that Shakespeare performed some of his plays here and it had several royal visitors including Edward VI, Elizabeth I and Charles I. The gardens are lovely to walk around in any time of year and the 13th-century tiles give a fascinating insight into the interior of this ancient building. Lovely walks along the river Meon to Titchfield Haven on the coast.

Take Junction 9 off M27 to join the A27 S towards Fareham. After the second roundabout, turn L into Mill La. Park in the garden centre car park on L, and walk into ruin via the path opposite the Fishermen's Rest pub.

50.8568, -1.2314, PO15 5RA

9 ST CATHERINE'S ORATORY

This rocket-shaped medieval building stands on one of the highest points of the island. The walk up to it can be a strenuous one but the views from this hilltop are simply amazing. The story goes that a local landowner, Walter de Godeton, was forced to build the oratory as a penance for stealing wine destined for a French monastery.

6 miles W of Ventnor off A3055. 1½ miles W of Niton, look for car park at 50.5881, -1.3079 . 10 mins strenuous walk to St Catherine's Oratory.

50.5931, -1.3030, PO38 2JB

9

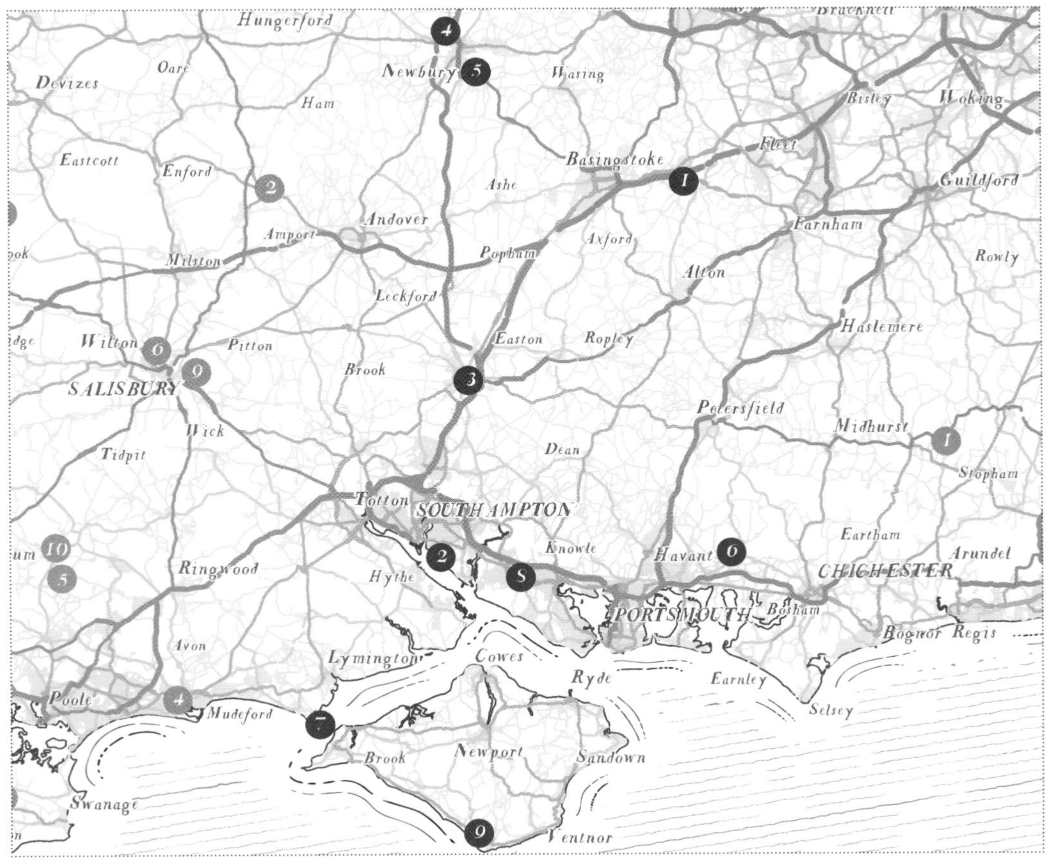
Hungerford
Newbury
Wasing
Devizes
Oare
Ham
Bisley
Woking
Fleet
Basingstoke
Eastcott
Enford
Ashe
Guildford
Andover
Amport
Axford
Farnham
Milston
Popham
Rowly
Alton
Leckford
Haslemere
Wilton
Pitton
Easton
Ropley
SALISBURY
Brook
Petersfield
Midhurst
Wick
Dean
Tidpit
Stopham
Totton
SOUTHAMPTON
Eartham
Knowle
Havant
Arundel
Ringwood
Hythe
CHICHESTER
PORTSMOUTH
Bosham
Avon
Bognor Regis
Lymington
Cowes
Ryde
Earnley
Poole
Mudeford
Selsey
Brook
Newport
Sandown
Swanage
Ventnor

CHAPTER 7

SUSSEX & THE HIGH WEALD

The High Weald stretches over the counties of Surrey, West Sussex, East Sussex and Kent. It is a vast medieval landscape protected for its forests and its unique heathland habitats. Nearly a quarter of the area is covered by ancient woodland making it one of the most forested areas of the country. Here dormice, deer and even a burgeoning population of wild boar have found a home. In the early spring the smell of wild garlic fills the air, followed by the later arrival of bluebells. When AA Milne wrote about the fictional, 100-acre wood in 'Winnie the Pooh' he took his inspiration from the Five Hundred Acre Wood, a very real corner of the Ashdown forest, part of the High Weald Area of Outstanding Natural Beauty. Visitors still flock to the area to get a glimpse of the small bear but it is thought he has become a recluse of late, only venturing out for essential supplies such as jars of honey or the odd Cottleston Pie.

The area has long since attracted wealthy landowners, such as the Richards family who owned the large spectacular ruin of Brambletye House. A ruin for hundreds of years, it has attracted artists since at least the 19th century, when they would come to paint the crumbling building as a romantic ruin. More recently, photography has brought people here to capture its decaying magnificence.

The Earls of Abergavenny (a somewhat geographically-displaced sounding family) are wealthy landowners who still live in the area; they own a vast estate at Eridge Park in Sussex. The 2nd Earl of Abergavenny seemed to have a penchant for tower follies. He built the remarkably intact Saxonbury Tower on an Iron Age hillfort and two more folly towers at Danegate.

1
2
6
5

1 BEDHAM CHURCH
BEDHAM

The enchanting ruin of Bedham church lies within the South Downs Area of Outstanding Natural Beauty between the bluebell woods at Flexham Park and the Sussex Wildlife Trust nature reserve called The Mens. Bedham Church was built in 1880 for a thriving community of charcoal burners who lived in the surrounding area. In Bedham, like many small communities at the time, in the absence of a local school it was down to the church to provide basic education. The church was used for worship and for education, and last thing on a Friday the chairs were turned away from the children's desks to face the altar.

Follow A272 out of Petworth as it heads N then E at mini-roadabout , take 4th R signposted Bedham, down single track road for ¾ mile, you may see it through the trees on your R. Pass the ruin and park in turning place/lay-by 50.9866, -0.5512, (sat nav to RH20 1JR but stay on lane, don't turn R) double back on yourself, pass the post box and look down to your L.

50.9882, -0.5534, RH20 1JR

2 BRAMBLETYE HOUSE
FOREST ROW

The three remaining towers of the 17th-century mansion at Brambletye, built by Sir Henry Compton, stand incongruously on a manicured lawn in the grounds of Brambletye Manor. During the late 17th century it was bought by Sir James Richards, a man of French extraction. There are inconclusive accounts of the life of Richards. Some stories claim that whilst he was out hunting, he heard word that he was wanted for treason, on account of arms having been found in his house. He immediately fled the country for Spain and his descendants were said to have taken up high ranks in the Spanish army. Historians have cast some doubt on this story, as the date of his departure to Spain 1683 came a year before Charles II of England awarded him the title of Baronet.

Head N from Forest Row on the A22 Lewes Rd. Just before the' reduce speed now' sign, take a L down Brambletye Rd. You can park here 51.1045, 0.0260 or follow the track down. Limited parking. The ruin is fenced off but there is plenty of it to see from this side of the fence.

51.1005, 0.0229, RH18 5EH

3 BRAMBER CASTLE
BRAMBER

Bramber Castle feels surprisingly hidden away, despite its proximity to the village of Bramber and the Steyning bypass. The remains of the stone keep are partially surrounded by trees and perch on the top of an earlier earthwork. Adding to the wild feel of the castle is the tree-lined protective ditch that surrounds the grounds. The whole site is a fun place to bring children with a sense of adventure and interest in history. The castle was founded in 1073 and held by William de Braose, and his descendants lived there until 1450.

Bramber is just off both the South Downs Way and the Monarch's Way long distance footpaths. Travelling N from Brighton on the A283, drive past the Upper Beeding turn off, stay on the A283 then take the next exit R down Castle Lane to car park. There are English Heritage signs to the castle.

50.8832, -0.3157, BN44 3XA

4 OLD KNEPP CASTLE
DIAL POST

Old Knepp Castle has been described as looking like a 'broken tooth' high on its mound overlooking the Worthing road. It is a good climb up to the single-arched remains which, for the best photographs, should be visited at dusk or dawn. References to a castle at Knepp date back to the mid-12th century. King John rebuilt the castle keep in stone in the early 12th century. It is suggested he would have stayed here leading up to his unsuccessful campaigns to regain lands in Normandy. As the small fields and heavy clay of Knepp estate mean it is not viable for any large scale arable farming, a unique conservation project is taking place there. Mixed farming of fallow deer, English longhorn cattle, Tamworth pigs and Dartmoor ponies (along with wild deer and rabbits) graze the land freely, creating a mosaic of habitats. This creates a viable alternative to crops whilst encouraging a diverse habitat for flora and fauna. The Countryman Inn, in nearby Shipley RH13 8PZ, is worth a stop off.

Heading N on A24 between Ashington and Horsham, just after Dial Post turn L down Castle Lane (just before the R turn to B2135). Park away from the driveways before the white gates. Walk through gates, across cattle grid and follow path up to R.

50.9758, -0.3448, RH13 8LH

5 DANEGATE TOWERS
ERIDGE PARK ESTATE

The Neville Family have owned land around the Eridge Park estate for more than 900 years, at which time their land stretched from there to the coast. When Henry Neville or the 2nd Earl of Abergavenny inherited the land in 1787 he wanted to make his mark. He demolished Eridge House and built a large Gothic-style castle from which he wanted to look out over follies and landscaped vistas, without an ugly building spoiling the view, so he had the two folly towers at Danegate and Saxonbury tower built. Please note that parts of the estate are private; Saxonbury Tower can only be viewed from Danegate road near Green Hedges Nursery.

Heading N from Crowborough on the A26 take a R after Eridge Station. Continue for approx. 1¾ miles past Sham Farm. Approx 230 metres after white semi-detached houses on R park on L 51.0754, 0.2332 postcode around TN3 9JA. Follow Sussex Border path until it branches R, continue forward to next field. Towers will be seen in clearing.

51.0800, 0.2370, TN3 9HU

6 MAD JACK'S FOLLIES
BRIGHTLING

At first sight Brightling looks like any pretty English village. It has a quaint collection of red brick houses, stone cottages, and a large manor house. There is also a large church with, in the churchyard, a large stone pyramid. The pyramid along with a temple, a ruined tower, an observatory, and large pointy building referred to as the Sugar Loaf are what makes Brightling a less than ordinary village. They were all the work of John Fuller, or Mad Jack as he became known. He was a Member of Parliament, a noted drunkard and a patron of the arts. Despite the nickname he was far from mad, for as an active philanthropist he financially supported the influential inventor Michael Faraday and bought Bodiam castle to save it from being demolished.

Travel S from Tunbridge Wells or N from Hastings on A21 to Robertsbridge. Head W past station, stay on the Brightling Rd until you reach the T-junction that marks the village of Brightling. There is a pull-in at 50.9633, 0.3986 just before the T. Pyramid 50.9636, 0.3964 in the churchyard, Temple 50.9578, 0.3911, Sugar Loaf 50.9512, 0.3750, Tower 50.9606, 0.4030. Off the road between Brightling and Twelve Oaks.

50.9636, 0.3964, TN32 5HJ

7 LEWES PRIORY
LEWES

Lewes Priory or The Priory of St Pancras, was founded in 1077 and was the first Cluniac Priory in the country. Up until this point monks had to participate in some form of hard labour, usually small-scale farming. The Cluniacs didn't like the sound of all this hard work and instead opted for a life of quiet contemplation, copying manuscripts and other such less physical tasks. The site was once much more extensive with a great church, larger than both Durham and Chichester cathedrals. A lot conspired against Lewes in subsequent years; the dissolution of the monasteries saw the demolishing of many of the buildings there. Later the railway from Lewes to Brighton destroyed the remains of the large church, along with associated buildings. The site was once so huge that, despite all of this, the remaining ruins are substantial. There are many information

5

panels that give you a more extended history of the site. The town of Lewes is worth a day out in itself. It has its own currency, the Lewes Pound, and many restaurants, cafés and independent shops in which to spend it.

Turn off the A27 onto A277 on the Brighton side of Lewes. After 1 mile turn R to Winterbourn Hollow, turn L on to Southover High St (B2193). Continue past Kings Head pub then follow 'Priory Parking' signs to Mountfield Rd car park 50.8693, 0.0110. Follow pedestrian signs to Priory Park.

50.8681, 0.0082, BN7 2XA

8 TIDE MILLS
NEWHAVEN

Tide Mills is a derelict coastal village in East Sussex, abandoned in the 1930s. Along with the foundations of the old hospital and scattered windswept coastal remains of homes, the ruins of the old tidal mill that gives the area its name can still be seen. It would have utilised water coming in from the sea through a sluice gate to a mill pond, and as the sea retreated the three mill wheels turned. A small community grew up around the mill when it was built in 1761. A small station and a hospital once existed in the village, the remains of which can still be seen. By 1939 the last resident had been evicted due to insanitary conditions; typically, the national press sensationalised the story dubbing the small community 'The Hamlet of Horror'. In a strange twist of fate, the empty village was later used by the army for street fighting training. The village was the setting for Lesley Thomson's book 'A Kind of Vanishing'. The story centres around a game of hide and seek where the seeker, Alice, instead of finding her friend Eleanor, disappears.

Tide Mills is situated off the Seaford Rd A259. Heading away from Newhaven the turning is on the R just before the boundary sign to Seaford. Small height-restricted car park just off road.

50.7824, 0.0699, BN25 2TW

9 NYMANS ESTATE
HANDCROSS

The once grand Gothic mansion house on the Nymans Estate is now a hollowed-out romantic ruin. Despite being gutted by fire, the gardens were maintained and at any time of year there is something to see in the grounds of this exceptional estate.

A wander into the woods is recommended and book lovers might find a bargain or two in the second-hand book shop. Along with the fantastic gardens, the grounds boast the tallest tree in Sussex.

51.0505, -0.1984, RH17 6EB

10 PEVENSEY CASTLE
PEVENSEY

As you enter the weathered remains of Pevensey Castle via the bridge across its moat you get a sense of the importance of this stronghold. Dating from the 4th century Pevensey is one of the last standing 'Saxon Shore' forts built by the Romans. The castle was the landing place of William the Conqueror's army. The dungeons, including the grated 'Oubliette' or forgotten place, show what a grim place this must have been to be imprisoned.

Castle Road, Pevensey, East Sussex

50.8193, 0.3339, BN24 5LE

10

S

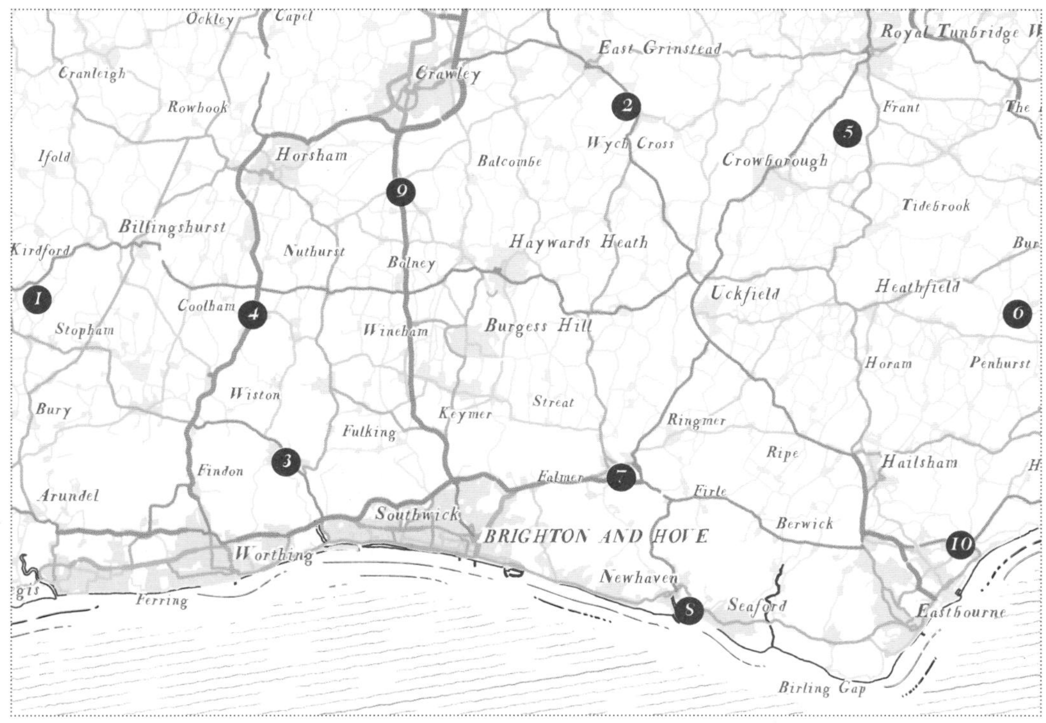
Ockley
Capel
Royal Tunbridge
East Grinstead
Cranleigh
Crawley
Rowhook
2
Frant
5
Ifold
Horsham
Balcombe
Wych Cross
Crowborough
9
Tidebrook
Billingshurst
Kirdford
Nuthurst
Bolney
Haywards Heath
1
Coolham
4
Uckfield
Heathfield
6
Stopham
Wineham
Burgess Hill
Horam
Penhurst
Wiston
Bury
Keymer
Streat
Ringmer
Fulking
Findon
3
Ripe
Hailsham
Arundel
Falmer
7
Firle
Southwick
Berwick
BRIGHTON AND HOVE
10
Worthing
Newhaven
Ferring
S
Seaford
Eastbourne
Birling Gap

CHAPTER 8

KENT & ESSEX

Estuaries, heritage coastline, big horizons, nature reserves and of course the chalk downs with rare orchids and unique birdlife make up the two large coastal counties of Kent and Essex. Within easy reach of the capital, they are perfect for a day trip or weekend away.

The position of these two counties, so close to France and flanking the Thames estuary, has meant they have been of strategic importance since Iron Age times. A line of defences dating from prehistory to the Second World War can still be seen across the shoreline. Other than earthworks there are few signs of the earliest of these but there are remains of a number of Roman forts such as Richborough and another at Reculver. Reculver later became home to the 12th century iconic towers of St Mary's Church but the Roman fort would have guarded the now silted up Wantsum channel which cut off the Isle of Thanet (where modern Ramsgate and Margate stand) from the Kent mainland.

Later large castles were built to defend these shores. One example is that of Hadleigh, built by Hubert de Burgh on the Thames estuary near Benfleet. Burgh was effectively governing the country at this time as Henry III was just nine years old when he came to power. With such a precarious reign Burgh had Hadleigh built as much a statement of power as a defensive structure.

During the First World War and interwar period, before the invention of radar, an early detection device was needed to warn of incoming enemy planes. The answer came in the shape of large concrete parabolic discs, known as sound mirrors. They were staffed by personnel with stethoscopes who would quite literally listen to what was flying in. As planes became faster these sound mirrors became obsolete, since once a plane was detected it was already over the head of the listener. Sadly many have fallen into disrepair or vanished completely but a large collection stands at Denge and a very accessible single mirror can be seen at Abbot's Cliff between Dover and Folkestone. Another, at Fan Hole on the iconic White Cliffs of Dover, has recently been discovered.

During the Second World War, civil engineer Guy Maunsell was commissioned to design a number of offshore forts to act as a stationary, first line of defence. They were vast steel and concrete constructions, the largest of which could accommodate up to 265 men. Four naval forts were constructed: Rough Sands, Sunk Head, Tongue Sands and Knock John plus three Army forts: Nore, Red Sands and Shivering Sands. The forts came into operation in 1943 and shot down 22 planes, 30 flying bombs and one U-boat during their service. Today you can take an adventurous boat trip and explore one of the remaining forts at Redsands.

1
3
2

1 HADLEIGH CASTLE
NEAR BENFLEET

Hadleigh dates back to 1230 when it was under the Stewardship of Hubert de Burgh. King Edward III later set about enlarging and refortifying the site in 1360-70. Rather than a castle built in the sand, Hadleigh Castle was built on London clay which is susceptible to landslides. By the 17th century a mixture of this unstable land, along with neglect, had all but left the castle in ruins. The 18th and 19th-century trend for romantic ruins meant the castle came back into its own and was painted by John Constable in 1829. Today just two large towers remain, along with fragmentary sections of wall. Visit towards the end of the summer and you'll find Hadleigh is a fantastic site for foraging, with rose-hips, haws and blackberries along with many coastal forageable goodies. The Salvation Army own nearby Hadleigh Farm and run a pleasant tea room near the site.

Hadleigh is 5 miles W of Southend-on-Sea. Take Chapel La off A13 in Hadleigh just past Morrisons heading NW, park at 51.5524, 0.5946 and walk from Hadleigh Country Park (1-2 miles depending on route taken). Or take Castle La, just off High St, opposite the green in centre of Hadleigh. Limited parking at end of Castle La. 51.5474, 0.6072.

51.5441, 0.6096, SS7 2AP

2 ST RADIGUND'S ABBEY
ALKHAM VALLEY

St Radigund's sits within the Alkham Valley, an Area of Outstanding Natural Beauty between Dover and Folkestone. The large gatehouse still has an imposing presence making this a worthwhile stop-off during a visit to the area. It was established in 1191 by Premonstratensians or White Canons. It took more than 50 years to build and by the reign of Edward I it would have been a site of national importance. Sadly, some 200 years later, things were a different story, for by 1500 John Newynton (or Newton), the abbot, had let things slide and it was falling into a ruinous state. He was in debt and it was said that he was found drinking in taverns and using bad language. There are self-catering converted barns at the abbey (Abbey Farm Holidays), with access to parts of the site otherwise only accessible on Heritage Open Days (heritageopendays.org.uk).

Alkham is 5 miles W of Dover. Head W from Buckland Hospital, Dover, at roundabout take 2nd exit, Barwick Rd for 1½ miles, then Abbey Rd to crossroads and postbox. Pull in on Minnis La or Abbey Rd itself. Avoid parking in front of local residents' gates.

51.1326, 1.2514, CT15 7DL

3 ST MARY'S
LITTLE CHART

The Church of St Mary is a rather lovely little ruined church set in the Kent countryside. The ivy-clad walls and large arched doorway make it a very photogenic site. It is in a very quiet and out-of-the-way area, making it a perfect place for a picnic. It dates from the mid-13th century but like many churches was added to. Construction was thought to have ended around the 16th century. It was once the private Anglican church of the Darell family. When the family line leaned more towards Catholicism in the 18th century, the church was neglected and left to fall into ruin. The already-depleted church fell into further ruin when it took a direct hit from a stray Second World War doodlebug.

Off the A20 at Charing, 6 miles NW of Ashford. Head S from Charing Station on Pluckley Rd for almost 2 miles. On L you'll see a sign to 'Chart Court Liveries', turn into church car park with noticeboard 51.1869, 0.7666 rather than into the farm.

51.1866, 0.7669, TN27 0QH

4 ST MARY'S
EASTWELL

The Church of St Mary Eastwell has one of the most impressive settings of any ruined church. It lies beside the largest lake in Kent in Eastwell Park. The church roof collapsed in 1951 and in 1981 it came under the care of the Friends of Friendless Churches. The 15th-century south wall and tower remain, alongside a mortuary chapel that dates from the 19th century. The church is just off the Pilgrim's Way and the North Downs Way long distance paths.

Head out of Ashford, N on A251. Follow signs to Potters Corner, down Sandyhurst La, take RH fork Lenacre St, follow for ¾ mile, then take the first R. Follow to a pull-in at approx. 51.1899, 0.8742 where the road is gated off.

51.1900, 0.8745, TN25 4JT

5 *OARE GUNPOWDER WORKS* FAVERSHAM

The ruins of Oare Gunpowder Works lie in a wooded glade with running leats, or ditches, and large open lakes. These may well be among the oldest gunpowder works in the country. In 1605 the works became notorious, for 36 barrels of gunpowder made there found their way to conspirator Guy Fawkes in his plot to blow up the Houses of Parliament. When John Hall & Son owned the factory in the Victorian era, the company had the ironic motto of 'in tumultibus me videbus', loosely translated as 'whenever there is trouble we are around'. There was indeed some truth in this motto as gunpowder produced here and at nearby Chart was used during the Opium Wars (a series of conflicts in the 19th century), at the battles of Trafalgar (1805) and Waterloo (1815) as well as during the First World War. The site of Oare Gunpowder Works is now a small country park to the north of Faversham.

From the A2 between Sittingbourne and Faversham take the exit on the roundabout signposted to Oare B2045. Take first L, Bysing Wood Rd, then turn R following signs into Oare Gunpowder Works. Or 333 Bus to Oare from Maidstone.

51.3247, 0.8718, ME13 7UD

6 *STONE CHAPEL* FAVERSHAM

On a summer's day, follow a path through waist-high corn to the ancient ruin of a stone chapel at Faversham. It lies in a field just off the old Roman Road of Watling Street, now the A2. The proximity to the Roman road is not by chance as this is a rare example of a Roman mausoleum (a tomb standing above ground) to be incorporated into a Christian church.

It is not far from Oare Gunpowder Works and is a little W of Faversham, just N of the A2 – well signposted from the road. Park before the bridge in lane adjacent to the field.

51.3161, 0.8565, ME13 0TR

7 *RECULVER TOWERS* AND ROMAN FORT

The ruined towers of St Mary's Church at Reculver sit high overlooking the sea just up from Herne Bay. The church was once at the head of the three-mile wide Wantsum Channel which cut off the Isle of Thanet, the area of land which is now Ramsgate, Margate and Broadstairs, from mainland England. The original building was built in 669AD almost entirely from pillaged stone from a nearby Roman fort. The dramatic two towers that you can see today were a later edition, in the 12th century. At sunset the site is at its most striking and on a clear day photographers flock to the site and tussle for the best vantage points for their shots. It is accessible by bike, just off the Oyster Bay Trail (regional route 15) a 7-mile linear route from Swalecliffe (Chesterfield & Swalecliffe station) to Reculver. The Thanet coastal path (Ramsgate to Herne Bay via Margate) also runs past the site.

5 miles E of Herne Bay. Take turning N of A299 up Brook La signposted Marshside, follow this until you see a sign to Reculver ¾ mile on the right. Follow lane past pub then park in Reculver Country Park car park.

51.3770, 1.1940, CT6 6SS

8 *SOUND MIRROR* ABBOT'S CLIFF

Not far from the White Cliffs of Dover, the Abbot's Cliff sound mirror is a fantastic example of eccentric technology. Before the advent of radar, large 'sound mirrors' were constructed on the shores of norht-east and southern Britain to warn of approaching enemy planes. There are also sound mirrors at Denge, on Romney Marsh near Dungeness, 20 miles to the west. The Romney Marsh Countryside Partnership (01797 367934) holds annual tours but they are off-limits for the rest of the year.

From A20 Dover-Folkestone take B2011 sign-posted Capel-le-Ferne. Park in first lay-by 51.1035, 1.2369 and walk alongside road until you reach the cycle path. Take the route marked Dover for about ½ mile.

51.1017, 1.2347, CT18 7HZ

9

10

9 OTFORD PALACE
OTFORD

Otford Palace is an interesting stop on the Pilgrim's Way/North Downs Way. The large weeping willow and grassy grounds on the approach to the palace make it a pleasant place for a picnic. Although you can't enter it you are able to peer into the building to get a sense of its past grandeur. It was built in 1514 by Archbishop Warham and was once a rival to Hampton Court. It played host to Edward I, Henry VII and Henry VIII. In fact Henry VIII liked it so much he took it for himself in 1538. Otford is tucked away, close to habitation but still out of the way enough to make it a pleasant place for a picnic.

Otford is on the A225, 3 miles N of Sevenoaks. Park off A225 near post office. Follow footpath behind post office.

51.3113, 0.1910, TN14 5PB

10 CLIFFE FORT
ROCHESTER

Cliffe Fort is a large Victorian fort built in the 1860s which has sadly now fallen into a state of disrepair. It was built on the Hoo peninsula to defend the Thames estuary. The fort had an early example of a land-to-sea torpedo and its steel chains and launch bay are still visible. Locals in the area talk of strange wildlife around the fort. Wild lynx have been spotted and from the mid-1970s a number of escaped flamingos would visit the site on an annual migration. Neither have been seen in recent years but Cliffe Pools is a great place for bird watching. The fort is fenced off but much of it can be seen from the footpath.

Park in car park at nearby Cliffe at 51.4614, 0.4970. Head up Butway La, take R then as the road runs out follow the Saxon Shore Way to coast and fort. 2 miles easy walk.

51.4636, 0.4557, ME3 7TG

11 MAUNSELL FORTS
THAMES ESTUARY

Visiting one of the Maunsell Forts is a real adventure. You'll take a boat ride over the waters of the Thames Estuary past wild seals and seabirds before climbing into these decaying capsules of history. During the beginning of the Second World War Britain was losing its battle to keep the Thames Estuary open for vital supplies. The Germans had invented the limpet mine, a magnetic mine that would stick to the steel hull of any passing ship. Guy Maunsell came up with the answer, lining the Thames with a number of stationary forts to act as a first line of defence. After decommission in the 1950s some of the forts became pirate radio stations including Screaming Lord Sutch's pirate radio station Sutch Radio on one of the Shivering Sands towers. The Rough Tower fort was bought by Paddy Roy Bates and became the disputed Principality of Sealand.

Trips to the Redsand army fort go from Queenborough, Isle of Sheppey, Kent and take an hour and 15 minutes with around 1 hour 30 minutes at the fort. Refreshments and toilet facilities provided (project-redsand.com).

51.4551, 1.1000, CT5 1AB

12 ST PETER'S CHURCH
ALRESFORD

North of the Colne Estuary and Brightlingsea, near Alresford in Essex, the ruins of St Peter's date back to 1300. The church was destroyed by fire in 1971 and it remains roofless to this day. It is a grade II listed building and said to be haunted.

Head south from Alresford for about a mile, church is on the RH side. Limited parking.

51.8464, 0.9960, CO7 8AZ

13 RICHBOROUGH
ROMAN FORT

The views from this large Roman fort and amphitheatre are simply spectacular. Despite its age the walls of the fort are remarkably high and you get a real sense of what life must have been like manning this ancient fort. It was one of the earliest forts built by the Romans and remained in use from 43AD to 410AD. For a real adventure catch a boat from nearby Sandwich.

Head for Sandwich, at the A256/A257 roundabout continue as for central Sandwich, then take the 1st L, Richborough Rd. Another mile will get you there.

51.2924, 1.3320, CT13 9JW

11

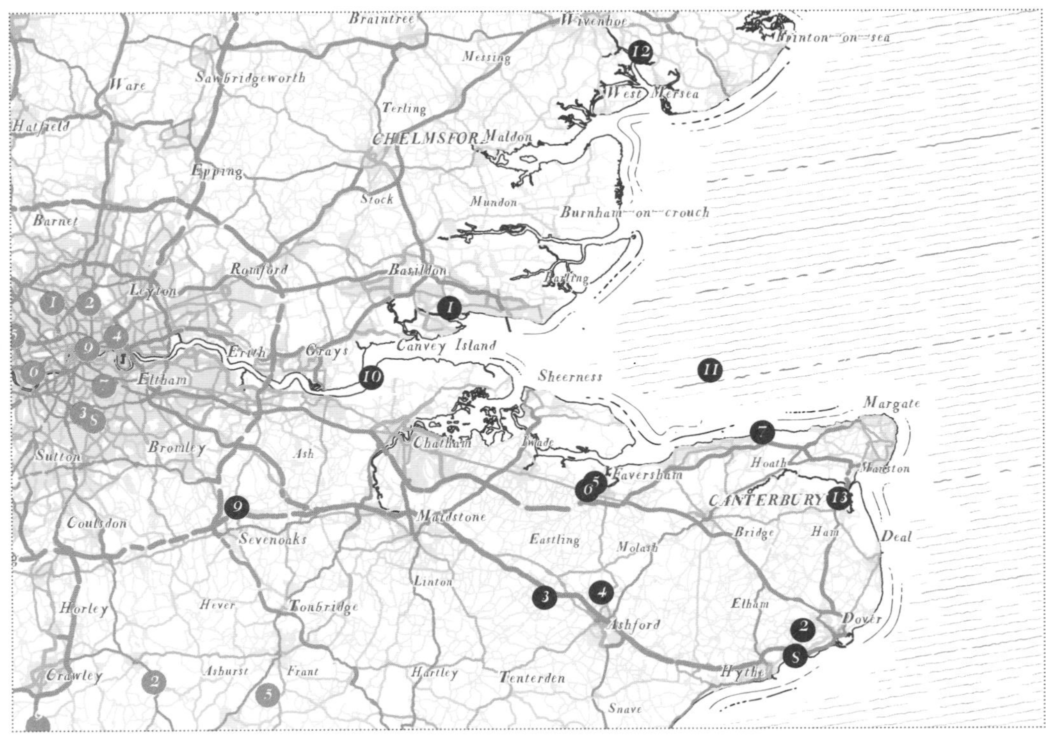
Braintree
Wivenhoe
Messing
Ware
Sawbridgeworth
West Mersea
Terling
Hatfield
CHELMSFOR
Maldon
Epping
Stock
Mundon
Burnham-on-crouch
Barnet
Romford
Basildon
Leyton
Erith
Grays
Canvey Island
Eltham
Sheerness
Margate
Chatham
Bromley
Ash
Sutton
Faversham
Hoath
CANTERBURY
Coulsdon
Maidstone
Sevenoaks
Eastling
Molash
Bridge
Ham
Deal
Linton
Horley
Hever
Tonbridge
Elham
Dover
Ashford
Crawley
Ashurst
Frant
Hartley
Tenterden
Hythe
Snave

CHAPTER 9

LONDON & SURROUNDS

1

It may seem strange to find London within the pages of a book of this kind. Yet in this overcrowded, polluted city, with such a densely packed population, the need to escape to wilder places is perhaps more pressing than in other parts of the UK.

Many of the large London graveyards are now nature reserves, offering a much-needed escape for the capital's wildlife population as much as its human one. The most important of these spaces are the large Victorian graveyards of Highgate, Nunhead, West Norwood, Kensal Green, Brompton, Abney Park and Bow Cemetery (now Tower Hamlets Cemetery Park). These make up what is now known as London's Magnificent Seven, a collection of cemeteries built to house the capital's dead. Before the Victorian age, London was treated as a collection of small, interconnected parishes, with the local dead being buried in local churchyards. The city was becoming overcrowded as much by its dead as by its living population. When the churchyards began to fill up, any scrap of land would suffice for burials – the land between pubs and houses, for example, or plots on street corners. As bodies became stacked on top of each other, there would be no room for the old, more forgotten corpses and there were even reports of these being flushed into the sewerage system.

Something clearly had to be done, as this was causing major health problems. The decaying bodies were contaminating water supplies and spreading diseases at an epidemic level. An Act of Parliament was passed and between 1832 and 1841 the seven cemeteries were built around the outskirts of London. It wasn't until the 1980s that they received their title the Magnificent Seven from architectural historian Hugh Meller.

The graveyards of the capital are not the only wild escape from this urban expanse. The bombed remains of St Dunstan's Church is a seldom-mentioned wilderness tucked away right in the heart of London. Slowly being reclaimed by a jungle of climbers and flowers, the natural world seems to be winning the battle of man versus nature.

On the southern side of town, the remains of a later Victorian ruin, that of the large Crystal Palace, play host to runners, walkers and day-trippers escaping the city. Incongruously, you can find a number of sphinxes and mock Greek statues here, overlooking the sprawl of the London basin.

1 HIGHGATE CEMETERY LONDON N6

Highgate is perhaps the grandest of the Magnificent Seven cemeteries. It is perhaps slightly more manicured and less wild in parts than many of the others. However, this should not put you off a visit to the site. Among the notable people buried here are the writer Douglas Adams, Karl Marx and the TV presenter Jeremy Beadle. Worth a special mention within the cemetery are the Circle of Lebanon and the Egyptian Avenue, and strange winding paths leading to tombs and vaults. They are in the West Cemetery, which can only be seen by paying to go on a guided tour, as the elaborate tombs and gravestones are monitored due to their delicate nature.

Archway tube station: Highgate Hill exit. Walk up Highgate Hill to Waterlow Park, then follow signs. 20 mins easy walk.

51.5669, -0.1470, N6 6PJ

2 ABNEY PARK LONDON N16

The suburb of Stoke Newington with its hipster coffee shops, yummy mummies and Turkish delis seems an odd place for a ruin. Yet in this trendy corner of London lies the large, neglected ruin of a funerary chapel designed by the influential Victorian architect William Hosking. The chapel sits in the centre of Abney Park, a Victorian graveyard turned nature reserve. Hosking, the first professor of architecture at Kings College London, designed this huge Gothic monument to be non-denominational. This was revolutionary in 1840 and it may have been the first non-denominational chapel in Europe, if not the world. Abney is one of the Magnificent Seven garden cemeteries of London. It is fantastically overgrown, like something out of a horror film: moss and lichen cover the graves and ivy-clad Victorian monuments lie in various states of disrepair. This urban oasis is an important conservation area and has become home to owls, sparrow hawks, woodpeckers and bats along with rare bees, bugs and butterflies. The site remains managed and open thanks to a team of volunteers (abneypark.org).

Main entrance is just off Stoke Newington High St, 5 mins S of Stoke Newington railway station, on opposite side of the road.

51.5649, -0.0781, N16 0LH

3 WEST NORWOOD CEMETERY LONDON SE27

West Norwood Cemetery has a collection of Gothic mausoleums and monuments. This is mixed with the more modern lawn cemetery on half of the site. It was said to be the first cemetery to be designed in the Gothic revival style, and as with much of this area, it has fantastic views over the city. The cemetery also contains a sizeable Greek Orthodox population set in its 40 acres. It is however the catacombs under the cemetery that are its main attraction. They are opened to the public sporadically and tours are only available to members (membership £5 per year, Friends of West Norwood Cemetery, fownc.org).

From West Norwood railway station head into Cotsowld St, L onto Norwood High St. Graveyard is 100 yards away, on the R. 2-3 mins easy walk.

51.4318, -0.0967, SE27 9JU

4 TOWER HAMLETS CEMETERY LONDON E3

Surrounded by flats, Bow Cemetery, now called Tower Hamlets Cemetery Park, appears at first to be native woodland, yet it is in the middle of a crowded urban space. The cemetery has been closed for burials since 1966 and is now a nature reserve, home to rare insect life and a diverse mix of flora. Among the notable people laid to rest in the cemetery are Dr Rees Ralph Llewellyn, who performed the autopsy on Mary Ann Nichols, Jack the Ripper's first victim; John Willis Jnr of the company John Willis and Sons, who owned the clipper Cutty Sark; and the notable trade unionist Will Crooks, who spent much of his life campaigning against inequality in this area notorious for its poverty. At one time 80 per cent of the graves were public; rather than being laid to rest individually, those people whose family was too poor to pay for a proper burial would have been put in one mass grave, perhaps 40 feet deep, which could have catered for up to 30 bodies.

From Mile End tube station exit L, take immediate L Eric Street, L into Hamlets Way to cemetery. 2 mins easy walk.

51.5236, -0.0272, E3 4PX

5 KENSAL GREEN CEMETERY LONDON W10

Not far from Portobello Market and Ladbroke Grove, Kensal Green Cemetery has much to see, both above and below ground; including Dissenters' and Anglican chapels, both of which have catacombs underneath. At present tours are only available under the Dissenters' Chapel every Sunday in the summer and every other Sunday in the winter. See kensalgreen.co.uk for more details. One of the most intriguing of the dead at Kensal Green is Doctor James 'Miranda' Barry. It wasn't until Dr James died in 1865 that it came to light that he was in fact a she. Born Margaret Ann Bulkley, it was doubtful that as a female she would have had such an illustrious career, first being able to train in medicine (unavailable to women at that period) then becoming inspector-general in charge of military hospitals. Rumour has it that 'he' would fight duels with anyone who dared criticise his/her voice.

Left out of Kensal Green tube station, R onto Harrow Rd, follow for 200 metres to entrance. 2 mins easy walk.

51.5286, -0.2241, W10 4RA

6 BROMPTON CEMETERY LONDON SW10

This comparatively small and rather uniform cemetery has two main entrances; one on the Fulham Road and the other on the Old Brompton Road. It has a very structured layout, but also has its share of reclaimed graves, mausoleums and large trees. The cemetery was originally designed by Benjamin Baud in 1839, and its prominent domed chapel was styled on St Peter's Basilica in Rome. One of the graveyard's most notable residents is the suffragette, Emmeline Pankhurst. Testament to her lasting influence and the admiration in which she is still held is the fact that her grave is never without flowers. It is also rumoured that writer Beatrix Potter may well have taken names for her characters from the headstones. Brompton is a stone's throw from the shops and cafes of the Kings Road.

From West Brompton tube station exit R. Cemetery is 100 metres up Old Brompton Rd. 1 min easy walk.

51.4831, -0.1876, SW10 9UQ

7 NUNHEAD CEMETERY LONDON SE15

Nunhead Cemetery is a fascinating place to visit. Like some of the others featured here it is now a nature reserve and has become a unique man-made wilderness. It is a huge site, the second largest of the Magnificent Seven. Much of the graveyard has been restored in recent years including Thomas Little's Anglican Chapel. Guided tours available: fonc.org.uk

Come out of Nunhead railway station and turn R to head S on Gibbon Road. Cross road into Barset Estate along the LH side of pavement. Walk up to alleyway/cut-through and follow this onto Linden Grove. Turn R and follow railings to entrance.

51.4644, -0.0534, SE15 3NA

8 CRYSTAL PALACE PARK LONDON SE19

The steps and footings of the old palace remain along with some rather curious large stone sphinxes and various mock ancient Greek statues. From the vantage point of the palace steps the London basin stretches out in front of you. The Crystal Palace was a large glass

DECEMBER
BERTHA

and structure, similar in appearance to the glasshouses at Kew. It was built to house the Great Exhibition of 1851 in Hyde Park. After the exhibition it was dismantled and rebuilt in its present home at Sydenham, now Crystal Palace, in 1854. In November 1936 a fire broke out in one of the offices within the palace. An estimated 100,000 people came to watch the blaze, the glow of which could be seen as far away as Brighton. The park houses the Crystal Palace dinosaurs, a collection of more than 30 large statues created in 1854. The 75-mile Capital Ring walk (often broken down into 15 one-day walks) goes through Crystal Palace and through many of London's large green spaces.

Turn right out of Crystal Palace overground station into the park. The dinosaur park is signposted towards the R and the site of the old palace, including the sphinxes, are on the L.

51.4223, -0.0758, SE19 2AZ

9 ST DUNSTAN
LONDON EC3

Perhaps it is the location of St Dunstan that makes it feel like such a romantic ruin. It is hidden away down a side street, not far from the Tower of London in the heart of the city. The remains of this bombed church have been planted with climbers, trees and shrubs giving it the look of a South American colonial ruin rather than a damaged British church. This 11th-century church was severely damaged in the Great Fire of London in 1666. It was later repaired before the great architect Christopher Wren designed a new steeple, built in 1695-1701. St Dunstan is the perfect place for a picnic lunch or as a place to escape the city as part of a romantic evening. Couples, children and those wishing a quiet spot to read all come to the church finding their own little corner among the gardens.

St Dunstan's Hill, EC3. From Monument tube station head up Fish St, R onto Eastcheap then fifth R down Idol Lane.

51.5097, -0.0827, EC3R 5DD

10 LEE HALL
SOPWELL NUNNERY

The ruins at Sopwell, just off Cottonmill Lane, are situated in an important nature reserve which provides a home to kingfishers, butterflies, slow worms and woodpeckers. To the south are walks along the River Ver and to the west it is possible to take in the ruins of the Roman Wall and the remains of Gorhambury House and its 16th-century parkland and woodland (51.7561, -0.3928). Henry VIII's dissolution of the monasteries in the 16th century came at a cost to more than 10,000 monks, canons, friars and nuns. Some became priests or were pensioned off but others were simply evicted or faced execution for their opposition to the king. For the rising middle class it was a property bonanza, as vast areas of land complete with building materials could be bought cheaply. On one such piece of land, Sir Richard Lee seized the opportunity to build Lee Hall in the grounds of the existing 12th-century nunnery. He paid just £13 and six shillings for the land which in modern terms would be around £5,500. Today all that is left of his Tudor mansion is a romantic ruin, with part of the gatehouse and kitchen wing remaining.

Park in Sainsburys at 51.7437, -0.3416 (charges may apply). R onto Holywell Hill, then 2nd R into Prospect Rd, cross road at end, head L to the ruins.

51.7441, -0.3347, AL1 2BN

10

9

Berkhamsted
ST ALBANS
Hatfield
Hoddesdon
10
Felden
Bedmond
Cheshunt
Epping
Potters Bar
Radlett
Watford
Barnet
Enfield
Coxtie Green
Bushey
Chigwell
Pinner
Kenton
Hendon
Hornsey
Romford
1
2
Leyton
Uxbridge
Barking
Hayes
Acton
5
London
4
9
WESTMINSTER
Poplar
Yiewsley
Erith
6
Putney
Brixton
7
Bexley
Feltham
Catford
Crayford
Egham
3
8
Ham
Merton
Bromley

CHAPTER 10

NORTH NORFOLK

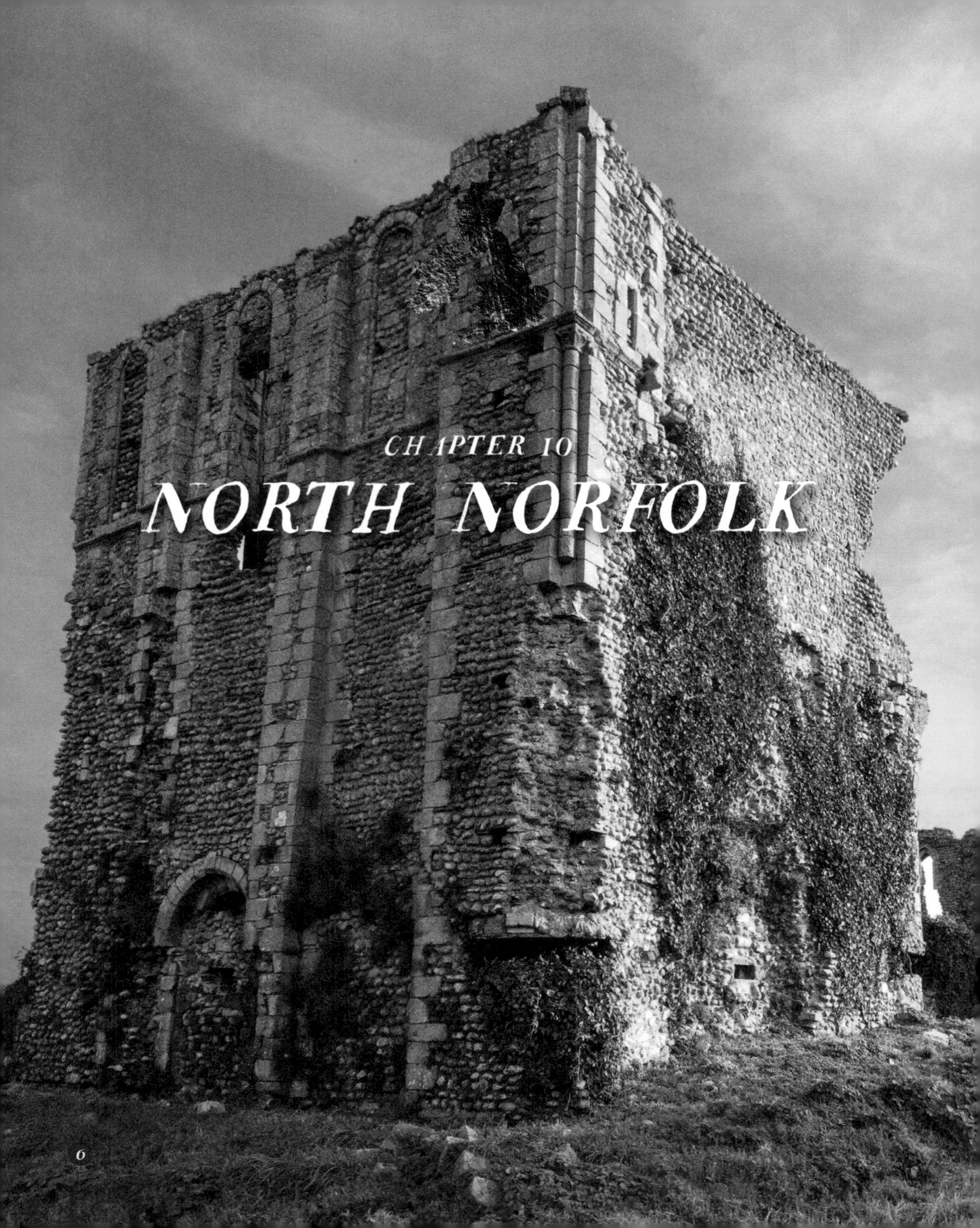

Each part of the country has its own characteristic set of ruins. For Scotland it is castles, Cornwall has its iconic, single-chimney engine houses, Wales its mines and of course Norfolk has its ruined churches. Having so many similar ruins in one place does tend to make you treat them a little like siblings of a close age. It is too easy to not see them for their own merits, instead comparing them to one another, perhaps sometimes unfairly. But as humans we like to characterise things, think in superlatives and make lists. We like to ask which are the two grandest castles or most picturesque engine houses in the region.

For Norfolk, we could find the most overgrown church; St Mary's in East Somerton and St John the Baptist in Croxton would be strong contenders. Each has become so engulfed by nature they seem more like a vine-covered Cambodian temple than any English country church. St Mary's is especially dramatic; the enormous cavernous yawn of its arched doorway, its ivy-clad walls which conceal it from the outside world. The tree growing in the centre of the church almost completes its near-assimilation by nature. Now, a newcomer to the church, not knowing it was once a Christian place of worship, may be fooled into thinking this is a place of pagan worship, somewhere the old gods of the land could be praised.

What others lack in drama they make up for in elegance, such as the Church of St Margaret's in the picturesque village of West Raynham. It doesn't scream or shout yet, much like St Peter's in Wiggenhall and the modest yet substantial ruin of the church in Oxwick, it is has a sublimely graceful presence. A gentle view of a bygone age, decaying in the flat fields of East Anglia.

Despite their differences, the churches have fundamental commonalities running between them. They would have been home to countless christenings, weddings and funerals. They would have been the focal point of the village, acting as the social hub where each week the people of the land would meet and catch up. They would have been places where friendships were made and gossip heard, as much as places of worship. With the villages all but gone, the crumbling walls now stand as a memorial to these inhabitants past, and a visit to them is a visit to the history of the ordinary working man.

1
3
2
4

1 ST JOHN THE BAPTIST
CROXTON

St John the Baptist in Croxton has all but been consumed by the surrounding undergrowth. It is easy to miss even when you are right on top of it and the graveyard has become almost invisible under an overgrown cherry laurel. During the 1880s when the Rector of St John the Baptist, found his church and neighbouring St Mary's, Fulmodeston (52.8309, 0.9561) falling into ruin he abandoned both and built a church between them. The church at Croxton has remained a ruin ever since.

Croxton is a couple of miles E of Fakenham. Turn R off A148 E-bound signed Kettlestone and Fulmodeston (Little Snoring Rd - seriously). Continue to Fulmodeston (Croxton) sign. Take first R past speed limit sign on a country lane and post-box and find a spot to park. Opposite the tennis courts you will see the church hidden in a thicket of trees.

52.8394, 0.9441, NR21 0NU

2 ST MARY'S ISLINGTON
NEAR TILNEY ALL SAINTS

The large church of St Mary's Islington is quite visible from the nearby A47 Kings Lynn Road. It certainly doesn't feel as remote as some of the other ruins, but there is still plenty to explore of this 13th-century construction.. Although the rest of the church is older, the tower was added later in the 15th century. This seems a common occurrence, perhaps as the result of years of generous donations on the collection plate (or many, many years of meagre donations). It fell into disrepair when attendances dropped then ultimately vanished, before the roof fell in and it was left to go to ruin in the early 1970s. The ruin can be reached from Wiggenhall St Germans if walking the Fen Rivers Way.

Heading towards Kings Lynn on the A47 you'll see a sign to Tilney All Saints; instead of turning L, head to the R down the no through road. The church is visible from the road and just a short walk from the track.

52.7267, 0.3247, PE34 4SB

3 ST MARGARET'S CHURCH
WEST RAYNHAM

West Raynham is a picture-perfect, chocolate-box village in the North Norfolk countryside. In the village is the large ruined 11th-century church of St Margaret's. Inside there is a wood stump carving of St Margaret of Antioc (Antioch), an early Christian martyr, with a dragon at her feet. St Margaret, or Margaret the Virgin, was tortured by a Roman governor after refusing his advances and was said to have banished Satan in the form of a dragon from her prison cell.

West Raynham is signposted off the A1065, 5 miles SW of Fakenham. Head through village, go past sign to church and hall on your right. The ruin is on a sharp bend to L. Limited parking outside.

52.7939, 0.7758 NR21 7EZ

4 OXWICK CHURCH
OXWICK

There is still much to see of All Saints church in Oxwick; superbly decorated grave stones with skull and crossbones, carved faces and of course, the large empty frame of the church itself. The church has been consolidated and cleared of overgrowth by the local council to prevent it falling into further decay. About 15-20 minutes' drive from the church, towards Fakenham, is the award winning Pensthorpe Natural Park, NR21 0LN, pensthorpe.com. The park has stunning gardens, lakeside and woodland works along with the WildRootz children's play area.

Oxwick is 5 miles S of Fakenham off the A1065. Turn E off A1065 to Whissonsett, at which turn L up London St. Take L to Oxwick, then L at next turn. Road veers slightly L, then R, you'll come to cottage R, a telegraph pole ahead with a footpath leading ahead and a bridleway to R. Park at roadside. Take the footpath for approx 50 yards to church on R.

52.7918, 0.8314, NR21 7HY

5 ST MARGARET'S
WOLTERTON HALL

The grounds of Wolterton Hall are a lovely place to walk, with large landscaped lake and views of the hall. The grounds also have a small adventure playground and many more extensive walks around the area linking with neighbouring Mannington Park (which also has a ruined church in the grounds). The medieval round tower of St Margaret's, within the grounds of Wolterton Hall, looks at first glance like a folly ruin, built for the enjoyment of the lord of the manor. However, up until the early 18th-century, the church was the focal point of Wolterton village. When Horatio Walpole, younger brother to the first Prime Minister, Sir Robert Walpole, wanted to build his grand house he demolished the village but decided to keep just the tower of the church to look out upon.

From the Erpingham Arms, Erpingham, NR11 7QA veer L to join The Street, continue on past the Saracen's Head then take the L turn into Wolterton Hall car park. Parking is £2 per car.

52.8424, 1.2110, NR11 7LY

6 BROMHOLM PRIORY
BACTON

There are some ruins that really make you wonder why more hasn't been made of them. The grand ruin of Bromholm Priory is one such building. Standing abandoned in a farmer's field not far from the Norfolk coast, Broomholm Priory is a tragic would-be tourist attraction. Its two abandoned gatehouses are easily as impressive as some of the more well known priories in East Anglia if not the rest of England. Underneath the 12th-century priory is a pillbox built into the structure during the Second World War. It is possible to crawl into this underground chamber from a gap at ground level. Founded in 1113, the priory lies on a pilgrimage route. In Chaucer's 'The Reeve's Tale' it was said it contained a piece of the true cross on which Jesus was crucified.

Take the Walcott road through Edingthorpe Green and Broomholm village. Go past the Bacton sign and thatched white cottage taking the next R signposted Parking. There should be plenty of spaces. Park up and head toward the Abbey Farm sign and take the footpath on the R. Half way up here you will see a gap in the hedge through which you can walk towards the priory.

52.8437, 1.4890, NR12 0HQ

7 ST MARY'S
EAST SOMERTON

The church of St Mary's in East Somerton is a huge, magnificent oddity. It has a vast, cathedral-like doorway, with a tree growing right in the centre of the church. Yet, despite its size, unless you are practically upon it, the ruined church is almost impossible to locate. It has been described as the most dramatic of all the ruins in East Anglia, part 15th-century church , part jungle!

At the Holy Trinity Church on Hemsby Rd, Winterton-on-Sea, take the L, Somerton Rd, then take the second R, then first L. Road bends to the R then to the L, go past the church conversion on the L and pull up 50 meters further along also on the L. The church will be alongside you in the trees.

52.7183, 1.6722, NR29 4DY

8 ST JAMES' CHURCH
BAWSEY

The iconic 'H'-shaped ruins of St James' Church, Bawsey stand slightly raised above the otherwise flat Norfolk landscape. It is a good walk or cycle along a dirt track road offering panoramic views across the region. The village of Bawsey was a thriving fishing village from Iron Age times right up until the 16th century. It began to fall into decline and a landlord saw an opportunity to switch to more profitable sheep farming, so demolished the remaining houses and kicked the residents out. All that remains now is the sad ruin of St James' church. This is a lovely spot for a picnic or a gentle afternoon stroll (just avoid the post-school invasion).

From Kings Lynn, take the A148 Gaywood/Lynn road E, at the Aldi supermarket turn R onto the A1076 Gayton Rd. Continue on the A1076 to towards the Queen Elizabeth Hospital. Head over the roundabout 2nd exit B1145, turn L after the crematorium. You'll come to some red brick farm buildings after about 1/3 of a mile. Park here and walk the remaining 300 meters or so to the ruin.

52.7592, 0.4623, PE32 1EU

9 ST PETER CHURCH
WIGGENHALL

This is a faded, red brick, ruined church with roofless nave and chancel but complete tower. The battlements on the top of the tower and large, glass-less Gothic windows give a cathedral like quality to this capacious ruin. It is maintained by the Norfolk Historic Churches trust, which has prevented it falling into further ruin. The grounds seem to be regularly maintained, making them a lovely place to stop for a picnic. The church makes a good first stop off point from the Fen Rivers Way, 4 miles after Kings Lynn.

From the Norfolk Arena S of King's Lynn, head S; 1st exit on the roundabout, and keep to this road as it veers R then L (becoming Tilegate La). Continue alongside the river to a T-junction. Here, turn R, cross the river; L and then L again to the church. There's no real parking on the site, so park sensibly where you can.

52.6932, 0.3725, PE34 3HF

10 ALL SAINTS CHURCH
PANXWORTH

All Saints Church is a pleasant walk or cycle, up a small hill, outside the quaint village of Panxworth. The church has a varied history: in the 1970s shortly after it fell into ruin, it became a place for Satan worship. They would congregate in the hilltop ruin and apparently conduct what were described as 'lurid' ceremonies. The church had been in ruins once before. An entry from The Norfolk Chronicle depicts a fundraiser in 1845 where £500 was needed to raise money to repair the church. As the building is a combination of earlier and Victorian architecture one can only assume they were successful. To the east of the church is the South Walsham Broad, dubbed the most picturesque of all the Norfolk Broads. The excellent Ship Inn (NR13 6DQ, 01603 270049), serving real ales and good food is a mile and a half walk away, in the village of South Walsham.

From Norwich take the Gurney Rd E for a mile until it becomes the Salhouse Rd, continue on for 6 miles through the village of Salhouse until you come to Paxworth itself. You should be able to see the tower from here. Take the L turn up Panxworth Church Rd to the tower. There is a small pull-in on the opposite side of the road to the tower.

52.6688, 1.4704, NR13 6JF

9

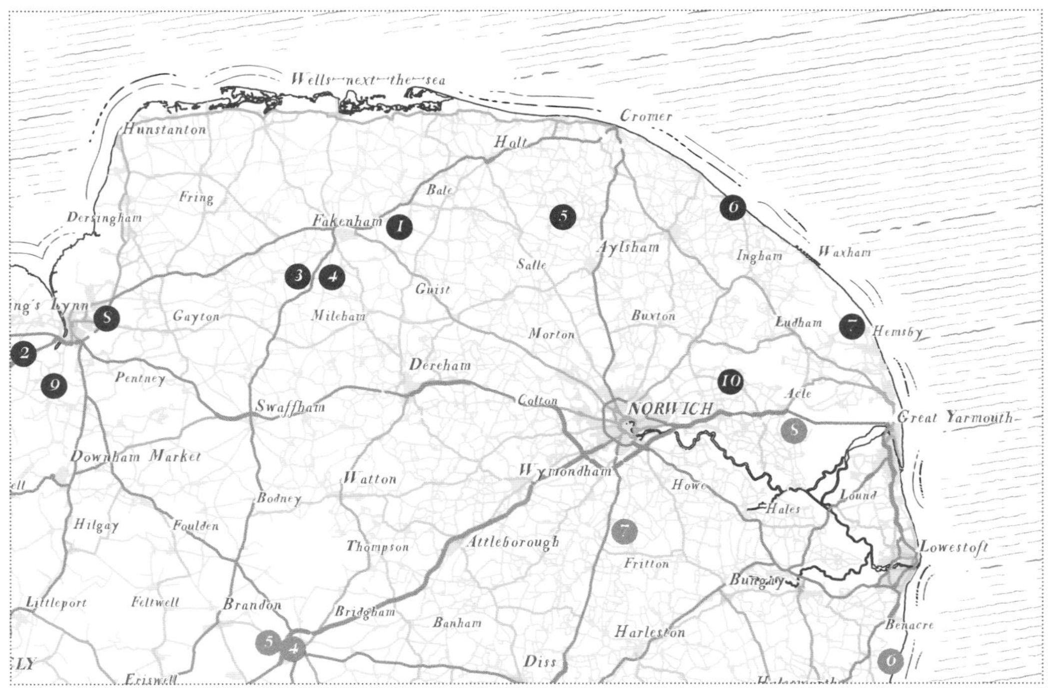
Wells-next-the-sea
Cromer
Hunstanton
Holt
Bale
Fring
Dersingham
Fakenham
Aylsham
Ingham
Waxham
Salle
Guist
Gayton
Mileham
Buxton
Ludham
Hemsby
Morton
Dereham
Pentney
Acle
Swaffham
Colton
NORWICH
Great Yarmouth
Downham Market
Wymondham
Watton
Howe
Lound
Hales
Bodney
Hilgay
Foulden
Attleborough
Thompson
Fritton
Lowestoft
Bungay
Littleport
Feltwell
Brandon
Bridgham
Banham
Harleston
Benacre
Diss

CHAPTER II

SUFFOLK & SOUTH NORFOLK

From the end of the 13th century and continuing into the 15th, England had begun growing rich on the wool trade. East Anglian manors were part of this thriving trade and the counties of Norfolk and Suffolk were both ranked among the richest in the land. Much of the wool would have been exported to foreign weavers in its raw state, as little woollen cloth was made in this country. Overseas, countries that included Flanders took on this raw product, and skilled artisans wove it into clothes and blankets. Rearing sheep, and exporting wool, was a thriving trade that helped the area's villages, towns and cities along, with religious institutions such as priories and abbeys, to prosper. The Cistercian Abbey of Sibton was one such institution. By the time it was sold off during Henry VIII's dissolution of the monasteries in the 16th century it made around £250 a year, which would have been a considerable amount in that period.

The village of Saxlingham Thorpe also thrived as a result of the booming wool trade in the 13th and 14th centuries and the church of St Mary's would have been vital for its growing population. However its prosperity was not to last as the Black Death swept through Saxlingham and the rest of Europe. The church and village never quite recovered and following the death blow of the Reformation in the 16th to 17th centuries, the church slowly but surely fell into ruin. Nowadays it is lies concealed in a wood not far from the village.

The town of Dunwich also thrived in the 13th century. It ranked as one of the ten largest towns in England, so large it could support eight churches! The fortunes of the town changed during the 13th century by what must have seemed like acts of a vengeful god to the pious citizens of medieval East Anglia. In 1286 a huge storm swept away Dunwich harbour and the lower part of the town. Another storm followed 42 years later and the town never fully recovered. For Dunwich and for nearby Covehithe, coastal erosion is still an on-going threat and both are shadows of their former selves. Some say Covehithe should be visited sooner rather than later as, with another big storm, the town could be lost forever.

1
7
4
3

1 *LABORATORY ONE*
ORFORD NESS

Orford Ness is not an easy site to reach. Only a sliver of land, south of Aldeburgh, prevents the River Ore from cutting this flat expanse of beach off from the mainland. During the inter-war period this was the location of early experiments into radar. Later, during the Cold War, the Atomic Weapons Research Establishment began to use the site to test their weapons, and today the remains of the buildings that they created look like eerie pagodas. It was always maintained that no nuclear material was used on the site. Even today the remains of countless bomb casings and other military debris litter the site. People have been largely excluded from this ex-military site and a unique wildlife habitat has developed. It is an atmospheric place, and fantastic for spotting birds. Access is limited to protect the fragile nature of the site and it can only be reached by ferry from Orford Quay.

The ferry to Orford Ness leaves from Orford Quay at the end of Quay St past the Jolly Sailor pub. There is parking on the quay.

52.0816, 1.5607, IP12 2NY

2 *GREYFRIARS FRIARY*
DUNWICH

The romantic ruin of Greyfriars Friary lies just to the south east of the quaint Suffolk village of Dunwich. By the 13th century much of the town, including eight churches, had fallen into the sea. So, due to fears of further coastal erosion, the priory was moved to its present home. The remaining walls, gatehouse and cloister buildings of this are just one of the pulls to this serene and tranquil coastline. Much of the area to the south of the ruin, including the stunning heather-topped cliffs, is managed by the National Trust. It has maintained three walks in order to take in the area's flora and fauna, where you will have a chance to see hen harriers and warblers along with rare coastal flora. Parking for Dunwich Heath NT is at IP17 3DJ (52.2522, 1.6265). The Ship Inn on St James St (IP17 3DT, 01728 648219) offers rooms and good food. The tea room at Bridge House Nurseries is also worth a visit.

From Yoxford head N on the A12 past the Satis House Restaurant and Hotel (IP17 3EX), take the 1st R to Dunwich. Continue through Westleton, veering L past the Crown, at some white cottages take a R to Dunwich Heath. In 2¾ miles you'll reach a triangle, veer L. 1st R to car park on the beach 52.2786 1.6326. Walkback the way you came. Ruin is on your left through a gate after 2 minutes easy walk.

52.2755, 1.6307, IP17 3DR

3 *SIBTON ABBEY*
SAXMUNDHAM, YOXFORD

The ruin of Sibton Abbey is overgrown with nettles and weeds and stands in a sad state of disrepair on private land owned by the Levett-Scrivener family. English Heritage are aware of the building's plight and it is on their buildings at risk register. The ruin is just about visible from the Yoxford road but there is no access to the site. There is a footpath running along the side of Abbey Wood near the ruin, but this is as near as you can legally get to it. There are occasional open days to raise money for the local church. Sibton Abbey was the only Cistercian abbey in East Anglia. It was founded in 1150 and although the Cistercian order was an austere one, the abbey became very rich through the wool trade. In the 16th century, during the dissolution of the monasteries, it was sold off, and today it's just a picturesque ruin.

Follow the A1120 NW of Yoxford, to the village of Peasenhall and park opposite Campaign Antiques, IP17 2HJ. (The Peasenhall Tearooms, IP17 2JE, are worth a visit). Carefully walk E on the verges of the main road for ½ a mile towards Sibton and Yoxford. Before you reach Sibton and its church you should see the abbey in the field to the R.

52.2755, 1.4655, IP17 2JG

4 *THETFORD PRIORY*
THETFORD

The large 'H' of the arched doorway and stairs leading to a long-collapsed tower rise above the expansive ruins of Thetford Priory. It is just a short walk from Thetford town centre and a good place to relax, walk the dog (on a lead) and have a picnic. This once grand building was founded in the very early 12th century by Cluniac monks. During the middle ages, it was the largest, richest and most important monastery in East Anglia. There is plenty to see and do in Thetford including the Dad's Army Museum behind the Guildhall, and the Ancient House Museum on White Hart Street. The Black Horse pub

on Magdalen Street (IP24 2BP), serves an excellent selection of real ales. In a park next to the large ruins of Thetford Priory are those of the 12th-century Church of the Holy Sepulchre. Situated just off Brandon Road, it is open 10am to 5pm.

Park in car park for Wilkinsons, etc in St Nicholas St, IP24 1BN, off London-Norwich Rd, N of Thetford centre. Walk back St Nicholas St, cross London Rd to Water La. Keep L to the end until you see a footpath to the priory. 2 mins easy walk.

52.4163, 0.7424, IP24 1AX

5 WARREN LODGE
THETFORD

Thetford Warren Lodge is a two storey, box-like ruin on the edge of the Thetford forest. It was built by the Prior of Thetford in the late 14th or early 15th century as a defensive structure against gangs of armed poachers. The size of the building indicates that hunting parties may well have also lodged there. The Forestry Commission has mapped out a number of walking trails around the woods, including a three-mile trail which passes the lodge. To the north west, Brandon Country Park, with tea rooms and lakeside walks, is a worthwhile stop off.

From A11, Thetford bypass, take B1107 W. Pass Thetford Golf Club, you will see an unmarked turn about 1 mile from the roundabout. Drive to the car park, 52.4239, 0.7070, and follow path W for about 2 mins.

52.4236, 0.7035, IP27 0AF

6 ST ANDREW'S
COVEHITHE

As you approach on the road to the coast, St Andrew's church is an imposing sight. It looks more like a vast bombed-out city church than a coastal ruin. Yet some intrinsic quality, impossible to put your finger on, links it with the surroundings. It feels right here, you get the sense that the sea air should have always blown through the large empty windows. It is a ruin at home, at peace in its surroundings. This large 15th-century church ruin houses a much newer 17th-century church within its walls. Gargoyles adorn the walls of both churches; the larger outer church has steps leading up to a gap in the wall, giving a bird's-eye view of the church. For a more detailed history there is a small booklet available in the newer church building.

From Lowestoft take the A12 S for 9 miles to Wrentham. In Wrentham pass a large red brick church on your R then L, then immediate L down Mill La. Continue for about 1½ miles towards the coast. Cars park right down this road, sometimes next to the church. 5 mins gentle walk.

52.3767, 1.7054, NR34 7JJ

7 ST MARY THE VIRGIN
SAXLINGHAM THORPE

I visited St Mary's with a photographer friend, and we got the sense of what this would have been like as a working church. Despite the church being in ruins you can imagine its congregation walking up with a sense of festivities to a wedding or christening on a bright spring day. It is quite hidden away in a small copse along a well trodden dirt path.

From Norwich, take the Ipswich road S for around 7 miles through Newton Flotman. After crossing the river, turn L and follow through to Saxlingham Nethergate. Through the village (pass Hall La on the L) until you reach Hill Cottage on your R. Follow the track R of the road (unsuitable for driving) and take the R fork in the path. The church is hidden among a clump of trees.

52.5216, 1.2867, NR15 1TE

8 ST PETER & ST PAUL
TUNSTALL

St Peter and St Paul at Tunstall is a working church within a ruin. The tower remains and the roof of the nave is missing but the chancel is still intact. Tunstall village lies within an area of beautiful lowland heath and just over a mile to the east is the large Tunstall pine forest. The whole area is a haven for wildlife and you may catch a glimpse of passing wild deer.

Tunstall is reached via Halvergate, just off the A47 9 miles W of Great Yarmouth. In Halvergate, pass Red Lion and School Lodge Country Guest House and take R up Tunstall Rd. At a triangular junction, church is on L fork slightly hidden in trees behind a post box. Park where you can without obstructing the traffic.

52.6160, 1.5688, NR13 3PS

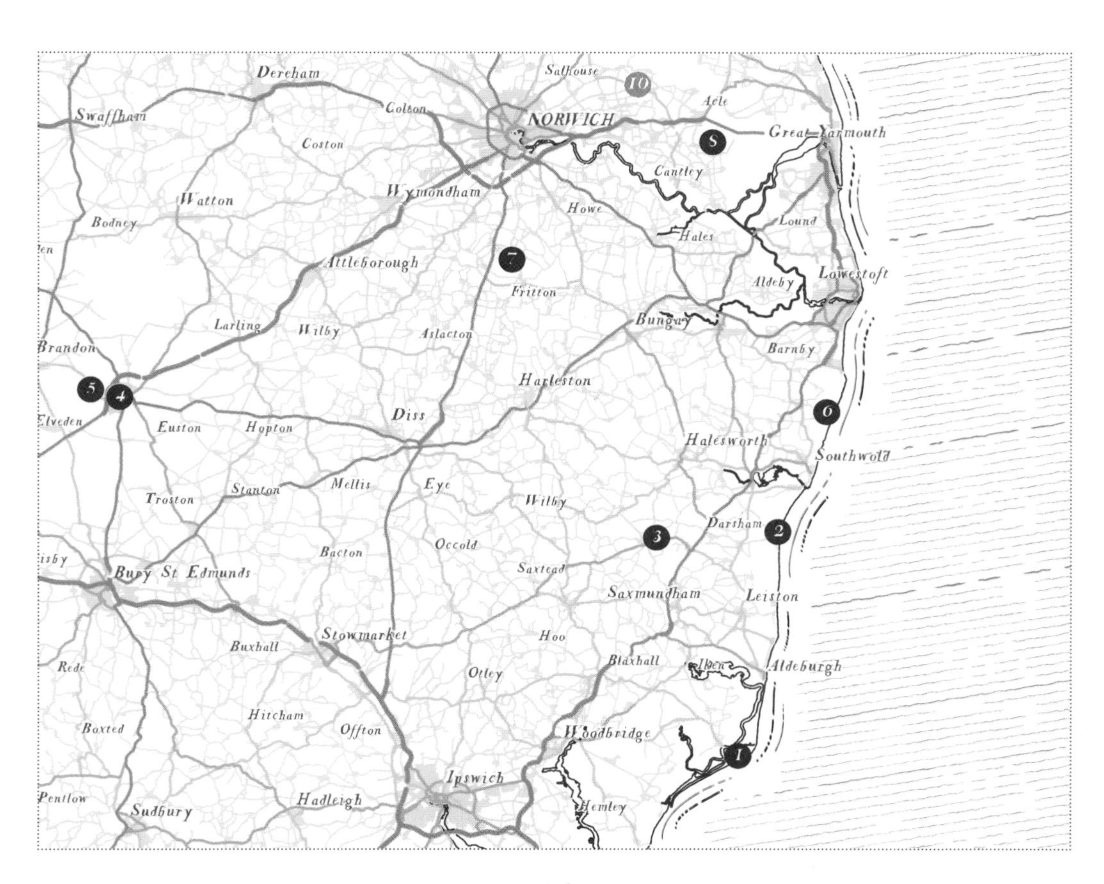

CHAPTER 12

SOUTH MIDLANDS

The farmland, parks, nature reserves and countryside of the South Midlands have historic churches, abandoned manor houses and halls to rival those anywhere in southern England. Many of the churches now lie in ruins, ivy-covered reminders of lost congregations. The roofless remains of Segenhoe Church, near Woburn Safari Park, would have been the hub of the community in the late Saxon times. Now it no longer serves the community as a place of worship but its isolated location, along with easy access, make it the perfect place for a summer picnic. Another ruined church, St Mary's, up from the village of Clophill, is an equally picturesque ruin for a summer stop-off, albeit one with a darker past. The church had a history of body-snatching, especially in Victorian times. More recently, in the early 1960s, two boys were found in the village playing with a human skull. The boys claimed to have found the skull, belonging to Jenny Humberstone who died in 1770 aged 22, in the church. Upon investigation, more of her remains were found set out in a ritualistic pattern along with cockerel feathers and two Maltese crosses. This led to the belief that the ruined church may have been the venue for some kind of satanic ritual.

Old St John's, in Boughton Green on the outskirts of Northampton, is home to further tales of superstition. Story has it that a ghostly figure, always of the opposite sex of the witness, appears and asks them for a kiss. If the witness submits and gives them a kiss they are said to die within a month. In the graveyard, on Christmas Eve 1875, a man by the name of William Parker kissed a red-headed girl, only for her to vanish in front of his eyes. On 24th January 1876 William died of unknown causes. It is hard to say if this was a case of ghostly happenings or a drunken incident and seriously dangerous infectious disease!

The year before this tale, on Christmas Eve in 1874, one of the worst rail disasters in English history took place at Shipton-on-Cherwell not far from the city of Oxford. A carriage put on in Oxford to deal with the extra Christmas passengers caused the London to Birkenhead train to derail, sending many of the carriages to plummet down the embankment. The stricken passengers called on the household at Hampton Gay to help and apparently they were reluctant to come to their aid (they did help later but sought to claim back any losses they made as a result of the crash). Instead Sir Randolph Churchill, celebrating his son Winston's christening at nearby Blenheim Palace, assisted along with fellow guests and staff. When Hampton Gay was gutted by a fire in 1887 some believed it was a curse as a result of that night - although others believe the house may have been subject to a far less supernatural arson attack.

1 THE DOWER HOUSE
FAWSLEY PARK, DAVENTRY

Built in Tudor red brick and local ironstone, the Fawsley Dower House, with its large turreted tower and spiralling chimney stacks, stands abandoned in the grand splendour of Fawsley Park. Built in the 16th century, it has the contested claim of being the first brick building in the country. It was home to Lady Ursula de Vere following the death of her second husband Sir Edmund Knightley. It has been uninhabited since 1704. The building is currently fenced off and undergoing repairs by English Heritage but there is still plenty to see and it is well worth a visit. The Plough Inn, in Everdon (NN11 3BL, 01327 361606) and the Maltsters, in Badby (NN11 3AF, 01327 702905) are perfect spots to rest weary legs and fill hungry bellies.

From the M1 get off at Junction 16 and take the A45 heading W to Flore, Weedon Bec and Daventry. Travel for 4½ miles heading through Flore and Weedon Beck. Turn L to Newnham B4037, go past the church and the school then take the L turn past the green. Continue for 1¾ miles and take a R turn at the staggered crossroads to Fawsley. Park in the pull-in by the church 52.2077, -1.1745. Cross the road, over the gate and follow the track to the Dower House.

52.2163, -1.1668, NN11 3BA

2 HAMPTON GAY MANOR

The abandoned grand house of Hampton Gay Manor stands in a thicket of trees among serene Oxfordshire countryside. Footpaths criss-cross the area; there are lovely walks to be had to nearby Hampton Poyle and Bletchingdon, or across the Cherwell to Shipton-on-Cherwell and further afield to Woodstock. The house, dating back to 1580, and nearby church are all that remain of Hampton Gay village. The information board near the entrance to the field will tell you a little more of the history of the place. The owner of Hampton Gay is keen that no-one enters the site of this derelict building. It should therefore only be viewed from the footpath. There is an excellent play park for younger children in nearby Bletchingdon, and The Bell at Hampton Pole (OX5 2QD 01865 376242) is highly recommended.

From Bletchingdon head S on the Oxford Rd to Hampton Poyle. Continue past the park and take the R turn, Hampton Gay Only. Follow the lane to the end and park where you can (do consider the local residents). Enter the field and follow the path to a fenced-off clump of trees where the ruin is situated.

51.8449, -1.2956, OX5 2QH

3 GODSTOW ABBEY
GODSTOW

If the crowds of Oxford get too much, a perfect Sunday escape can be had along the pleasant two-mile stroll across Port Meadow along the Thames Path to Godstow. Enter via Walton Well Road in Jericho (where there is parking) and follow the path over the Thames. Just off the path The Perch Inn (OX2 0NG 01865 728891) has a large garden suitable for children and serves excellent food (booking advised). Legend has it that Dame Ediva, widow of Sir William Launcelene, followed a voice telling her to establish a nunnery for 24 "of the most gentyl women that ye can find" at Godstow where she had seen a beam of light touching the ground from heaven. Godstow is the burial place of Rosamund Clifford, a great beauty of her day and the mistress of Henry II.

Follow the Godstow Rd west through past White Hart and Red Lion pubs. Free car park on the L after grey brick flats. Walk through the village, over the bridges, past the Trout Inn to Godstow Abbey on the L.

51.7782, -1.2993, OX2 8PN

4 MINSTER LOVELL HALL NEAR BURFORD

Take a picnic under the shade of the trees by the flowing river Windrush by the romantic ruins of Minster Lovell as the kids run around on the large open lawns. Rumour has it that Francis, Lord Lovell, went into hiding at Minster Lovell Hall in 1487. He hid as a result of his support for the Yorkist imposter Lambert Simnel and his challenge to Henry VII's weak Lancastrian claim to the throne. When the servant who fed him died, Lord Lovell was himself thought to have slowly died of starvation.

If travelling via Oxford, try to avoid the A34 Oxford by-pass at peak times. From the roundabout A40/A361 S of Burford (Travelodge and Little Chef OX18 4JF), take the A40 E towards Oxford for 2 ½ miles. At the roundabout take the 1st exit onto

Burford Rd, B4047 for 2 ¼ miles to Minster Lovell. Go through the village then take the L Minster Lovell Hall. Turn R across the bridge, next R, park in the car park to the R. Follow this road down for 2 mins easy walk to the Hall.

51.7995, -1.5307, OX29 0RR

5 ALL SAINTS, DENTON
PETERBOROUGH

Mentioned as far back as the Domesday Book, All Saints is an intriguing little ruin. Although roofless, much of it remains so there is still a substantial amount to see. To the knowing eye, the church might seem like a contradictory mix of architectural styles. It was mostly rebuilt in the 16th century but in a medieval revivalist manner, fusing contemporary and older designs. The Addison Arms in Glatton (PE28 5RZ) is a lovely family pub with a large play area in the garden. It is a good place to begin or end a walk to the ruin. From the pub walk past the church and join the track at Mill Hill to Denton. Nearby Stilton village, birthplace of the cheese, is worth a stop off.

Leave the A1(M) at junction 16, and take the exit from the roundabout signed to Stilton. In the centre of the village, turn R and head towards Caldecote. In Caldecote hamlet, turn L for Denton, L again in the village and you will see the ruin on the R. Parking on bank by side of road.

52.4765, -0.3079, PE7 3SD

6 ST JAMES'S CHURCH
MIDDLE ASSENDON

The ruin of St James's Church is famous for appearing in the 1971 classic Folk Horror film, 'Blood on Satan's Claw'. The church was abandoned in 1875 and only the outer shell remains. It has recently undergone renovation work to secure the masonry and clear it of ivy. It is not far from the bluebell wood of the Warburg Nature Reserve.

From Middle Assendon take the L turn at the end of the village past the Tennis Courts. Turn R after ¾ mile, Bix Bottom. Pass a large old redbrick farm, a redbrick house on your L, you'll come to a track running L - the church is in that clump of trees. Park a few yards further on, on the RH side.

51.5769, -0.9534, RG9 6BJ

7 SEGENHOE CHURCH
RIDGMONT

On a summer's day, the stone floor and overgrown interior of Segenhoe Church have an almost Mediterranean feel. The patchwork remains of this roofless church reflect the mix of architectural styles used to enlarge or renovate the church from its 11th (or arguably 12th) century origins until its abandonment in the mid-19th century. A mix of brown cobbles, the characteristic local ironstone, have been used in the construction. Part of the Greensand Ridge Walk and John Bunyan Trail are nearby.

Leave the M1 at junction 13, and follow signs for A507. R onto A4012, cross the motorway then soon L into Station Rd. At T-junction, R then soon L into Eversholt Rd. L into Segenhoe Manor Rd. Continue to church, and find parking.

52.0119, -0.5718, MK43 0XW

8 HOUGHTON HOUSE
AMPTHILL

As you approach Houghton House from its tight turn north of Ampthill, there is little to suggest the red brick grandeur soon to unfold in front of you. With so much of the building still standing there is much to explore of this grand house. It is a fun place for children to run from room to room around its hollow interior. The views both looking down on the ruin and from its grounds are simply stunning. The house was built around 1615 for the wealthy dowager and literary patron, Mary Herbert (formerly Sidney), Countess of Pembroke. It has been suggested that Mary may have completed some of Shakespeare's unfinished plays. Mary unfortunately died of smallpox not long after Houghton House was completed.

Leave the M1 at Junction 13 and follow signs to the A507 Ampthill. Continue 5 miles to Ampthill. Take 1st exit on both mini-roundabouts. Continue N up Bedford St past Waitrose. As the road bends round at the top of the hill take the tricky turn on the R to Houghton House. Follow this to the car park on the L. Walk down the hill, 5 mins moderate walk.

52.0440, -0.4862, MK45 2EZ

9 KENILWORTH CASTLE
KENILWORTH

In 2014 English Heritage completed their series of staircases and platforms to allow you to climb right up to the top of this grand Elizabethan ruin. Now you can peek into the chambers and rooms that Robert Dudley, Earl of Leicester, constructed within his grand tower - built to win the heart of Elizabeth I. The queen visited a number of times but sadly for Dudley she never yielded to his offers of marriage. You can easily spend two hours plus wandering around the extensive ruins of Kenilworth Castle and its recreated Elizabethan gardens. Regular events take place there too.

Signposted from Kenilworth. Bus Johnsons of Henley 539; Travel West Midlands 11 & 11X; Stagecoach U12.

52.3492, -1.5916, CV8 1NE

10 ST JOHN THE BAPTIST CHURCH

The captivating little ironstone ruin of this old church has almost succumbed to encroaching ivy. Although the churchyard is still in use, its weeds can grow above knee height. Underneath the rear window, there is a square hole marking the entrance to the holy well or sacred spring at the back of the church. A church may have stood on this site since 1201 but the present building dates to the mid-14th century. At that time it would have been part of a medieval village.

From Moulton village head W on West St past Moulton College to join the Boughton Rd. After a mile or so the road bends round to the L, take the R turn when you come out of the bend, then take 2nd R to the car park/lay-by. Walk ahead through stone pillars to the church.

52.2836, -0.8802, NN2 8RE

11 ST MARY THE VIRGIN
CLOPHILL

A pleasant walk up the lane from the village of Clophill is this little church. Climb to the top of the restored spiral staircase for stunning views of the countryside. Built around 1350, old St Mary's has been subject to body snatchers and satanic rituals (see chapter introduction). The ruin can be taken in as part of the 40-mile Greensand Ridge Walk across the pleasant Bedfordshire clay vales from Leighton Buzzard to Gamlingay (greensandridgewalk.co.uk). Just 15 minutes away is the toddler-friendly Summerfields Miniature Railway and Art Gallery, in Hammer Hill, Haynes, MK45 3BH.

From Clophill village, head to the High St and find a spot to park by the side of the road (locals seem to park near new St Mary's on the R). Walk up Great La ½ mile to the footpath, cross the field to Church La, you should see the church ahead, 10-15 minutes moderate walk.

52.0337, -0.4095, MK45 4BP

12 HEMINGTON CHURCH
LOCKINGTON

Hemington Church is now in someone's garden, but can be easily seen from the footpath running to nearby Lockington, which is a ½ mile/10 minute easy walk away. The church was built in the 14th century but abandoned by the late 16th. The large square tower of the church collapsed as late as the 1980s.

From Hemington head S past the Jolly Sailor pub. At the red phone box at the S of the village take the next L onto Church La. Park by the side of the road before the road runs out. A footpath runs nearer to the ruin at the back and to the L.

52.8454, -1.3241, DE74 2SF

11

9

12

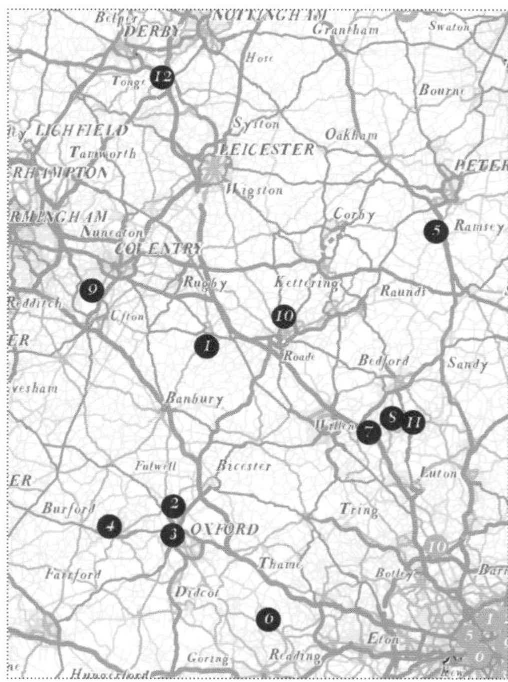
Belper
DERBY
Grantham
Swaton
Bourne
LICHFIELD
Tamworth
Syston
Oakham
LEICESTER
Wigston
Nuneaton
Corby
Ramsey
Rugby
Kettering
Raunds
Ufton
Roade
Bedford
Sandy
Banbury
Bicester
Luton
Burford
Tring
OXFORD
Thame
Fairford
Didcot
Eton
Goring
Reading

CHAPTER 13

LINCOLNSHIRE

The Viking Way long distance footpath runs from the Humber Bridge in the north to Oakham, Rutland in the south. It runs for a total of 147 miles (or 140 depending on sources – why can they never quite agree on the length of long distance paths?) snaking through a large proportion of Lincolnshire, including the stunning Lincolnshire Wolds, an Area of Outstanding Natural Beauty. The path leaves the city of Lincoln along the path of the River Witham and into the Witham valley to the east of the city. In late the 11th and early 12th centuries the banks of the Witham were home to no less than nine monasteries. Their position, almost overlooking each other, is not accidental. The monasteries of the valley grew rich on sheep farming and the river would have been vital for transport to the port of Boston. From there, the monks exported the wool, trading with wealthy European wool merchants. Around eight miles from Lincoln the Viking Way reaches the first of the three abbeys with any significant remains, the lonely single wall of 12th-century Barlings Abbey. The brethren of Barlings were model citizens with only one recorded deviation from the rules of the strict order: it seems in 1494 one brave canon had the audacity to wear slippers. The path heads north from here, passing Bardney limewoods (Hardy Gang Wood), a Site of Special Scientific Interest. It has been managed as a coppice since the time of the abbeys in the 11th century. Four miles further on and you reach the earthworks and scant remains of Bardney Abbey. In the 7th century the monks there refused a request to house the bones of King Oswald within the abbey and instead they locked the coffin outside. During the night a large beam of light was said to have shone from it to the heavens. Seeing this as an act of God, the monks decided they had made a mistake. They brought in the coffin and removed the abbey door to prevent it happening again. From then on when someone left a door open, people would utter the phrase "Were you born in Bardney?" eventually corrupting to our modern "Were you born in a barn?".

The final abbey of the three, and the most complete, is Tupholme, home to the 1972 Festival where the Beach Boys, Joe Cocker, Genesis, The Faces, Roxy Music, Slade and even Monty Python's Flying Circus all performed.

Lincolnshire is a vast, flat, rural county making it a perfect place for walks and cycling. For the keen ruin hunter, the vanished medieval villages of Calceby, the large ruined Jacobean hall at Nocton, the sprawling remains of the Bass Maltings and the historic Bolingbroke Castle are just some of the attractions.

1
7
4
3

1 OLD ST PETER
SALTFLEETBY

'The leaning tower of Lincoln' or the 'Stump' as it is known locally is all that remains of St Peter's - its oddly shaped tower. The church was rebuilt following subsidence in the late 19th century and the wonky tower was corrected at the church end of the ruin. The result of this is quite extraordinary: one side looks completely straight and the other has a very visible lean. Around 7 miles drive from the ruin is the Seal Sanctuary at Mablethorpe (LN12 1QG, 01507 473346).

Follow B1200 from Louth, E for about 8 miles to Saltfleetby St Peter. Turn L by the new church of St Peter's, and you will see the tower on your R.

53.3867, 0.1571, LN11 7TB

2 BASS MALTINGS
SLEAFORD

This sprawling mass of red brick buildings was built by Bass Breweries in the early 1900s. The maltings are unfortunately off-limits but their sheer size means they are actually easier viewed from afar. For photographers, the best views are to be had to the south of the site, on the footpath running east from Mareham Lane at 52.9912,-0.4016. The maltings have recently been bought by a developer who plans to turn them into shops, office space and housing. The maltings were built in Lincolnshire because the county was well-suited for growing the barley needed for the malting process, and Sleaford offered good transport links to the rest of the country. In 1973 the building ceased operation as a malting house and was damaged by fire the following year.

From Sleaford Station, turn R (S) along Mareham La, then first L into the industrial estate where you will see the Maltings.

52.9940, -0.4017, NG34 7BT

3 BARLINGS ABBEY
BARLINGS

The only above-ground reminder of Barlings Abbey is a sliver of the old nave wall, looking like a large raised fin in the Lincolnshire countryside. From some angles, this ruin looks bizarrely like a finger pointing to the sky. The views from the ruin are far-reaching and panoramic. Earthworks mark out the location of the rest of the abbey and a number of ancient fish ponds still exist on the site. Barlings would make a good place to pause if walking the Viking Way long distance path, which runs very near here (see Introduction).

North of Fiskerton, 2 miles off Sustrans Route 1 National Cycle Path. Heading NE from Lincoln on A158, turn R at Langworth onto Barlings Lane. 1 mile S of Barlings village, reach Low Barlings farm. Park on roadside here and follow footpath to abbey in field L.

53.2480, -0.3688, LN8 5JH

4 BARDNEY ABBEY
BARDNEY

Although little remains of Bardney Abbey, there has been a great deal of money spent turning this into a bit of tourist attraction. It might not be to everyone's taste but few would disagree that the work has improved a site which looks like nothing more than a few bumps in the ground! Numerous information boards circle the location of the old abbey and a carved wooden monk is happy to chat away with a pre-programmed history of the site. As with Barlings to the north and Tupholme to the south, Bardney can be taken in as part of the Viking Way (see Introduction).

½ mile north of Bardney village off off Sustrans route 1 National Cycle Path. 12 miles E of Lincoln off B1190. Once in Bardney turn N, follow road round past the Nag's Head and continue on Abbey Rd to farm buildings. Limited parking by roadside. Ruins are in field directly ahead of farm.

53.2204, -0.3336, LN3 5XD

5 TUPHOLME ABBEY
SOUTHREY

Of the three remaining abbeys in the Witham valley this is perhaps the most universally appealing. There is still much to explore and it was a personal favourite of mine. Its appeal was in part thanks to the sheep grazing the grounds; they were endearingly comical, inquisitive yet timid, adding real character to the site. The large open space at Tupholme meant it was a perfect spot to host a rock festival in the 1970s. What made for a good rock festival then now makes for an excellent spot for a summer picnic. There is plenty of space for kids to run around here, but do leave dogs in the car especially during lambing season.

South of Bardney just off Sustrans route 1 National Cycle Path. 14 miles E of Lincoln off B1190. Heading S on B1190 Horncastle Road, 1¾ miles after Bardney look for large red brick farmhouse just before road veers L. Ruin is in field on R. There is a pull in space outside.

53.1988, -0.2881, LN3 5TQ

6 *NOCTON HALL*
NOCTON

Nocton Hall is a grand Jacobean mansion hidden among overgrown trees and shrubs. The large chestnut tree in the garden is said to have been planted by Katherine Howard, fifth wife of Henry VIII, during a royal visit in 1541. Despite its position behind a safety fence, this architectural masterpiece is a must-see in the area. It was built in 1841, adding to older buildings dating back to 1530. It was used as a convalescent home for American soldiers in the First World War. From the Second World War until its closure in the 1990s it alternated between an American and an RAF hospital. It remained empty for several years before being devastated by fire in 2004.

8 miles SE of Lincoln. Heading S on B1188, pass Branston and take fourth L onto B1202 signed Nocton. At Nocton pass the Green and park in All Saints Church parking. Follow path in trees NE to Nocton Hall. Or walk back up the Green, take path on the R to join the Avenue, then R at crossroads, walk down to residential care home and Nocton Hall. Several buses between Lincoln and Nocton.

53.1658, -0.4136, LN4 2BQ

7 *BOLINGBROKE CASTLE*
OLD BOLINGBROKE

If you were going to paint the perfect Lincolnshire village, you wouldn't have to travel much further than Old Bolingbroke. Its red brick houses all seem to have immaculate gardens, the green is equally pristine and the 14th-century Black Horse Inn (PE23 4HH) serves a fantastic vegetarian curry. The castle is another pull to the area; it makes for a good 45 minute or so stop-off as you wander round the ramparts and down the few remaining stairs. With little of the height of the walls remaining, the castle stands as a perfect hexagonal enclosure around a wide open space for children to run around in. It was the birthplace of the future Henry IV in 1367 and was taken by Cromwell in 1643 during the Civil Wars.

Take the A158 E from Horncastle and continue for 3 miles. Take a R (B1195) towards Snipe Dales Nature Reserve. Continue past petrol station then take the R turn to Old Bolingbroke and Asgarby. Continue to Bolingbroke village where English Heritage signs direct you the remainder of the way.

53.1651, 0.0169, PE23 4HH

8 *CALCEBY CHURCH AND VILLAGE*
ALFORD

In the southern half of the picturesque Lincolnshire Wolds, a field slightly raised from the road contains the single-arched ruin of St Andrew's Church. The village it once served has all but vanished and the church, last used in 1692, is not far behind! There are lovely walks all over the area and the gentle hills in this part of Lincolnshire give outstanding views across the countryside. Every July the market town of Alford, 5 miles drive from Calceby to the east, puts on a Jazz, Folk and Classical music festival. Bikes can also be hired in the town at James Cycles on West Street (LN13 9DG, 01507 463329).

Calceby is 9 miles SE of Louth on the A16. From A16 head S, at large sign indicating Driby and Calceby R (and South Thoresby L), turn R to Calceby. Pass two red brick houses L and come to a noticeboard and lay-by R. Pull in here. Walk down to the gate to enter the field with the ruins.

53.2602, 0.0820, LN13 0AX

S

6

6

5

Redbourne
Caistor
Croxby
Ludney
Fulstow
Kirkby
Gainsborough
Market Rasen
Louth
Saxby
Mablethorpe
Knaith
Stow
Welton
Rand
Sotby
Haugham
Aby
Alford
LINCOLN
Apley
Hogsthorpe
Harby
Horncastle
North Hykeham
Spilsby
Eagle
Woodhall Spa
Skegness
Coleby
Brough
Croft
Medlam
Eastville
Gibraltar
Digby
Dogdyke
Fenton
Wrangle
Cranwell
Langrick
Evedon
Wilsford
Foston
Boston
Leverton Lucasgate
Swaton
Bicker
Kirton
1
2
3
4
5
6
7
8

CHAPTER 14

PEAK DISTRICT & NORTH WEST MIDLANDS

Within easy reach of the cities of Manchester, Sheffield, Leeds and Nottingham, the Peak District is a rare mix of accessibility and wilderness. Although the natural beauty of this area, shaped by the last ice-age, has always been attractive to walkers, it has not always been open to the public. In 1932 an act of mass trespass took place on the moorland plateau of Kinder Scout, in the Peak District, to protest against the lack of access to areas of open countryside. This act of civil disobedience led to the National Parks legislation in 1949 and the creation of the Peak District National Park in 1951, the first National Park in the country.

Long before its status as a National Park the mineral-rich Peak District had a life as an industrial landscape. Where walkers now tread, workers would have made their way to work in the mills, mines, quarries and kilns of the area. An old lead mine, near Sheldon, four miles to the west of Bakewell, is one such remnant from this time. The romantically named Magpie Mine began operation as early as 1740 and continued to operate into the region's time as a national park, finally closing in the 1950s. Based on Cornish design, Magpie is not the only mine of this ilk in the area. The remains of Mandale Mine can be found in the woods at Lathkill Dale. The mine was home to one of the largest waterwheels in mining, a fact that seems hard to believe now as the river all but dries up every summer.

Towering above the Monsal Trail, a cycle track and footpath, the vast buttresses of the twin lime kilns constructed by the East Buxton Lime Works are a totally surreal sight. Neatly lodged into a Derbyshire hillside, they tower above the landscape like a section of a space station or the home of a super-villain. Their purpose was to make quicklime for the then-burgeoning chemical and steel industries. There would have been little joy working in these kilns; the top would have been a relentless feed of coal and lime and at the bottom a man, or sometimes even child, would have removed the caustic quicklime with very little in the way of safety equipment - injuries would have been frequent and no doubt very painful!

3
5
2
6

1 EAST BUXTON AND MILLER'S DALE

The two large lime kilns just off the former Midland Railway line are an awesome site. A footpath leads to the top of the East Buxton Kiln, where you'll find spectacular views as well as an old cart that was once used to fill this vast structure with alternating lime and coal. The 8½ mile-long Monsal Trail, running between Blackwell Mill in Chee Dale, and Coombs Road at Bakewell, passes this site. It is suitable for walkers and cyclists of all ages.

7 miles E of Buxton. Turn N from A6 onto B6049. Immediately after crossing River Wye, turn L to Miller's Dale, under the bridge, and then L towards Monsal Trail parking.

53.2566,- 1.8031, SK17 8SN

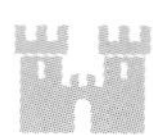

2 PEVERIL CASTLE
CASTLETON

With its breath-taking vistas out to the surrounding Hope Valley, you'll be glad you made the very steep climb up to the medieval fortress of Peveril Castle. Film fans might recall it as the location where Wesley and Buttercup roll down the hill after each other. The structure visible today was built by Henry II in 1176 but the site predates this by around a century. Full facilities including picnic area and visitor centre. The castle marks the start of the 46-mile Limestone Way which finishes in Rochester in Staffordshire. Ye Olde Nags Head, a 17th-century coaching inn on Cross Street, Castleton S33 8WH offers stone-baked pizza, Derbyshire breakfast and four-poster beds (01433 620248). Nearby Peak Cavern can be a costly but worthwhile boat trip into underground mines.

In Castleton follow signs to car park (up to £6 per car!) From here the castle is signposted.

53.3399, -1.7774, S33 8WQ

3 MAGPIE MINE
SHELDON

The old lead mining works at Magpie Mine consists of a near-complete Cornish engine house along with a winch that has its original cabling. It is a short pleasant walk over pasture land just south of the village of Sheldon. In the 1830s Magpie had an ongoing rivalry with neighbouring Maypitt Mine, which worked the same vein. In 1833, 24 Magpie Mine workers were put on trial for the murder of three Maypitt workers who died of suffocation from the fumes emanating from an underground fire that was started deliberately.

From Bakewell, head W of B5055. Take R turn signed Sheldon, Flagg, Chelmorton. Keep L at next junction, then drive to a pull-in by a track R to the old mine. It is an easy 5-10 min walk from here.

53.2105, -1.7439, DE45 1QU

4 MANDALE MINE ENGINE HOUSE

Tucked away in the woods at Lathkill Dale you'll find the remains of a Cornish engine house, the ruins of Thomas Bateman's house (the mine's 19th-century owner) and some of the old 'soughs' or drainage passageways allowing water to drain from the mine. The soughs can be explored using a head torch along with a good pair of wellies. For the really adventurous, many of the area's mine shafts can be explored with the help of a potholing expert (try outdoorinstruction.co.uk or focusactivities.co.uk).

A couple of miles S of Bakewell near Over Haddon. From Over Haddon car park head down to the river. Follow the footpath to the right along the river before branching right after ½ mile/10 minutes walk.

53.1925, -1.7082, DE45 1HZ

5 SUTTON SCARSDALE HALL

Set amid a manicured lawn, on a hillside with the backdrop of the Derbyshire countryside, this roofless Georgian mansion has plenty to explore. Fireplaces, chimneys and traces of the old plasterwork can still be seen as you wander round the red brick interior. It is a tranquil place, suitable for quiet contemplation or for a family picnic. Built in 1724-29 by the Earl of Scarsdale, the hall was eventually bought by the Arkwrights, a notable family of industrialists in the 19th century. Frances Kemble, the wife of Richard Arkwright, loved entertaining at the house and held many lavish parties. About a mile to the south, along the footpath passing through Owlcotes, are the ruins of Heath Old Church 53.1992, -1.3239, the last remaining building of the deserted village of Lound.

Approx. 3 miles from M1. From M1, junction 29, exit onto A6175 then take 2nd R to Sutton Scarsdale. Cross over the main road then, just after the road dog-legs to the L, follow English Heritage sign to hall and car park.

53.2153, -1.3410, S44 5UR

6 HARDWICK OLD HALL
CHESTERFIELD

Visitors can climb the four storeys to the top of this imposing ruin for far-reaching views out across the surrounding hills of the Derbyshire landscape. Much of the original plasterwork can still be seen and an audio tour tells you a little more of the history of the site. Bess of Hardwick, one of the most influential and successful women of the Tudor age, constructed both the New and the Old Halls along with nearby Chatsworth House. From a humble birth, each of her four marriages saw her rise up the social ladder until she reached the ranks of Countess of Shrewsbury.

Leave M1 at junction 29 and take the A6175, take first L Stainsby, Hardwick Hall, take the L under the motorway to Stainsby Mill and Hardwick Hall. Veer R past the Mill and follow signs to Hardwick Hall and car park. Hardwick Old Hall (English Heritage) is just behind Hardwick New Hall (National Trust) and you can pay for a discounted ticket for both or just visit just the Old Hall.

53.1665,- 1.3099, S44 5QJ

7 CODNOR CASTLE
RIPLEY

Half way down a pot-holed lane behind an overgrown hedge in a field full of thistles, north of Langley Mill lies the ruin of Codnor Castle. Despite its forlorn appearance, Codnor is a beguiling ruin; you'll find yourself circling the site finding a new perspective with each step. It is fenced off most of the week but open by volunteers some Sundays between 11am and 3pm (codnorcastle.co.uk). There is some evidence that an older motte-and-bailey castle existed on the site in the 11th century. However the present castle was built by Henry de Grey around 1210.

Codnor is 2 miles SE of Ripley. At Codnor, park in car park near Poet and Castle pub. Walk up Alfreton Rd, to N, away from town. After pavement runs out turn R down New Rd. Take next R, the road dog-legs to L, take R turn. Pass white cottage then look for the stile in hedge to your L opposite derelict farm. Enter field for the castle.

53.0450, -1.3547, NG16 5PQ

8 TRINITY CHAPEL
ALFRETON

The bell tower is hidden under a thick layer of ivy. The walls that once supported this remote church's roof now support an ecosystem of mosses, ivy, trees and shrubs. The whole building seems to be slowly sinking into the leaf litter surround the building; this is truly a building merging with the world around it. The chapel was mentioned in the Domesday book and completely rebuilt in the 16th century. Due to its remote location, the building was rarely regularly used throughout its history, but on Trinity Sunday crowds would flock here in such great numbers they would fill the hillsides surrounding the area. The Plough Inn in Brackenfield has an excellent selection of local micro-brewed ales, good food and fine wines (DE55 6DD 01629 534437).

Head E from the Plough Inn, Brackenfield, L off main road, veer E up the hill/ Cold Harbour La and keep going until you find a convenient place to park without obstructing traffic. Where Berridge La splits off from this lane, go over the stone stile in the drystone wall R. Follow the tree-lined walk, pass through a gate, the church is in the conifer wood.

53.1296 -1.4664, DE55 6EE

6

9 BONE MILL ON THE WYE
ASHFORD IN THE WATER

Next to the River Wye, the old mill at Great Shacklow Wood is a picture postcard ruin. The mill had a rather macabre use as bones were sent here from around the country to crush down and use as a calcium-rich fertiliser. Just past the twin stone cottages of Lower Farm, to the east of Sheldon village, a footpath runs past Little Shacklow Wood (another runs through it) and along the river to the mill. A route can be navigated along from the mill, up the hill and through Great Shacklow Wood back to Sheldon. This circular walk is a total of 2½ miles and strenuous at times.

Take the A6 north of Bakewell, and continue for 2½ miles passing the turn to Ashford in the Water. As you come out of a sharp bend to the L you'll see a straight track leading to the woods on the L followed by a lay-by to the R. Park here and walk down the track and over the bridge to the mill.

53.2235, -1.7285, DE45 1QP

10 WINGFIELD MANOR
SOUTH WINGFIELD

Wingfield Manor is a large ruined medieval manor house built in the mid-15th century. Its sinister silhouette can be seen for miles around during the winter. Conversely in the summer months it is almost completely hidden amongst the tree line. You can still climb up to the top of its tower for spectacular views across the area. The manor house was once used as a prison and during its history it had imprisoned Mary Queen of Scots three times.

The manor is only available to visit by pre-booked guided tours only 0370 3331181 and it is recommended you call well in advance. No parking on the site, park in the lay-by.

53.0912, -1.4424, DE55 7NH

11 THROWLEY OLD HALL

The substantial ruins of Throwley Old Hall seem to have been hidden almost completely away from public view for centuries. Today's hall was built from local limestone by Sir Samson Meverell in 1503. Meverell had the impressive title of Constable of England and had survived 11 battles in just two years during the wars with France. Throwley Hall is best walked to rather than getting to by car. It is situated not far from the Manifold river and the Manifold Way. From Ilam Country Park, DE6 2AZ, walk to the north west from the car park, past Rushley Farm to join the country lane to the ruin.

From Peveril of the Peak Hotel in Thorpe (DE6 2AW) follow the road to the R/SW. Continue on to Ilam, turn R, past monument, then take the next R up Ilam Moor La past the Warringtons Coaches. Veer L onto Lodge La, turn R after a mile then a mile later the ruins will be on your R next to the farm buildings. Side of road parking only.

53.0693, -1.8345, DE6 2BA

10

9

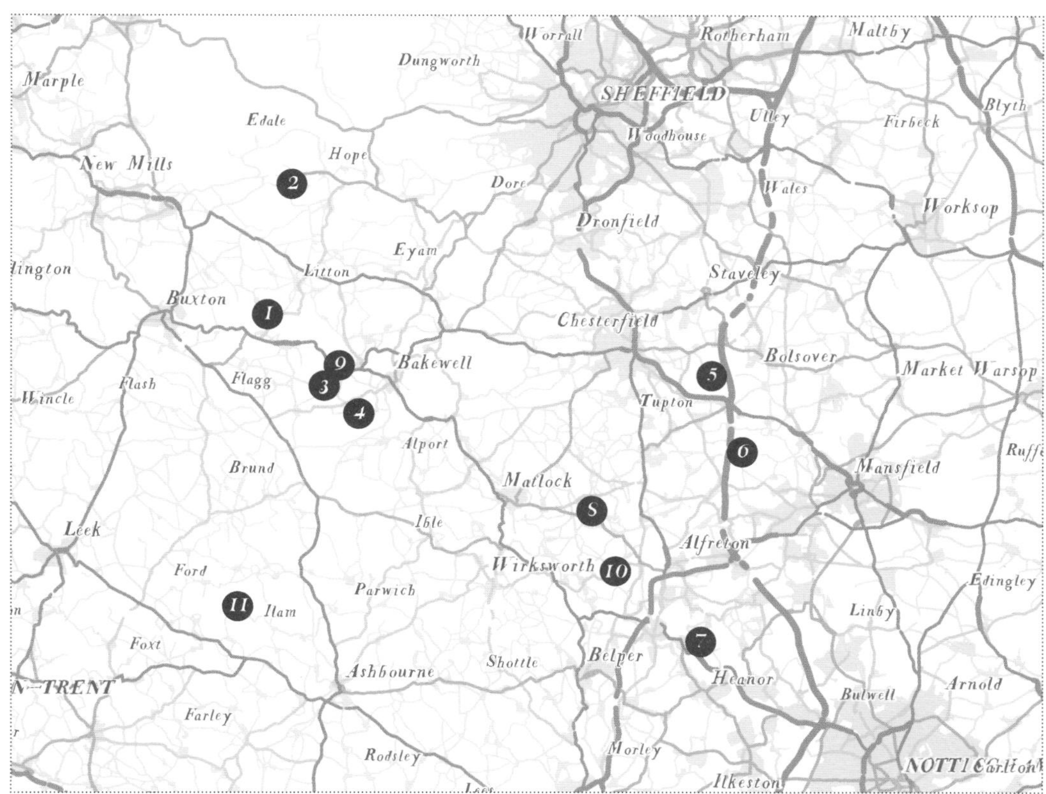
Worrall
Rotherham
Maltby
Dungworth
Marple
SHEFFIELD
Blyth
Edale
Ulley
Firbeck
Woodhouse
Hope
New Mills
2
Dore
Wales
Worksop
Dronfield
Eyam
Litton
Staveley
Buxton
1
Chesterfield
Bolsover
9
Bakewell
5
Market Warsop
Flash
Flagg
3
Wincle
4
Tupton
Alport
6
Brund
Mansfield
Matlock
8
Ible
Leek
Alfreton
Wirksworth
10
Edingley
Ford
Parwich
11
Ilam
Linby
Foxt
7
Belper
Shottle
Ashbourne
Heanor
Arnold
Bulwell
Farley
Morley
Rodsley
Ilkeston
Carlton

CHAPTER 15

WELSH BORDERS

The rolling hills, large open plains, woodlands, valleys and flowing rivers of the Welsh Marches are one of Britain's best-kept secrets. The region's historic towns such as Leominster, Hereford and Shrewsbury have a relaxed, almost sleepy feel to them, perfect for an afternoon pottering in and out of charity shops, cafés and antique shops. At its heart are the stunning Shropshire Hills, an Area of Outstanding Natural Beauty, and the area is a traditional a getaway for the big conurbations of the West Midlands.

However, the area has not always been a sleepy one, for the number of hill forts along the border show that these lands have been fought over, tooth and claw, for centuries. Perhaps the bloodiest of these times was when William the Conqueror came to power. The independent Welsh very quickly proved themselves to be a thorn in his side. The troubles had started in the years leading up to the Norman invasion. Gruffydd ap Llywelyn had united the independent states of Wales into one kingdom. Until his death in 1063, he launched aggressive attacks on his English neighbours. When William arrived in England three years later, his first job was to crush resistance and to secure his borders with Wales and Scotland. He needed castles as a place to garrison his men and protect his lands. He commanded his most loyal supporters, including William FitzOsbern, to build a line of castles down the Welsh border and granted them lands there. The castles they built eventually became vast, extravagant structures, as much a show of strength as defensive buildings. The region became known as the Welsh Marches, a semi-autonomous land, acting as a buffer between England and Wales. Clun Castle, within the Shropshire Hills, was one such castle. Another castle at Wigmore demonstrates, even hundreds of years after it was built, the wealth that many of the Norman lords of this area had at their disposal.

1
3
4
2

1 LILLESHALL ABBEY
NR TELFORD

The scale and beauty of Lilleshall Abbey is staggering, easily comparing with many of the more well-known abbeys both within the area and further afield. A short climb up the dark, narrow, spiral staircase will reward you with breathtaking and vertigo-inducing views of the abbey and surrounding area. Lilleshall was an Augustinian abbey, founded in the late 12th century. It prospered until the 14th century when it began to struggle. There were many pressures on the abbey including an obligation to pay dues to retired abbots. Some of these dues were reasonable, such as food and clothes, but others may have been considered extravagances, such as servants or money for upkeep of large estates. Retired abbott John of Chetwynd clearly did not believe his dues to be adequate and he pillaged the abbey with a gang of armed men to regain the value of goods he felt he deserved!

Exit the M54 at junction 3 take the A41 towards Wolverhampton. Stay on the A41 for 4¼ miles heading over the A5roundabout, turn left Lilleshall Abbey and Corner Farm Antiques. L at the T-junction, then R continue 2 miles, turn R, head through the gates to abbey car park (limited parking).

52.7249, -2.3898, TF10 9HW

2 HAUGHMOND ABBEY
UPTON MAGNA

The picturesque remains of the 12th-century Haughmond Abbey lie on the side of Haughmond Hill, around 15 minutes drive to the south of Moreton Corbet Hall. The ruin is a pleasant, easy, four-mile (1-1½ hour) walk from Shrewsbury station along The Hollies or Shropshire Way. This Augustinian priory was built in the early 12th century and grew to be one of the most prosperous and influential in the region. The abbey is not far from Douglas's Leap, the supposed area where the Earl of Douglas, in flight from the Battle of Shrewsbury in a rebellion against the Henry VI in 1403, was thrown from his horse and seized by the king's soldiers .

From Shrewsbury, take the B5062 E. After the bypass, A49, continue to the treeline, where you turn L (English Heritage sign).

52.7321,- 2.6801, SY4 4RW

3 ACTON BURNELL CASTLE

All that remains of this 13th-century former fortified manor house is the red sandstone shell of the outer walls. There are plenty of doorways to run in and out of, making it a fun place for kids (and adults who refuse to grow up). It is tucked away in its own grounds surrounded by trees next to the rather less ruined 13th-century Church of St Mary. Within the school grounds adjacent to the castle, you can see the two gable end remains of Parliament Barn. It was here for the first time that commoners were allowed to speak about matters of state with the king and the ruling barons in the late 13th century.

Signed from the A49, 10 miles S of Shrewsbury.

52.6129, -2.6897, SY5 7PE

4 MORETON CORBET HALL & CASTLE

The grounds of this grand Elizabethan mansion and medieval castle are perfect for a family visit. It is a great site to explore, with its large gatehouse, courtyard, keep and manor remains. The brave-hearted might want to descend the steps to the dark and reportedly haunted cellar! Although Moreton Corbet dates back to Saxon times the stone castle was not constructed until the turn of the 13th century by Bartholomew Torret. At this time the castle was known as Morton Torret but changed to the present name when it passed down by marriage to the Corbet family. During the 16th century, strongly influenced by his travels through Europe, Robert Corbet began work on the grand Elizabethan house we see today. Unfortunately he died of the plague just five years into construction and it was down to his brothers to complete the work. Just off National Cycle Route 45 and the Shropshire Way. The Stanton Arms in Stanton Upon Hine Heath, SY4 4LR, 01939 250221, a mile from the ruin, serves real ale and reasonably-priced food.

N of Shrewsbury off the A53. From Battlefield Island Services (where A49/A53 and A5124 meet), take the A53 heading E towards Market Drayton and Stoke-on-Trent for 4 miles. At Shawbury pass the garage and take the next L towards RAF Shawbury. Continue for 1 mile, go past the airbase and take the R signposted to the castle (easy to miss). Turn L and park by road.

52.8045, -2.6524, SY4 4DW

5 BEESTON CASTLE
BEESTON

The steep climb to the top of this castle offers spectacular views over the vast Cheshire Plains and the surrounding eight counties. With vistas such as this you can see why there has been a stronghold on the site of Beeston Castle since Iron Age times. The site is a great place to bring kids as there is plenty to explore at this medieval fortress. It is easy to lose an afternoon exploring this imposing ruin or playing hide and seek around the remains.

Off National Cycle Route 45 and the Sandstone Way long distance footpath. From the Red Fox pub where the A51 and A49 meet take the A49 southwest. Go over the canal then take a R onto Dean Bank. Take a L and continue to the pay and display car park opposite the castle entrance.

53.1284, -2.6922, CW6 9TX

6 WIGMORE CASTLE
WIGMORE

Wigmore Castle has become so overgrown it feels as if it may have risen organically from the wooded hillside that it sits upon. The towers, curtain wall and the gatehouse spring up from the hillside like something from a fairytale. Continue on the path from the church to the castle to climb the 945ft (288m) up the hill, Wigmore Rolls. Along with castles such as Monmouth, Clifford and Chepstow, Wigmore was built by William FitzOsbern between 1067 and 1071 as part of his programme of building new castles or refortifying old ones. Wigmore changed hands many times and even spent part of its time as a prison. It has lain in ruin since the Civil War in the mid-17th century.

Head W out from Leominster past Morrisons on Bargates/Baron's Cross Rd. Stay on the road/B4360 across the roundabout past the Baron's Cross Inn. After 1¼ miles take the R turn B4360 towards Kingsland. Take the L past the post box toward Wigmore. R on A4110 continue to Wigmore. Follow signs to the R towards the village hall and parking. From here it is 15 minutes moderate to strenuous walk to the castle.

52.3184, -2.8696, HR6 9UB

7 WHITE LADIES PRIORY
COSFORD

The ruin of White Ladies Priory lies at the end of a tree-lined path in a field knee-high with weeds. Despite being just a mile from a motorway and close to large urban areas, it feels quiet and out of the way and does not see a huge volume of visitors. It lies just off the Monarch's Way long distance path. Despite the name, the priory itself has vanished and the ruins we see today are the remains of the medieval church. Unlike some of the larger houses, White Ladies never prospered, with an annual income of just £17, the modern equivalent of £5,300 in 1535. King Charles II hid here following his defeat at the Battle of Worcester in 1651.

Between Telford and Wolverhampton. Leave the M54 at junction 3 to head S on the A41 towards Wolverhampton and RAF Cosford. Stay in the L lane and take 1st L, take the L (not the no-through road) onto Shackerley La. Stay on this road for 1¾ miles to a pull in on the L. Follow English Heritage signs to the L down the path/lane - 2 minutes easy walk.

52.6657, -2.2584, ST19 9AR

6

4

8 WROXETER ROMAN CITY

A replica Roman town house sits alongside the remains of the public baths of Wroxeter Roman City, which was the fourth largest city in Roman Britain. The replica, using traditional Roman methods, was built as part of Channel 4's programme 'Rome wasn't built in a day', in conjunction with English Heritage. There is an audio tour and a small museum on site.

From the W end of M54 stay on the A5. At the roundabout before Telford, take the first exit, staying on the A5 for another mile.

52.6741,- 2.6444, SY5 6PH

9 WENLOCK PRIORY MUCH WENLOCK

The topiary gardens are the perfect place for a tranquil afternoon stroll. The priory at Wenlock dates back to the 7th century when an Anglo-Saxon monastery was founded here. The remains we see today are of the much later 12th-century Cluniac priory. The priory lies just off the Shropshire Way long distance path. In 1850 Dr William Penny Brookes set up the Wenlock Olympian Games here "for the promotion of the moral, physical and intellectual improvement" of the inhabitants of Wenlock. The idea went on to inspire the modern Olympic Games and in the 2012 games one of the Olympic mascots was called Wenlock in tribute.

Take the A458 SE from Shrewsbury for 10 miles through Cross House and Cressage to Much Wenlock. Take L at the Gaskell Arms Hotel go down the High St and turn L signposted Abbey Ruins. Go past the church and turn R. Car park is on the L.

52.5973, -2.5553, TF13 6HS

10 CLUN CASTLE

Paddle in the river, climb up the steep hill to Clun Castle and relax in one of the many pubs or cafés in the village of Clun. Built in the 11th century, the powerful Marcher castle defended the English-Welsh border during the Norman occupation. Much of the large keep still stands high on this naturally occurring knoll overlooking the Saxon village. It's also not too far from the Offa's Dyke Path and the Shropshire Way walking routes.

Clun is between Bishop's Castle and Knighton on the A488. There are two car parks in the village and the castle is a short, moderate-to-difficult walk from the town centre.

52.4222 -3.0330, SY7 8JR

11 TITTERSTONE CLEE HILL

The climb to the concrete quarry remains and working radar station on the summit of Titterstone Clee Hill, some 1,749ft or 533m high, is a vigorous but rewarding one. From this vantage point, within the Shropshire Area of Outstanding Natural Beauty, you can see as far as the Black Mountains in Wales and the Malvern Hills. For the less active it is possible to drive to the summit and park next to the remains of the quarry buildings. Titterstone has been in use since the Bronze and Iron Age, and some of the earthworks of the old fort can still be seen. A railway once ran to the top of Clee Hill to carry down the raw materials of coal and dhustone or dolerite, which was mined and quarried here. Many of the buildings date from this time including the series of small square rooms which made up the old loading bays. The no-thrills Kremlin Inn, SY8 3NZ, on the hill itself, has the claim of being the highest pub in Shropshire.

From Ludlow take B4364 and then R onto A4117. Turn L Dhutone, Titterston Clee Summit and carry on for 1 ½ miles to the summit where there is parking.

52.3955,- 2.6000, SY8 3NY

11

9

2

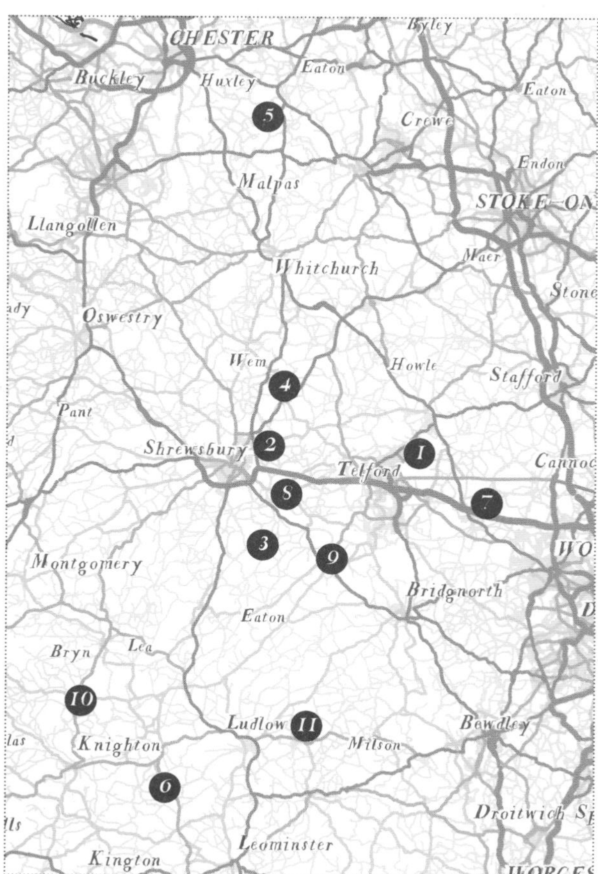
CHESTER
Byley
Buckley
Huxley
Eaton
Eaton
5
Crewe
Endon
Malpas
Llangollen
Whitchurch
Maer
Oswestry
Wem
4
Howle
Stafford
Pant
Shrewsbury
2
1
Telford
8
7
3
9
Montgomery
Bridgnorth
Eaton
Bryn
Lea
10
Ludlow
11
Bewdley
Knighton
Milson
6
Leominster
Kington

10

CHAPTER 16

SOUTH WALES

South Wales is a land without pretence, a place where immense beauty and heavy industry sit side by side. Much of the industry has now departed, leaving nothing but the odd relic among the hills, valleys and harbours. On the shores of Abercastle the remains of an old grain store look out to sea from the cliff-side. Once trading ships filled the harbour, yet now pleasure boats and tourists flock to this remote, unspoilt part of Wales. To the east of Hafodyrynys village another industrial relic, the last remnant of the Hafodyrynys Colliery, can be seen just off the main Newbridge to Pontypool road. At its peak in the 1920s the mine employed approaching a thousand men, yet despite the prediction of a bright future, geological problems caused it to close in the mid-1960s. The mine and its infrastructure have all but vanished. All that remains is what appears to be a modern day folly, the large circular building that acted as a washery, once used to clean slurry coal .

The castles built by the Welsh stand as relics of a more distant era. During the middle ages, the territory on either side of the Welsh/English border became known as the Welsh Marches; it was a warring land, ruled by princes and kings. Rhys ap Gruffydd, Lord Rhys, was a notable 12th-century Welsh leader, instrumental in fending of the Anglo-Norman army and reuniting the kingdom of Deheubarth - an area now comprising mainly Pembrokeshire and Carmarthenshire along with parts of Cardiganshire. The stunning Carreg Cennen Castle (meaning Castle on the Rock) was built by Lord Rhys in the late 12th century and passed down to his son Rhys Fychan. The Rhys family didn't prove to be a harmonious one when it came to the castle. Rhys the Younger's own mother betrayed him by passing it over to English rule. He soon regained control of the castle in 1248 only to have his uncle take it away from him!

As the ruling class, the Normans often had more money than the native Welsh, a fact never more apparent than in the construction of their castles. Raglan, Llawhaden, Llansteffan and Ogmore Castle are all impressive Norman strongholds, the remains of which are no less impressive than in their day.

1
3
4
7

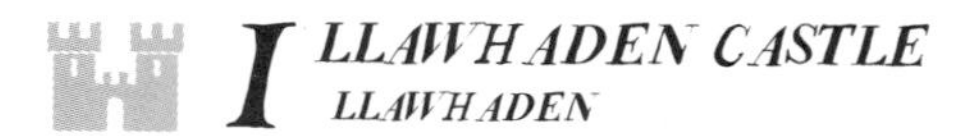

1 LLAWHADEN CASTLE
LLAWHADEN

Llawhaden is a bit of a gem; there is plenty to explore, large towers to climb, a well to make wishes in and rooms and passageways to get lost in. It is not really on any tourist trail so even during the summer you may be the only ones exploring these ruins. It was built as a stronghold for the Norman bishops of St David's. Many bishops would live in fortified palaces, but few would have had castles. This is perhaps testament to the bitter feelings towards the bishops from the suppressed Welsh population but also speaks of the wealth and power they commanded.

From Haverfordwest travel about 9 miles E on the A40 to Canaston Bridge roundabout and then take the 1st exit B4314 Robeston, Wathen and Llawhaden. Or from Narberth, head N for 1 ½ miles following Cadw signs to a small car park with a noticeboard located in the middle of LLawhaden. The path to the castle is just a 1 minute walk from here.

51.8223,- 4.7976, SA67 8HL

2 DRYSLWYN CASTLE
CARMARTHEN

Dryslwyn is a very atmospheric castle, associated with Lord Rhys in the 12th century. From high on the battlements there are broad and far-reaching views of the surrounding landscape. A site with a pretty view today would have been originally chosen for its strategic importance. Another of Lord Rhys's castles is that of Dinefwr, about 15 minutes' drive (40 mins cycle) to the east, around a mile from Llandeilo. Dinefwr is a National Trust property which includes Newton House and Dinefwr park. There are great walks to be had in the area. Three miles to the southeast of Dryslwyn Castle is the mansion house (not ruined) and woods of Gelli Aur Country Park (parking at 51.8585, -4.0411). North of the castle, on the other side of the A40 is the volunteer-run Dryslwyn local shop (SA32 8QX) which sells fresh local produce.

From the A40, the turning to Dryslwyn is 2¾ miles E of Llanegwad and 1½ W of Broad Oak. Head S here following the signs to Felindre and Dryslwyn on the B4297. Head straight across two sets of crossroads to find a parking and picnic site signposted on the R. Cross the road to the castle. It is a 5–10 mins strenuous walk.

51.8624, -4.1013, SA32 8JQ

3 GRAIN STORE
ABERCASTLE

Abercastle is a harbour off the beaten track, visited by walkers, divers and boat owners. Its jagged rocky shore is enveloped with multi-coloured seaweed and rock pools beckoning inspection from young enquiring minds. Abercastle was once a busy trading port throughout the 18th and 19th centuries. Boats would have sailed out from the harbour and traded with England, Ireland and Europe. The ruined grain store, situated on the cliff overlooking the harbour, is all that reminds us of that time. Alfred Johnson, a fisherman living in Massachusetts, made an historic landing in Abercastle on 12th August 1876. He was the first to sail single-handed across the Atlantic and did so in a small fishing boat after a dare during a card game.

Head to Mathry on the A487, 9¼ miles E of St David's, 6½ miles W of Fishguard. Head NW to Abercastle and park at the head of the bay. Follow the footpath R of the bay for the grain store, 5mins walk. Carreg Sampson, an ancient megalithic tomb, is along the footpath to the L. Several buses from Fishguard and St David's.

51.9611, -5.1277, SA62 5HJ

4 ROSEBUSH QUARRY
ROSEBUSH

It is easy to lose a day when visiting Rosebush. The quarry buildings are just one small part of this large abandoned quarry. On top of the mounds to the right of the path there are enough bilberries to stain your fingers and tongue, while filling your belly. The large quarry hole, now filled with crystal blue water, is perfect for a wild swim. There is also an intriguing tunnel arch in the side of the mound, which looks like it could be a home for pixies or elves. In the early 19th century, Rosebush and neighbouring Bellstone were small quarries surrounded by wilderness. In the late 1860s Edward Cropper bought the site for £3,750 (£230,000 in today's money) and expanded both with typical Victorian zeal. He put his stepson, Joseph Macaulay, in charge and built links to the outside world via the Narbeth Road and Maenclochog Railway (which linked with the Great Western Railway). Despite their enthusiasm and enterprise, the site never really prospered as the price of slate collapsed in 1877 and the railway closed in 1882.

Between Fishguard and Narbeth on B4313. Turn into Rosebush village at the pink corrugated traditional Tafarn Sinc inn (01437 532214). Walk up the dead-end lane past cottages to the ruined quarry building. Continue up to the R for the swimming lake.

51.9349, -4.7984, SA66 7QX

5 *CARREG CENNEN CASTLE*

Carreg Cennen Castle was once voted the most romantic ruin in Wales. Its name translates as 'Castle on the Rock' and it sits on top of a remote limestone cliff within the Brecon Beacons. On a winter's day, the hill next to the castle is perfect for a spot of sledging! However, it is the underground caves that make this castle so unique. A vaulted passageway leads from the castle to the caves, which are natural, not man-made. Bring a torch along to help guide the way!

The castle is situated E of Llandovery and W of Carmarthen. 4½ miles SE of Llandeilo. From the A483 S of Llandeilo, take the minor road E, opposite the A476. Cross the railway, then R and follow to Trapp. In Trapp, continue 1 mile E, following brown signs, until you reach Carreg Cennen Castle.

51.8545, -3.9354, SA19 6UA

6 *OGMORE CASTLE NEAR BIRIDGEND*

When the Normans seized control of this region within the Vale of Glamorgan they built three castles to secure their power. Coity Castle, the Newcastle and perhaps the best located of the three, the picturesque castle of Ogmore on the banks of the River Ewenny. Ogmore was built by William de Londres, a follower of Robert Fitzhamon and one of the Twelve Knights of Glamorgan. It is a great site for children as they can run up and down the large waterless moat that surrounds the castle. Wild horses regularly graze this area while the nearby riding school, Ogmore Farm Riding Centre (01656 880856, rideonthebeach.co.uk), leads much tamer horses on 1-2 hour treks over the ford. Tearooms, an ice cream van and the nearby pub offer refreshments for the weary traveller. You can walk from Ogmore to Candleston Castle – see entry for Candleston for directions.

Exit M4 at junction 35 (Crossroads Services), for A473 S-bound. Straight over 4 roundabouts (the road will become the A48); at the 5th roundabout turn L to B4265, signed Ewenny. At Ewenny take the B4524 to Ogmore (not Ogmore-by-Sea). 1st R after reaching the castle, and follow the lane to the car park. Coity Castle (CF35 6BH; 51.5219, -3.553) is NE of Bridgend, off A4061. Newcastle (CF31 4JN; 51.5088, -3.5830) is in Bridgend itself, 10 mins walk from the station.

51.4805, -3.6121, CF32 0QP

7 *NEATH ABBEY*

The substantial remains of Neath Abbey lie on the banks of the gentle flowing waters of the Tennant Canal. It was a favourite of the Romantics and is still a very beautiful place to have a picnic. It was founded in the year 1130, and absorbed by the Cistercian order in 1147. At one time it would have been one of the largest and most powerful abbeys in Wales. You can see the extensive remains of the abbey and a 16th-century mansion.

The Abbey is located 1 mile W of Neath town centre, off the A465.

51.6610, -3.8261, SA10 7DW

8 *RAGLAN CASTLE*

Dubbed as one of the best-kept secrets in Wales, this castle still has a lot of the original features intact and is a fascinating place to explore. There is a large moat and plenty of room for kids to run around. Raglan was built in the 1430s. It held off Parliamentary forces for 13 weeks in 1646, during the Civil War. Once finally taken the castle was 'slighted' – put to ruin so it would no longer serve any military purpose. There are a gift shop and toilets at the castle.

Raglan Castle has CADW signs from the A40. You may need to swing around the roundabout nearby, depending on the direction you are travelling.

51.7702, -2.8500, NP15 2BT

S

5

9

13

9 LLANTHONY PRIORY
ABERGAVENNY

Llanthony Priory is one of the most striking ruins South Wales has to offer. It is well worth the diversion off the Offa's Dyke long distance footpath where it can be seen from the high ridge of the path as you pass from Pandy to Hay-on-Wye. The location of Llanthony Priory proved to be both a blessing and a curse throughout its history. This Norman, Augustinian priory is situated in a remote valley, the Vale of Ewyas, in the middle of the Brecon Beacons National Park. The 12th-century Welsh historian Giraldus Cambrensis, or Gerald of Wales, described it as being "fixed amongst a barbarous people" due to the regular attacks made on the priory by the local Welsh population. Because of these attacks, Miles de Gloucester, the 1st Earl of Hereford, eventually founded Llanthony Secunda Priory as a retreat for the monks of Llanthony. What makes this site special is there is a pub selling real ales and Thatcher's cider along with teas, coffees and ice cream.

From Abergavenny head N on A465, through Llantilio Pertholey. At Llanfihangel Crucorney, turn L after the Skirrid Inn, veer L before the river, and then stay on the road through Llanthony to the priory. It is signposted well in the area, and you will just have to trust the signs as they can seem few and far between. There is on-site parking.

51.9449, -3.0365, NP7 7NN

10 CANDLESTON CASTLE
MERTHYR MAWR

The fortified manor house of Candleston stands just on the edge of the large sand dunes at Merthyr Mawr National Nature Reserve. The site was occupied from the 12th century but the present castle is thought to have been built in the 14th. The ruins could be unstable so take care when visiting. The castle is wild and abandoned, nothing like its tourist-friendly neighbour at Ogmore, which you can walk to from here: head down into the village, take a right at the triangle to the swing bridge, follow the footpath to Ogmore and cross the stepping stones - it's 15 minutes easy walk. The Pelican in her Piety pub (CF32 0QP, 01656 880049) at Ogmore is worth the walk from Candleston alone. Frequented by locals and tourists alike, it serves afternoon tea, real ales and good food.

Exit M4 at junction 35 (Crossroads Services), for A473 S-bound. Straight over 5 roundabouts (the road will become the A48); after the 5th roundabout turn L to small Merthyr Mawr Rd. Continue straight to the end, and park in dunes car park. Castle is up a small track in the trees to the L of the car park (facing away from the dunes).

51.4820 -3.6262, CF32 0DT

11 HAFODYRYNYS MINE WASHERY

As you speed past Hafodyrynys on the A472 you can't help but notice the space age looking building on the side of the road. It looks like some sort of derelict futuristic mansion at first glance but it is in fact a mine washery and would have been used to clean coal slurry. It is the last remnant of the Hafodyrynys mine which closed in the 1960s. The building is on private land but plenty of it can be seen from the road.

Junction 25A M4 head N on the A4042, bypassing Oakfiled, Cwmbran and Pontrhydrun. On the 6th roundabout take the 2nd exit to Pontypool A472. Don't turn to Pontypool at the next roundabout but instead take the 1st exit to A472. Continue for just under 3 miles past Caerphilly County Borough sign (look to your right and you may see the ruin) then take R turn. Head up road until you see a pull in on the R. Just 2mins easy walk up the road.

51.6849, -3.0952, NP4 6UA

12 MYNYDD NANT-Y-BAE
OLD FARM RUIN

Within the Afan Forest Park, hidden amongst the trees, just off the St Illtyd's Walk footpath is the extensive ruin of an old farm complex. Not much is known about the farm but it is thought it may have pre-dated the Forestry Commission's ownership of the land. Bike hire is available at Glyncorrwg Mountain Bike Centre SA13 3EA and the Afan Forest Park Visitor Centre, SA13 3HG. From these two locations you can navigate your way onto the Afan Valley Cycle Way before following trails to the ruin.

Off the St. Illtyd's Walk footpath. Join the path N of Abercregan and walk approx two miles W along St Illtyds Walk.

51.6537, -3.6903, SA13 3HA

13 RUPERRA CASTLE NR CAERPHILLY

Ruperra is not a true castle but a grand house or 'mock' castle built in 1626 by Thomas Morgan. It has been damaged by fire twice in its history. The first fire, in 1785 resulted in a rebuild but the second in the early 1940's proved to be the final blow to a then already declining building. It is an impressive ivy-clad ruin within landscaped gardens just off the Rymney Valley Way, situated on private land but easily visible. The surrounding area is semi-ancient woodland managed by the Craig Ruperra Conservation trust. There are numerous walks around the woods and views as far as the Bristol Chanel on clear days. The building is home to greater and lesser horseshoe bats which has put pay to development of the site.

Take the Rymney Valley way footpath from the Hollybush Inn, Draethen.

51.5703, -3.1272, NP10 8GG

14 LLANSTEFFAN CASTLE

The stunning Llansteffan Castle is a 12th-century Norman castle overlooking the Tywi estuary. It is a large spacious ruin, perfect for children to run around, explore and play hide and seek. It was voted the 6th most romantic ruin in the country and the second most romantic ruin in Wales after Carreg Cennen. From the castle there is a lovely half a mile walk to Scott's Bay.

The turning to the castle is off the A40 E of St Clears and W of Carmarthen. 10 minutes/ ½ mile strenuous walk through woodland to the castle.

51.7656, -4.3906, SA33 5JG

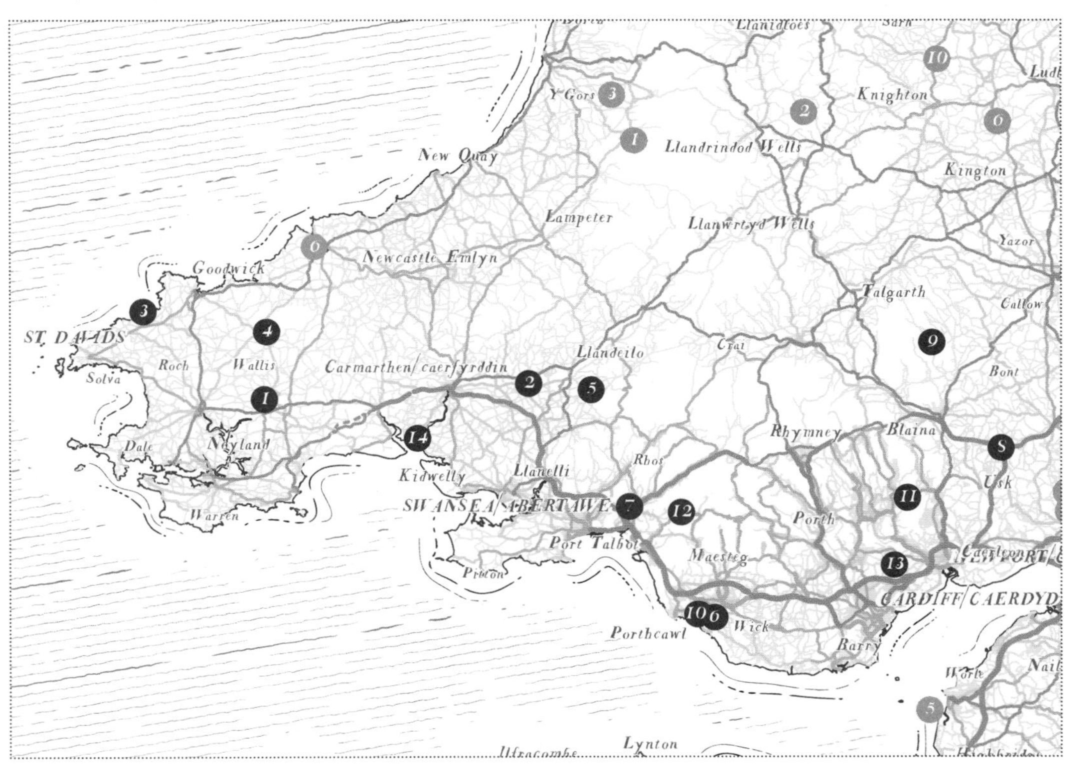

CHAPTER 17

MID WALES

Mid Wales is a vast area of upland sheep farms, isolated communities, reservoirs, mountains and forests. In the 19th century English travellers called the area around the Cambrian Mountains 'the green desert of Wales'. The term goes some way to describe this area but it underestimates the stark beauty within the region. We drove through during the low tourist season and on many occasions felt that ours was the only car around for miles. Sheep graze by the side of the road, sometimes wandering in front of cars or sitting, quite contently chewing the cud, in the path of on-coming traffic. It is quite unlike anywhere in the British Isles, it feels untouched and truly wild.

It would have been this remoteness that attracted monks to build their abbeys in this part of the country during the 12th and 13th centuries. On this impoverished nutrient-poor land, the monks at Strata Florida Abbey, Abbey Cwm Hir and Cymer Abbey would have grazed sheep in much the same way as farmers do today. They were of the Cistercian order, following an austere, self-sufficient lifestyle befitting their surroundings. Here the world outside would have been as much an area of contemplation and worship as the buildings in which they lived and prayed. Walking around the hills and valleys of Mid-Wales, you can see why. With a bit of brooding Welsh sky to add some drama, it is a truly breathtaking region.

Farming is now one of the main industries of Mid-Wales but this wasn't always the case. A century ago this would have been a hive of productivity with zinc, lead, slate and coal mines operating right across the region. Now the remains of this industrial past can sometimes seem like they have been dropped from the sky as you stumble across them in fields or at roadsides. Unlike other parts of the country where ruins become engulfed by weeds, saplings and ivy, those of Mid-Wales take time to heal. The terrain can be exposed so its ruins become weathered and worn by strong winds and rain. In this way they are turning back into the rock and slate they once were and are re-joining the Welsh hillside from where they came.

1
3
2
4

1 STRATA FLORIDA ABBEY
NEAR PONTRHYDFENDIGAID

The name of this 12th-century Cistercian abbey is a Latin corruption of the evocative Welsh name for the site of the abbey, 'Ystrad Fflur', valley of the flowers. The most substantial of all the remains is the large carved doorway, which gives some indication of the great building that once stood here. The site is one of national pride and importance for many reasons: a large yew tree marks the last resting place of the medieval Welsh poet Dafydd ap Gwilym at the abbey. The Brut y Tywysogion, a document chronicling Welsh history from the 7th to the 14th centuries was said to have been written here. Adding to the site's importance, Llywelyn ap Gruffudd, the last king of Wales, held a council of Welsh princes here where they agreed to name his son as their rightful leader. The promise wasn't kept for long and the princes continued to battle once the king was dead.

From A44 at Ponterwyd, head S on A4120 to Devil's Bridge. There, take the B4343 S to Pontrhydfendigaid. Through the village, then L to Strata Florida and the abbey.

52.2756, -3.8386, SY25 6ES

2 CWM HIR ABBEY
NEAR LLANDRINDOD

Cwm Hir Abbey translates as abbey of the long valley. Monks here led a simple life and along with sheep they farmed fish and improved the land to grow all their own produce. Despite their self-sufficiency they would have not existed in isolation in the community, taking their social responsibilities very seriously. They would have acted as a form of social care, looking after the sick and injured, giving them a warm bed, a meal and medicinal herbs if necessary. The abbey is the disputed resting place of the last king of Wales, Llywelyn ap Gruffudd and a memorial to him lies within the ruins. There are many footpaths criss-crossing this wooded valley including the long distance Glyndwr's Way, which passes alongside the ruins.

Between Newtown and Llandrindod Wells off A483. From Llandrindod Wells head N through Crossgates over A44. Approx 1¼ mile from A44 take L signed Abbey Cwm Hir for 4 miles.

52.3298, -3.3873, LD1 6PH

3 PONT CEUNANT GENERATOR
NR DEVIL'S BRIDGE

Between a stream and a wooded, winding road, in the middle of a sheep field, you'll find the giant stone ruins of Pont Ceunant Generating Station. This was designed and built in 1899 by Italian engineer Bernardino Nogara to provide electrical power for Frongoch Mine. It was the first use of such technology in Mid-Wales and would have used water from the hills above to turn a cupped water wheel, or turbine, within the building to generate electricity. The mine had already been in operation for 150 years when the Belgian company, Société Anonyme Métallurgique bought it up and built the station. Sadly their expense would be short-lived as the mine closed operations, selling all the machinery, in 1903. Bernardino was to return to his native Italy where he landed the lucrative position of secretary of the Vatican Bank.

From A44 at Ponterwyd, head S on A4120 to Devil's Bridge; then S on B4343. In Pont-rhyd-y-groes turn R by grey slate garage/shop (with antique pumps). Continue for 3 miles past various mining remains. Park at 52.3508, -3.9057 and walk down road to see the ruin across the fence, as it is on private land.

52.3517, -3.9009, SY23 4RR

4 DARREN SLATE QUARRY
PANTPERTHOG, MACHYNLLETH

Uncut slates lie in rows as if the slate workers had just downed tools and left in the middle of a job. The story has it that if it weren't for opportunists walking up the hillside and pilfering the slates for their roofs, a lot more would line the hill. There is much to see here, among the mountains with the ascent to the site as an enjoyable part of the whole experience. The old slate workers' buildings are in a state of decay but surprisingly complete. Take care, as there are abandoned mine workings here.

Pantperthog is on the A487. A little S of the village and of the Centre for Alternative Technology, park on R at 52.6219, -3.8480, next to phone box. Head back past bus stops to a turning on R marked by a tree with ribbons on. Walk up forester's track marked 'no cars or bikes' to hairpin bend. A footpath heads off main track through edge of Esgair Forest. Follow path over hill to reach quarry buildings. From the village it's a 1-2 hour strenuous walk. Buses to Pantperthog from Machynlleth.

52.6326, -3.8890, SY20 9AU

5 BRONWYDD HOUSE
NEAR ABERBANC

Bronwydd Houyse was built in the Gothic Revival style, which back in the 1850s would have been as fashionable as any modern steel and glass building of today. The house was owned by the Lloyd Baronets of Bronwydd, a benign but wealthy family of landowners. When the 2nd Baronet, Sir Marteine Owen Lloyd died in 1933, the house went to his daughter, who lived only for another four years. On her death, the house and grounds were sold, briefly being a boarding school during the war. The house then fell into ruin and, by 1983, both the roof and floors had fallen in.

From Aber-banc head N on B4334. Road veers to R then to L. Take no-through road on L after white farm buildings and a corrugated black barn. Bus 460, Cardigan-Newcastle Emlyn-Carmarthen passes Aberbanc.

52.0628,- 4.4036, SA44 5LY

6 ST DOGMAELS ABBEY
NEAR CARDIGAN

The Abbey at St Dogmaels was founded by Tironian monks in 1115. This austere monastic sect believed not only in a vow of silence but that all monks in the order should be skilled craftsmen. One has to wonder how the skills were taught and how silent they really were each time they slipped with a hammer and hit their thumb. The traffic can be slow moving in St Dogmaels as ducks, chickens and geese all wander into the road from the nearby millpond. The cafe has a relaxed but efficient atmosphere and I strongly recommend the Welsh cakes. It is a fantastic place to bring children and there are regular plays and community events on at the abbey.

Off B4546 at St Dogmaels, 1 mile W of Cardigan. Signposted from St Dogmaels town centre. Park outside the abbey or on roadside up the hill. Bus 407 from Cardigan.

52.0805, -4.6807, SA43 3EB

7 CASTELL Y BERE
NEAR ABERGYNOLWYN

Castell y Bere was an impressive stronghold built for Welsh princes, in a fantastic defensive position perched on a steep-sided rocky plateau with great views towards Cadr Idris. The castle fell to Edward I in 1283 and has been a ruin for 600 years. The castle is towards the southern boundary of Snowdonia National Park, at the end of a long and winding road, up in the hills overlooking the village of Abergynolwyn. In the village is the excellent Caffi'r Ceunant restaurant and nearby you can see the area in the best possible way by hiring bicycles at Brid Rock cycle hire, Llanegryn, near Tywyn (01654 712193).

From the village of Abergynolwyn, B4405, opposite café and community centre, head on road up hill past Railway Inn. After a mile turn R at staggered crossroads, past phone box and down no-through road. Park ½ mile on L. The castle is a 2-3 mins.

52.6582, -3.9713, LL36 9TP

8 CYMER ABBEY
LLANELLTYD

The Cistercians at Cymer Abbey, founded in 1198, were rather different to other monks. In this tranquil spot they ran a stud farm breeding horses for the nobility of Gwynedd. It seems unlikely that they became rich from this enterprising sideline but the discovery of a hidden silver plate near the site shows they may have had a little bit to spare. Some of the walls stand up to 20 feet high and there are impressive arches along the aisle. The area is great for walking; the abbey is on the circular route of the well-known three-mile Precipice Walk (walkers usually start from Dolgellau). It takes you up just over a mile to the Llyn Cynwch reservoir, a popular haunt for local fishermen.

7

Join A470 just N of Dolgellau and take signposted R turn before Llanelltyd. Follow signs to Vanner along no-through road, which branches off R to abbey.

52.7583, -3.8962, LL40 2HE

9 ESGAIR HIR MINE
NEAR TALYBONT

Arguably nowhere symbolises the bleak, barren beauty of Mid-Wales more than the Esgair Hir Mine. The elements have been at play here and what little does remain is quickly re-joining the Welsh hillside. Any exploration of this area should be carried out with extreme care as there are open shafts all over the site. Along with the shafts it is possible to see the crumbling ruins of an old office block, a crusher house, a barracks and the remains of the school for the miner's children. Esgair Hir was in operation from the late 17th century following a rich discovery of ore. To boost its attraction to investors, in the 1850s it was renamed Welsh Potosi as at this time the majority of the world's silver was produced by the famously rich Potosi silver mines in Peru. The mine features in George Borrow's book 'Wild Wales' (published 1862), about his famous walk across Wales.

Head S along New Street Talybont, past post office and turn L at White Lion Pub, continue to T-junction and take L at Black Lion pub. Veer to R at post box, take L at yellow grit box and continue for 5 miles. The road forks here, there is little in the way of landmarks other than a few telegraph poles. Take L (east) dirt road and continue for a mile until you see the ruins. Parking at 52.5038 -3.8676. From Esgair Hir walk along the track heading east (passing through the forestry gate) for half a mile to arrive at the mine's close neighbour Esgair Fraith Mine.

52.5041,- 3.8663, SY24 5HL

10 HAFOTTYFACH FARMHOUSE

The farmhouse at Hafottyfach is a substantial ruined complex to the south east of Barmouth, a town with a spectacular location between a mountain range and the sea on the mouth of the River Mawddach in North Wales. If the weather is good it is a perfect area to spend the day, or even a week traversing the many cycle tracks and footpaths in the region.

Approx 1 mile from car park at Llynnau Cregennen, Cregennen Lakes, 52.7098, -3.9885. Walk R from car park, then R.

52.7022, -3.9845, LL39 1LX

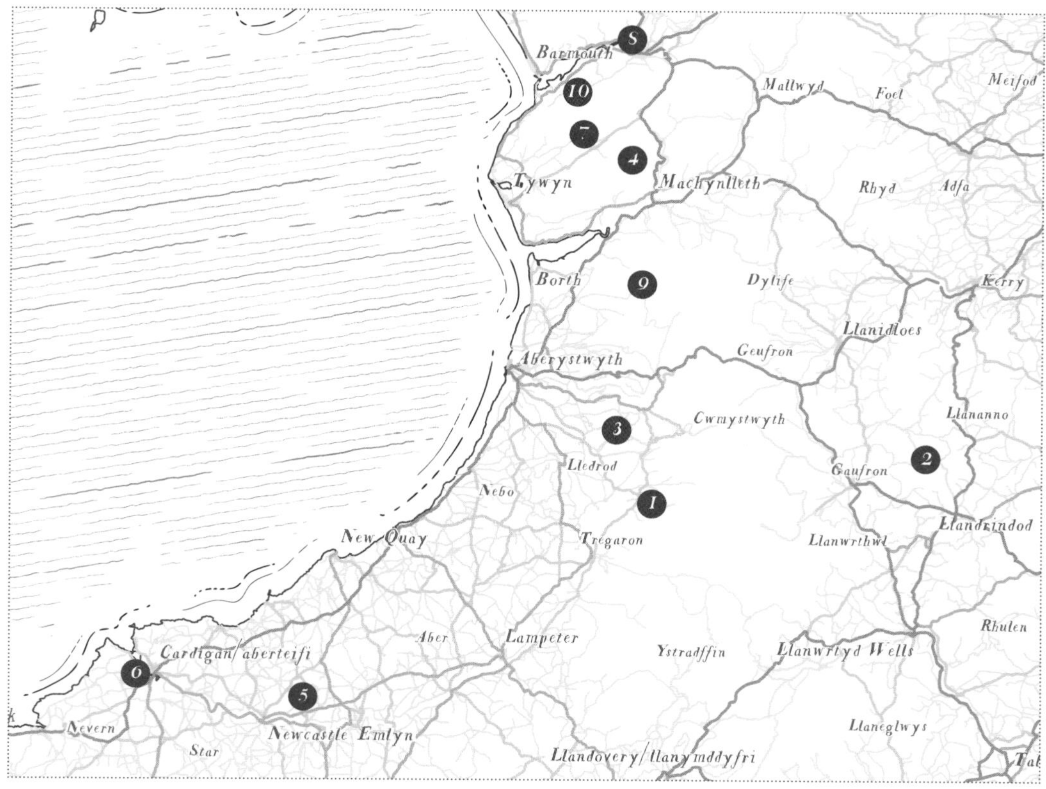
8
Barmouth
10
Mallwyd
Foel
Meifod
7
4
Tywyn
Machynlleth
Rhyd
Adfa
Borth
9
Dylife
Kerry
Llanidloes
Aberystwyth
Geufron
3
Cwmystwyth
Llananno
Lledrod
2
Gaufron
Nebo
1
New Quay
Tregaron
Llanwrthwl
Llandrindod
Aber
Lampeter
Rhulen
Cardigan/aberteifi
Ystradffin
Llanwrtyd Wells
6
5
Nevern
Newcastle Emlyn
Llaneglwys
Star
Llandovery/llanymddyfri

CHAPTER 18

NORTH WALES

Growing up in the Midlands, family holidays to Wales were my first real taste of wild Britain. Most summers we would strap the large family tent to the roof rack of my Dad's Vauxhall Viva and hit the road. More like a mini-bungalow, with separate canvas rooms including a dining area big enough to stand up in, the tent acted as a great base of operations. From there we made forays to explore castles (Gwrych Castle, Dolbadarn), slate quarries (Ynys y Pandy Slate Mill, Cwm Llan quarry) and derelict houses (Gwaen-ydog). As well as all this, the region offered streams in which to build dams and paddle, beaches that were great for sandcastles and plenty of hills to climb. As a Dad myself now I can appreciate what a fantastic playground Wales can be.

The twin rows of roofless houses near the National Slate Museum in Llanberis, ruins known as Anglesey Barracks, are a playground that never fails to fascinate young minds. Life must have been hard for the quarry workers living in these tiny cottages, consisting of a living room and a bedroom. Four men would have been crammed into each one with no running water, no soft mattresses and no electricity. As you wend your way up the path leading to the barracks you can also see the ruins of Dolbadarn Castle across the waters of Llyn Peris. There is much to do in this area and the ruins of the castle and barracks act as a good and free stop-off point if visiting the Slate Museum or embarking up the hillside by the steam driven Snowdon Mountain Railway.

There are plenty of spectacular walks to be had in North Wales, especially in and around Snowdonia National Park. The name Snowdon derives from the Saxon 'Snow Dun' meaning snow hill - but the Welsh translation 'home of the eagles' is equally evocative of a wild place. The mountain dominates the area, and there are a number of paths up it, ranging from those suitable for the whole family to those that require ropes, crampons and mountaineering experience. The most scenic of them all has to be the Watkin Path, a former donkey track on the southern side of the mountain. The route is like a microcosm of Welsh ruins, as you pass mining remains, old farmhouses and decayed buildings from the slate industry. There are many visitors to North Wales yet the large expanses of this edge of the British Isles mean you can always find a hidden corner for yourself.

1 ANGLESEY BARRACKS
DINORWIC QUARRY

The two rows of roofless slate houses, sprouting ferns and short grasses, blend seamlessly into the green and grey of the Welsh hillside. The ruins are unstaffed and completely open to the public making them a fascinating interactive museum and a fun place to explore. They are situated just up from the National Slate Museum in Llanberis LL55 4TY (serving refreshments) with views across the valley from the tower of nearby Dolbardarn Castle. Most of the 3,000 strong workforce at the Dinorwic slate quarry travelled in from the surrounding area. However, a proportion of the workforce came from further afield, including Anglesey. The two rows of houses known as Anglesey Barracks were built to accommodate them and did so until a visit from a health inspector condemned the buildings in 1948.

From the mining museum 53.1216, -4.1161 (free to enter but fee for parking), head back out down the road towards the quarry's barriers. Take path on L behind power company sign and map. Pass ruined winch, and cross bridge. Keep to the blue path and barracks will be on R near a green sign.

53.1205, -4.1092, LL55 4TY

2 TRE'R CEIRI
NEAR LLANAELHAEARN

On the southern slope of Yr Eifl, a mountain on the north coast of the Llyn peninsula, this is one of the best preserved and most dramatic hillforts in Europe. Many of the houses are near-intact which, considering both the site's age and exposed position, is remarkable. It is thought that settlement on this remote spot dates from at least the Iron Age (the period from around 800BC to the Roman conquest in AD43) and probably before that. The climb up the hill is well worth it both for the ruins and for the spectacular views of the surrounding area. The name, Tre'r Ceiri, roughly translates as 'Home of the Giants'.

From Llanaelhaearn on the A499 head SW on B4417. After ½ a mile ignore large lay-by on R, park in next smaller one at 52.9707, -4.4155. Follow footpath as it snakes to L and comes in at back of the fort.

52.9744, -4.4243, LL54 5BB

3 CWM LLAN QUARRY
& HAFOD-Y-LLAN MINE

The Watkin Path is a breathtaking four-mile hike up the southern path to the summit of Mount Snowdon. It is littered with ruined buildings from the slate quarrying, copper mining and farming industries. At times the path gets a little tricky, as it fragments into nothing more than a precarious scree trail. The crystal-blue pools, fed by white rushing waterfalls, are worth dipping your toes into if it all gets to much (located at 53.0441, -4.0551). If you are lucky you may get a glimpse of the wild mountain goats that inhabit this area, and in the spring the wooded part of the walk flushes blue with a carpet of bluebells. A selection of the many buildings are near the waterfalls at 53.0478, -4.0579 and 53.0484, -4.0599, further up the hill near the path at 53.0508, -4.0702 and off the path at 53.0508, -4.0729. The YHA hostel at Bryn Gwynant has dorms, twin and single rooms at reasonable prices. There is also camping at the north end of the lake, Llyn Gwynant. The Gwynant Chapel Cafe is a great place to refuel before or after your ascent.

From Beddgelert head N, parking is just off A498 past Gwynant Chapel Café (LL55 4NL). From here head S to start of path.

53.0508, -4.0702, LL55 4NR

4 DOLWYDDELAN CASTLE
BLAENAU FFESTINIOG

The castle dates back to the 13th century and is the contested birth place Llywelyn the Great, a notable Welsh prince who's military campaigns and diplomacy united Wales. The remains consist of two towers; one ruinous and the other more complete, having been restored in the 19th century. It's a short, steep climb to the castle's remains but once up the hill the views down the Afon Lledr valley below are stunning. To gain an even better vantage point, climb up to the battlements of the restored tower and imagine yourself as a Welsh Prince preparing to do battle with English troops. No dogs.

1 mile W of Dolwyddelan on A470 (there's also a train station here). The castle's car-park is signed on the R. 5-10 mins walk uphill. There is a simple campsite at the farm here and a lake near the car park.

53.0530, -3.9084, LL25 0JD

5 GWYLFA HIRAETHOG
PLAS PREN

This shooting lodge held claim to two superlatives: it was both the highest inhabited house in Wales and it had the widest views of anywhere in the UK. The ruin has a sinister feel to it and locals have attached all kinds of stories to the site, claiming to have seen glowing skeletons and heard strange noises. The name translates as 'watch tower' or perhaps more aptly 'watch ruin of Denbigh Moors'. Locals know it as Plas Pren after the older wooden structure that once stood here.

At time of writing nearby Sportsman's Arms, once the highest pub in Wales, was closed and for sale. The white building still makes for a good landmark when locating the ruin. Between Betws-y-Coed and Llangollen ¼ E of Pentrefoelas turn off A5 and head N signed Dinbych/Denbigh on A543. Continue for 7 miles and park in Sportsman's Arms (roughly LL16 5SW). Head up footpath from back of pub grounds, turn off main footpath to track leading to ruin. ½ mile moderate to strenuous walk.

53.1184, -3.5745, LL16 5SW

6 DOLBADARN CASTLE
LLANBERIS

Dolbadarn seems an archetypal romantic ruin, one of the most beautiful of all Welsh castles. It overlooks the deep waters of Llyn Peris which was formed as the last glaciers retreated. Today access to the tower is restricted but you can still climb up the outside to gain a vantage point over the spectacular surrounding area. The castle is a rare example of a proper Welsh castle rather than one built by English invaders under Edward I. It was constructed in the 13th century by Llywelyn the Great and would have guarded the Llanberis Pass.

Head S from Llanberis on A4086 and follow signs.

53.1164, -4.1140, LL55 4UB

7 GWRYCH CASTLE
ABERGELE

It is not hard to see why Gwrych Castle has inspired such immense local interest. This mass of towers, turrets, battlements and ornate windows sprawls across a wooded hillside. With views stretching out over the Irish sea, Gwrych is a must-see romantic, fairy tale castle. Currently the only access is available through the Trust ,and people wanting tours or wishing to volunteer should contact them via their website gwrychtrust.co.uk. Work began on the castle in 1812 and it took ten years to build; improvements were made right up until the 1870s. The house was used to house Jewish refugees during the Second World War.

The castle is accessible via a private road off the A547, W of Aberele, past the Manorafan Farm Touring and Camping site.

53.2832,- 3.6089, LL22 8ET

8 GWAEN-YDOG
FARMHOUSE, MYNDD MECHELL

Set between the gentle whir of a wind-farm and low lying heathland hills stands the remote ruin of Gwaen-ydog. This large farmhouse is completely gutted, with balls of ivy pouring from the windows and tree-filled interior. It was once home to Hugh Owen a notable translator of Christian texts into Welsh.

From Llanfachraeth, nr Holyhead head NW on A5025 for 5 miles through Llanfaethlu onto Llanrhyddlad. Go past the bus stop and turn R just before a large church on you left. Turn L at next T-junction, R at next 3 forks to find ruin on your R.

53.3667,- 4.4562, LL68 0TD

9 LLYS EURYN MANSION
COLWYN BAY

Llys Euryn Mansion is situated in the centre of Bryn Euryn nature reserve on a hillside overlooking Colwyn Bay. It is a very unusual looking ruin with only two large outer walls remaining along with the large fireplace and chimney. This is a Site of Special Scientific Interest due to the rare limestone grassland which is home to many flowers and butterflies. The grand house of Llys Euryn was built on the site of a much earlier hillfort, Bryn Euryn. Like many grand houses at the time, Llys Euryn had to be fortified as it was built in the 15th century during the turbulent Wars of the Roses.

Exit A55 Junction 20 and take the B5115 north to Panrhyn Bay and Llandudno. Cross roundabout then take 2nd L at lights, Rhos Rd. Continue to end to nature reserve. Park on R. Walk up steps from car park, then down RH path past Llyn Euryn Cottage, through kissing gate and down path to R.

53.3060, -3.7526, LL28 4TJ

7

10 YNYS Y PANDY SLATE MILL

This large three-storey slate-processing plant dominates the local landscape. Its windowless and roofless shell resembles more a textile mill than anything attached to the slate industry. Stone steps lead up to the ruin from the banks of a brook that once served the building. Dating from 1855, it specialised in the production of slate slabs used as flooring and for the farming industry. During peak production in 1860, it was producing more than 2,000 tons of slate every year before closing in 1871. Later the building was used as a centre for the local eisteddfod, a Welsh tradition of song, poetry and dancing.

Head W from Porthmadog on A487 through Penmorfa, R signed 'Hostel, Golan and Woollen Mill', R past row of cottages to Cwm Ystradllyn, continue straight on the road until you see the ruin.

52.9680, -4.1607, LL51 9AZ

11 RHOSYDD QUARRY TANYGRISIAU

The breathtaking scenery and remoteness of this abandoned slate quarry near the Blaenau Ffestiniog railway make it a must-see for those visiting the area. Ruined quarry buildings litter this stunning Welsh hillside and waterfalls feed into the picturesque expanse of the Tanygrisiau Reserviour. To the west a road leads on to the Llyn Stwlan Reservoir. It winds up the hillside with a series of hair-raising hairpin bends and has been voted one of the most dangerous roads in the country!

Head through the town of Tanygrisiau, Blaenau Ffestiniog off the A496, and up into a no through road. Park and follow the footpath to the ruins by the side of the road, and walk up the road to the ruins.

52.9966, -3.9905, LL41 3ST

11

1

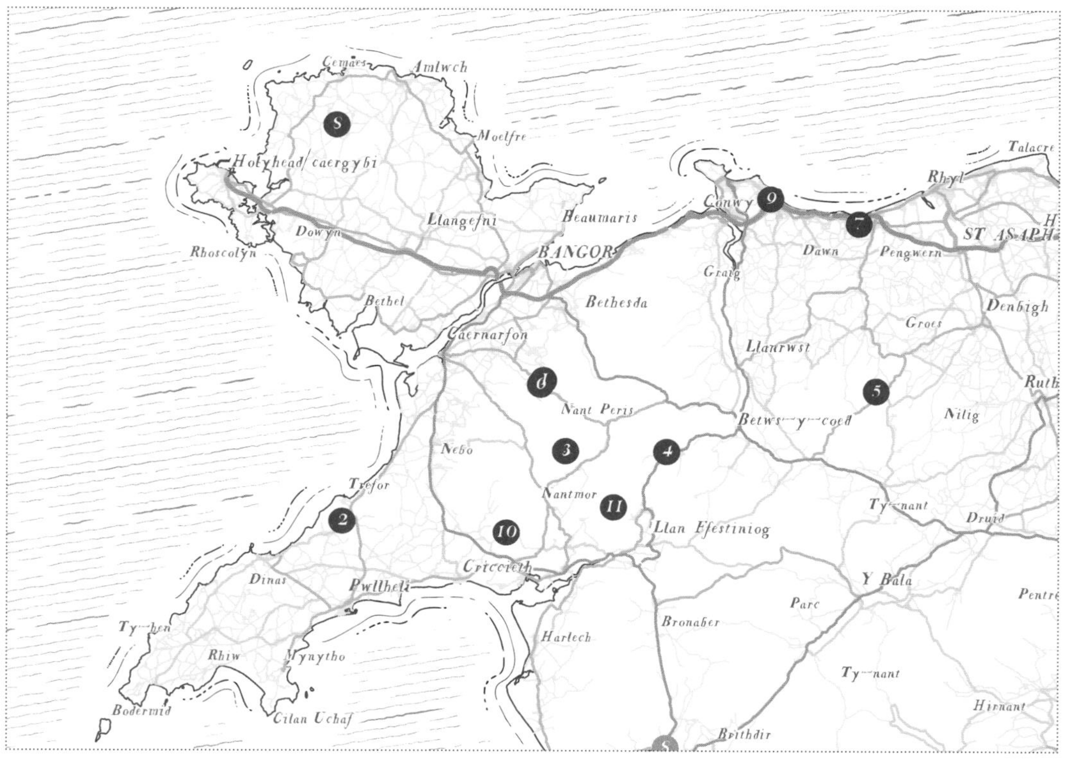
Cemaes
Amlwch
8
Moelfre
Holyhead/caergybi
Talacre
Rhyl
Conwy
9
7
Llangefni
Beaumaris
ST ASAPH
Dowyn
Rhoscolyn
BANGOR
Dawn
Pengwern
Graig
Bethel
Bethesda
Denbigh
Groes
Caernarfon
Llanrwst
6
5
Nant Peris
Betws-y-coed
Nilig
Nebo
3
4
Trefor
Nantmor
11
Ty-nant
Druid
2
10
Llan Ffestiniog
Criccieth
Dinas
Pwllheli
Y Bala
Parc
Bronaber
Ty-hen
Harlech
Rhiw
Mynytho
Ty-nant
Bodermid
Cilan Uchaf
Hirnant
Brithdir

CHAPTER 19

NORTH YORK MOORS & MIDDLESBROUGH

Middlesbrough and the North Yorkshire Moors are home to a diverse mix of industrial and romantic ruins. The ruined Guibal Fan House, known locally as 'the SS castle', is one of my favourite ruins of the area. It was built to house a mineshaft ventilation fan (of a type known as a Guibal fan, after its inventor), and its local name is not a reference to the Nazis, but to the S-shaped wall ties installed to strengthen the building. Nearby a very similar structure, another Guibal fan house, stands off the Cleveden Way. Perhaps not everyone 'gets' these ruins, and certainly they aren't as romantic as some of the others of the area. Yet, as testament to their appeal, when a large part of the Eston Hills came up for sale, many petitioned and raised money to save this industrial relic. Like so many of the buildings in this book, the SS castle is a very personal ruin to so many people. Without their work, many of these landmarks of our industrial heritage, along with castles, grand houses, mills, mines and abbeys would all but disappear.

The SS castle is by no means the only ruin in the area with which people have developed a relationship. In Georgian times, during the Romantic era, many of the ruins of Yorkshire began to attract poets, artists and tourists in increasing numbers. At the time ruins such as Whitby Abbey, along with Rievaulx Abbey, Gisborough Priory, Mount Grace Priory and Byland Abbey, were all committed to canvas by Romantic artists. Romanticism was seen very much as a reaction to the Industrial Revolution, as much a social movement as an artistic and literary one. It drew on myths and legends, hankering for a pre-industrial past that critics say may have never existed.

Today Whitby has famously become home to the Gothic subculture, a trend which one might arguably call the modern revival of the Romantic movement, albeit with a much darker edge. Twice a year the town is home to Whitby Goth Weekend, a music and fringe festival that sees thousands of Goths descend on the town. If you miss the festival but want a taste of the Gothic (quite literally), then why not try a 'Gothic Top' ice-cream from the van outside the Abbey!

1
4
5
2

1 WHITBY ABBEY
WHITBY

Whitby Abbey is an effortless romantic ruin perched on the North Yorkshire coast. It is a large, managed property, with gift shop, museum, picnic areas and a café. The audio-tours talk through the history of the abbey and various events take place on the site. The current abbey dates from the 13th century and took the place of the much earlier Streonæshalch Abbey, founded by St Hilda in the 7th century. The romantic past of Whitby is a long standing one. During the 7th century a monk by the name of Caedmon, often described as England's first poet, lived in Streonæshalch Abbey. It is said he was inspired to write following a dream and a memorial to him stands in the churchyard of St Mary's in Whitby. The novelist Bram Stoker found inspiration for 'Dracula' after a visit to Whitby in 1890. The Ditto Restaurant on Skinner Street, Whitby, YO21 3AJ, 01947 601404 caters for vegetarian and coeliac diets. Cheap accommodation at YHA Boggle Hole, YO22 4UQ, 0845 3719504.

From the A171 S of Whitby cross bridge over River Esk heading E away from the town. Turn L into Spital Br, R to Whitby Abbey and Youth Hostel. turn onto Green La, after 1/2 mile turn L to Abbey La, follow to car park. 5-10 mins easy walk.

54.4883, -0.6078, YO22 4JT

2 ROSEDALE LIME KILNS

You can still see the vast multi-arched lime kilns in the hillside, along with wash houses and other scattered remains, that once made this area an important part of our industrial past. A mineral railway ran right through the valley taking materials from here up to industrial Teesside. The route of the old railway is popular for walkers and cyclists and makes for easy exploration of the ruins.

From Wrelton, W of Pickering on A170, take the road N for Rosedale Abbey. Follow signs for Castleton, then keep R at the fork (Daleside Rd). Near Hill Cottages park on R at 54.3679, -0.9037. Walk up road towards Ebenezer Methodist Church, just before take track R by noticeboard. Follow track then L along old railway line to kilns. 1 mile, 25 mins moderate to difficult walk.

54.3743, -0.9154, YO18 8RH

3 BYLAND ABBEY

Romantic Romanesque ruin amid stunning Yorkshire moorland. There is a lot more to the Abbey than first appears by the roadside, including a little museum and information boards depicting its history. The early Gothic architecture of the abbey inspired many ecclesiastical buildings in the area including parts of the great York Minster. Excellent walks to be had in the area with summer teas served in the Abbey Inn opposite the ruin (YO61 4BD, 01347 868204).

From Thirsk take Sutton Road/A170 E through Hambleton for 9 miles. Take R to Wass, Ampleforth, Coxwold and Byland Abbey. Continue to abbey for 2¼ miles. 31X bus from York.

54.2034, -1.1586, YO61 4BD

4 SS CASTLE
ESTON HILLS

A superb, almost sinister ruin. This graffiti-covered, mid to late 19th-century concrete fan house was used to ventilate the shafts of the Eston mining complex. Scant remains of the mining complex can be seen throughout the area by following the track that once made up the old railway. The fan house has a large square tower with a series of three crescent moon insets at regular intervals on the outfacing wall along with the characteristic two metal S-shaped wall ties that give it its local name. Behind stand the two large gables between which the Guibal fan, named after its Belgian inventor, would have hung. On a clear day, from the vantage point of the 'nab' (the hill), you can look north out over the fast-disappearing industrial landscape of Teesmouth, all the way up to Sunderland. To the south, the contrasting views of the vast Yorkshire moors make Eston Hills a truly unique experience.

From Eston take the High St E, cross the roundabout 2nd exit to join the A174 towards Redcar and Saltburn. At the next roundabout take the 4th exit, doubling back onto the A174. 1/2 mile on your L pull into a large lay-by. Follow path, bear L following edge of golf course. Walk over bridge and immediately drop down steps to the L. 15 mins moderate walk.

54.5617, -1.1039, TS14 6QZ

5 RIEVAULX ABBEY
HELMSLEY

The Cistercians always seemed to pick stunning locations to place their masterpieces and Rievaulx is no exception. As you head down the steep wooded hills into the valley, and see the ruin towering above the banks of the River Rye, you soon realise why this place has attracted visitors for more than two centuries. The remote location would have been perfect for Rievaulx's founding monks in the 1130s. During the 12th century it was one of the richest of all the Cistercian Abbeys in England, supporting a population of 140 monks and many lay-brothers. This was to be the high point for Rievaulx, as from the 13th century it was cash-strapped and the numbers of monks and lay-brothers dwindled. Its fortunes rose and fell until the dissolution of the monasteries in the 16th century, when the roof was taken down. A private company took over the monks' ironworks, turning it into a profitable business. As a large managed ruin it has all the usual facilities, café, toilets, car-parking, shop and museum. Rievaulx makes a good walk from nearby Helmsley about three miles to the east.

From Helmsley follow High St to N past Feversham Arms Hotel for 2 miles. Take L to Rievaulx and Abbey.

54.2572,- 1.1174, YO62 5LB

6 BROTTON FAN HOUSE
SALTBURN-BY-THE SEA

A very similar structure to the SS Castle, this Guibal fan house stands in a windswept location next to the railway, off a stunning coastal section of the Cleveland Way long distance path (110 miles, Helmsley to Filey). You can crawl in through a tunnel at the back of the building to come out in a large pit in the interior of the building. The large fan mechanism housed here would have drawn up stale air from the mine below pushing it outside by means of centrifugal force.

Park in Hunley Hotel golf course car-park (TS12 2FT) and follow the track to the N along the edge of the golf course. From here cross the field to the ruin, 10mins moderate to strenuous walk. Alternatively park in Skinningrove and take the Clevedon Way Path for 1 ½ miles. 20 mins easy walk.

54.5833, -0.9226, TS12 2FT

7 RAVENSCAR ALUM WORKS

The ruins of Ravenscar Alum Works lie strewn across the hillside, three miles walk from Robin Hood Bay. Although the ruins aren't very tall, the site is extensive and it is easy to spend an hour or two reading all the different information boards about the works. Alum for the textile industry was produced here from mined alum shale. Urine was an essential ingredient, and Ravenscar would have needed the equivalent of 1,000 people's yearly urine to complete the process, a demand they met by importing the wee from as far away as Newcastle and London. In Victorian times there was a scheme to turn this dramatic stretch of Yorkshire Coast, overlooking the North Sea, into a tourist rival to Blackpool. However, with steep cliffs and no beach to speak of, few invested in it and the company responsible quickly went bust. A 10-mile stretch of the Cleveland Way long distance footpath runs from Robin Hood Bay in the north to Cloughton in the south, taking in Ravenscar. Look out for the abandoned radar station!

Off A171, 8 miles N of Scarborough. Turn off A171 following signs to Staintondale and Ravenscar. After 1½ miles, turn L to Ravenscar and Coastal Centre. Pass ruined Beacon Mill following road as it veers R. Follow to the end, park on road by Ravenscar Visitor Centre (National Trust). Follow footpath past centre to works. 15 mins moderate to difficult walk.

54.4056, -0.5018, YO13 0ET

8 GISBOROUGH PRIORY
GUISBOROUGH

Gisborough Priory is best visited in the spring when a dusting of spring flowers brightens up this field. Three large arches that once made up the windows to the east end of this Augustinian priory tower into the sky, dwarfing nearby trees. Be sure to have a look at the priory gardens during your visit.

Guisborough is off the A171. Priory is on Church St. Car park 500 metres away in Guisborough town centre, disabled parking next to site.

54.5363, -1.0491, TS14 6HG

5

9 OLD MULGRAVE NR SANDSEND, WHITBY

The keep of Old Mulgrave Castle stands raised up on an escarpment, flanked by the old curtain wall. It is set in a clearing about a mile and half though the tranquil woodland of the Mulgrave Estate (access permitted Weds, Sat & Sun only, closed May: mulgrave-estate.co.uk). When the tide is low it is possible to walk the 2-mile stretch of beach from Sandsend to Whitby. The Runcible Spoon café and deli in nearby Hinderwell, TS13 5JH is a friendly place and highly recommended, with a good selection of cakes and lunches.

Sandsend is 3 miles N of Whitby on A174. At Sandsend pass the Beach Hotel, turn L to Mulgrave Estate car park or Beach Side car park. From the rear of the estate car park take path past sawmill, for 30-40 mins moderate walk. Number 4 Bus from Whitby.

54.4935, -0.7055, YO21 3TN

10 MOUNT GRACE PRIORY

A romantic ruin just off the A19, Mount Grace Priory offers a real glimpse into the past with a reconstructed monk's cell and herb plot. The Cleveland Way passes the woods to the back of the priory. Mount Grace was a Carthusian monastery (or Charterhouse) dating back to around the turn of the 15th century. It is the most complete of all the Carthusian monasteries in the country. Monks here would have led mostly solitary lives and would have been reasonably self-sufficient in food. The 14th-century ruined gatehouse of Whorlton Castle, DL6 3HT near the picturesque village of Swainby is off the A172, four miles north of Mount Grace Priory. The Blacksmith Arms in Swainby serves some of the best food in the area (DL6 3EW, 01642 700303).

Off the A19, 9 miles N of Thirsk. Just N of junction with A684, take small road to E signed Mount Grace Priory.

54.3798, -1.3101, DL6 3JG

9

10

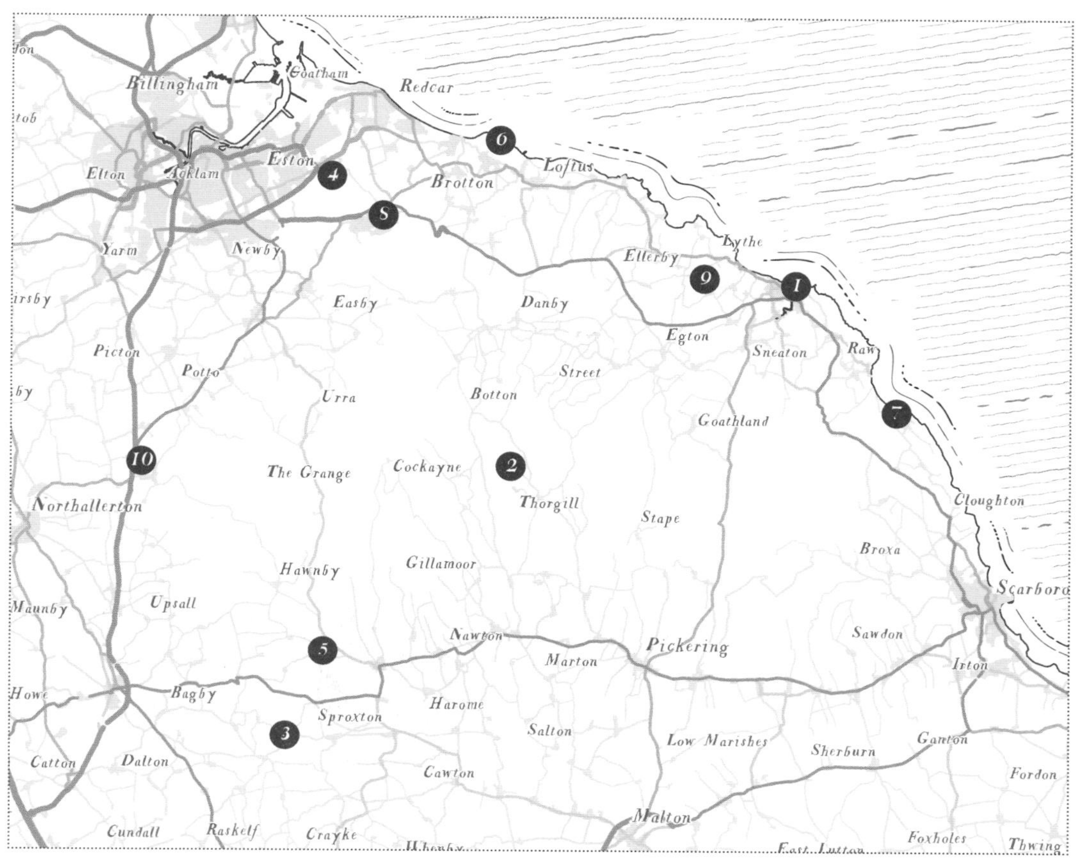
Billingham
Coatham
Redcar
Elton
Acklam
Eston
Brotton
Loftus
Yarm
Newby
Lythe
Ellerby
Easby
Danby
Egton
Sneaton
Picton
Potto
Street
Urra
Botton
Goathland
The Grange
Cockayne
Thorgill
Stape
Northallerton
Cloughton
Broxa
Hawnby
Gillamoor
Upsall
Maunby
Nawton
Pickering
Marton
Sawdon
Irton
Bagby
Harome
Sproxton
Salton
Low Marishes
Sherburn
Ganton
Catton
Dalton
Cawton
Fordon
Malton
Cundall
Raskelf
Crayke
Foxholes
Thwing
1
2
3
4
5
6
7
8
9
10

CHAPTER 20

BRONTE COUNTRY

More than 150 years after his creation, Emily Brontë's wild, untameable anti-hero Heathcliff and his moorland home of Wuthering Heights are still able to strike a chord with the reader. His lasting reputation is no doubt, in part, thanks to the landscape in which his creator chose to put her character. This wild part of the country between Leeds, Blackburn, Skipton and Oldham is where Emily lived with her sisters Charlotte and Anne. The three sought inspiration from the area, basing many of their fictional characters in this part of the world which we now, in tribute, call Brontë country.

Since Emily wrote 'Wuthering Heights' it has been a hotly debated subject where exactly she chose to base the fictional home of Heathcliff. The most recent and arguably the most viable location is that of Top Withens, an Elizabethan farmhouse, now a ruin, not far from the town of Haworth in West Yorkshire where the sisters lived. 'Withens' easily corrupts into 'Wuthering' and the word 'Top' depicting the house's hillside location easily translates to the word 'Heights'.

The true setting of Ferndean Manor, the second home of Mr Rochester in Charlotte Brontë's 'Jane Eyre' is perhaps even more contested. The ruinous Wycoller Hall, in the country park of the same name, has long been the favourite contender. However in recent years Moor Lodge, above Scar Top, has started to lay claim to this fictional building. Moor Lodge may or may not be the true home of Mr Rochester; but one thing is for certain, it does serve an excellent hot chocolate!

Although the landscape away from the large cities hasn't fundamentally changed, socially there have been some huge changes to the area. Industry has declined or vanished, with many of the old mills either renovated as apartments or offices or sadly falling into decline and ruin. Some of the mills took on a new life altogether, albeit for a short amount of time. The cotton mill at Brock Bottom, for example, functioned as a dance hall before falling into ruin in the 1930s.

Not all the ruins of this region are quite what they seem. Mowbray Castle and Yorke's Folly are both folly ruins commissioned by wealthy landowners as extravagant additions to their garden. Yorke's Folly and the Druid's Temple at Ilton were built during the height of the post-Napoleonic Wars depression. There would have been little work around and seemingly benevolent land-owners employed a local workforce to labour with these huge pieces of rock in remote locations for one shilling a day.

1 TOP WITHENS
HAWORTH

Many take the pilgrimage from Haworth, home of the Brontë sisters, to the high hill ruin Top Withens, thought to be the inspiration for Emily Brontë's *Wuthering Heights*. A seven-mile or so round trip can be taken along the Brontë Way from the car park at Penistone Hill Country Park. The path is easy to navigate, with signs in both English and Japanese! It passes over the Brontë Bridge and past Brontë Waterfalls (beginning to see a theme here?) offering fantastic moorland views throughout. The Elizabethan farmhouse was first used as a dairy farm before its abandonment in the mid to late 19th century. It was briefly taken on as a chicken farm in the 1920s before being left to fall into ruin in the 1930s. In recent years the brickwork has been secured to ensure it has a long lifespan.

Park in the car park for Penistone Hill Country Park to the SW of Haworth, off the road between Lower Laith Reservoir and Oxenhope. From here cross the road and follow the footpath past the Brontë Waterfalls to the ruin for 2½ miles, moderate to strenuous walk.

53.8147, -2.0299, HX7 8RP

2 WYCOLLER HALL
NEAR COLNE

The village of Wycoller is reason enough to travel to Wycoller Country Park and its ruined Hall. The shallow River Beck is a good place to paddle or sit next to while having a picnic. Wycoller Hall is a 16th-century manor house and the contested second home of Mr Rochester in Charlotte Brontë's 'Jane Eyre'. Wycoller Country Park is just off the 44-mile long Brontë Way long distance path (running from Birstall near Dewsbury to Padiham west of Burnley).

From Colne take the A56/A6088 E. At a roundabout, turn S onto B6250 signed Trawden, and brown sign to Wycoller Country Park. Stay on main road as it winds through Winewall, then take L signposted to the park. Continue to car park on the L, 53.8518, -2.1137. Walk along road into the village to the ruin, ½ mile 10 mins easy walk.

53.8491,- 2.1038, BB8 8SY

3 YORKE'S FOLLY
PATELEY BRIDGE

The twin pillars of Yorke's Folly have been a landmark of the area for around two centuries. Originally there were three pillars, but strong winds during the late 19th-century brought the third down. This wasn't a building with a purpose - it was simply built as a folly. John Yorke of Bewerley Hall commissioned its construction during the Post-Napoleonic Wars depression of 1812-21 to give local men employment. They were paid a loaf of bread and a shilling a day or around £2 in today's money. The path on from the ruin can be precarious at times but it rewards you with spectacular views of the surrounding dales. Nearby, the enormous art installation of The Coldstones Cut, two miles west of Pateley Bridge on the B6265, is not to be missed. The ruins of Merryfield lead mine are to the north west of Coldstones Cut off Ashfield Side Beck.

From Bewerley, south of Pateley Bridge head south in the direction of Otley. After a mile until you'll reach a parking place to the right of the road on hair pin bend 54.0692,-1.7635. From here cross the road and follow the track 5 minutes, strenuous walk, to the folly. For Coldstones Cut, park in Toft Gate Lime Kiln car park, 54.0753, -1.8044 off the B6265.

54.0674,- 1.7591, HG3 5JA

4 SAWLEY ABBEY
SAWLEY

Within the Forest of Bowland Area of Outstanding Natural Beauty lie the fragmented remains of a Cistercian Abbey founded in1147-48. The abbey is set on the banks of the River Ribble, with dramatic hills seen in the distance. It was dissolved in the 16th century, and for the next 300 years its stone was plundered to build local farms and houses. The Ribble Way long distance path passes by the ruin. For food, the Spread Eagle Inn has a good reputation in the area.

Sawley is 5 miles NE of Clitheroe and is signed off the A59. Continue to Sawley village; the ruins are on the R. Park by side of road on L.

53.9135,- 2.3415, BB7 4NH

5 DRUID'S TEMPLE
ILTON, RIPON

A folly Druid's Temple in the middle of a conifer wood. This is a great place to visit with children, as there are two caves to explore, along with a hundred-foot-long stone circle. William Danby of Swinton Hall commissioned the building of the temple in 1820. There are some lovely walks to be had in this area. The Ripon Rowel Walk runs nearby, overlooking the Leighton Reservoir. To the south west of the temple overlooking the reservoir you will find the enormous and somewhat surreal Colsterdale Sighting tower, used in the construction of the reservoir 54.1884, -1.7576.

From the red phone box in Ilton, head NW and take the first R, Knowle La. This leads to a car park. Follow footpath, 5 mins easy walk.

54.2037, -1.7347, HG4 4JZ

6 MILL AT BROCK BOTTOM

This tranquil stretch of ancient woodland was once home to a bustling community of around 20 houses servicing a cotton spinning mill. The mill remains are quite substantial but you will have to explore the area much harder to see any remains of the houses. When the mill closed in the 1930s it functioned for a time as a cafe and a dance hall at weekends.

Take the road heading east across the motorway between Bilsborrow and Catterall then turn R. Take the next L and continue for 2 miles to a T-junction. Turn R and continue as the road bends round to the Brock Mill Bottoms car park at 53.8817, -2.6879. Follow the footpath out from the E of the car park to join the banks of the river. Head S here (away from the road), follow the footpath for about ½ mile. 10 mins easy walk to the ruins.

53.8731, -2.6946, PR3 0PP

7 LEAD MINES CLOUGH

There is much to explore on the path from Anglezarke Reservoir, as you walk your way to the lonely ruined farm house. If you delve around in the shale rocks around the lower waterfall at Lead Mines Clough you may find ancient marine fossils! You'll also pass the pit of the old waterwheel and you might want to bring a torch to peer into the old lead mine adits (or entrances). Tragedy struck this area on 16th November 1943 as during a training exercise a Wellington Bomber came crashing into the hillside, killing all on board. A memorial to the crew stands at the top of Lead Mines Clough valley.

Leave the M61 Junction 8 and head E on the A674 towards Blackburn. 1st exit next roundabout continuing on the A674, take a R at the lights onto Blackburn Rd. L just before the mini-roundabout onto Knowley Brow. Veer L onto Heapey Rd, take 2nd R, and continue on this road (Higher House La, then Moor Rd) for a further 2 ¾ miles past the large white house, a grey cottage next to reddish bungalow, around the top of the reservoir, past the lay-by and viewpoint, park in the Anglezarke Reservoir car park at 53.6399, -2.5755. From here walk down to the triangle, take the L to the bridge and the Danger Deep Water sign. Follow the path through the woods, along the stream until it branches to the R, continue on for 1 mile to the ruined house.

53.6527, -2.5523, PR6 9DN

8 HACKFALL
GREWELTHORPE

There is some bitter irony at play when folly ruins fall into ruins themselves. After falling into decline in the 1930s, the follies and landscaped grounds of Hackfall were in danger of being lost forever. Fifty years after being all but abandoned, the Woodland and Hackfall Trusts stepped in and began to restore this man-made wilderness. There are many buildings to see as you wander around the grounds, including the folly Temple, Fisher's Hall, the rebuilt Grotto, the now restored Banqueting House and William Aislabie's 18th-century folly ruin of Mowbray Castle. The latter was in danger of collapse until renovations took place in 2007. Grewelthorpe Village Hall Community Café, HG4 3BU, is open in the middle of the day for lunches, teas and coffee.

Grewelthorpe is 8 miles NW of Ripon. Drive past the Grewelthorpe Village Hall Community Cafe and continue on the road as it veers R for ½ mile until you reach car park R. Follow path to woods. Allow two hours to see all the ruins, moderate (occasionally) strenuous walk.

54.1882,- 1.6406, HG4 3DE

5

9

9 FOUNTAINS ABBEY
STUDLEY WATER GARDENS

It is easy to spend an entire afternoon at the UNESCO World Heritage site of Fountains Abbey. Along with the abbey you can explore Studley Water Gardens with its lakes and follies, the medieval deer park and nearby St Mary's Park. There is a restaurant, along with a shop and plant centre. Wander through the Serpentine Tunnel, designed to frighten visitors, to the gardens. Fountains Abbey was founded by Benedictine monks expelled from St Mary's Abbey in York in the early 12th century. The monks converted to the Cistercian order and built what was to become one of the largest and most prosperous and powerful abbeys in England. The abbey was bought by Willam Aislabie in 1767 who incorporated it as a romantic ruin into the gardens he inherited from his father.

Well signed 4 miles SW of Ripon off the B6265.

54.1095, -1.5818, HG4 3DY

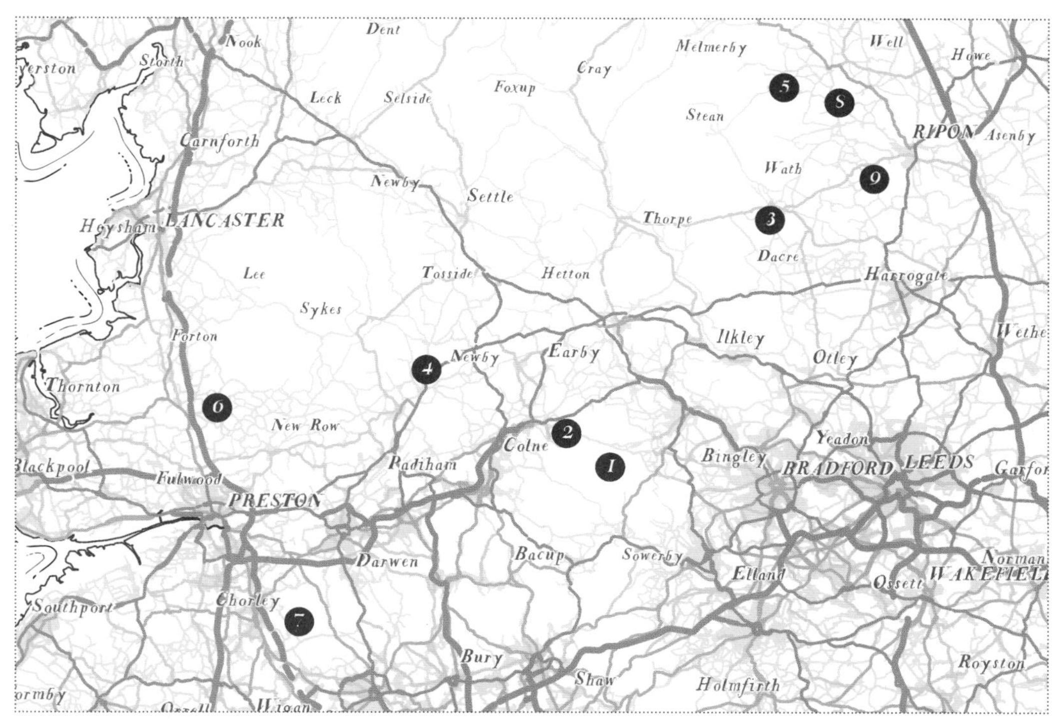

CHAPTER 21

NORTHUMBERLAND & THE NORTH EAST

When the ancient continents of Laurentia and Avalonia collided 400 million years ago it triggered volcanic activity right across the collision point. These ancient volcanoes helped shaped the heather-clad mountains and hills of the Scottish and English border. Perhaps this birth by fire was somewhat prophetic as the history of this region has long been a troubled one. During the Roman occupation it is said that the invading army used more force trying to keep the Scottish under control than it did invading the whole of England and Wales. After many failed attempts Hadrian built his vast wall to keep the invading Scots out. Centuries after the Romans left, fighting began again in the region as the border wars raged between the 14th and 16th centuries. This was a time of lawlessness, when pledging allegiance to a distant crown in Edinburgh or London would not win you any favour with neighbouring tribes. English raiders attacked the Scots and their own countrymen too, while Scots clansmen followed suit.

Travelling around this landscape you get a real sense of how hard life must have been. At the height of the troubles many turned to reiving, essentially a life of crime over and above that of the Mafioso. They would steal livestock, burn crops and houses and take prisoners for ransom. Fortified Peel-houses and bastle houses, such as Black Middens, were built to protect both livestock and people. Existing castles like Edlingham and Dunstanburgh Castle would have had to have been refortified to withstand the invaders.

Not all of the history of the area was fierce and warlike. The ruins of Low Roses Bower not far from the town of Stonehaugh have a far more romantic history. The buildings here are thought to have been built in the early 16th century, as a secret place of rendezvous between a local woman called Rosamund Dodd and her chieftain lover. Even the name 'bower' means secluded place, a very apt description of this remote location by the fast-flowing waters of Wark Burn. Across the water and down from the bower you'll find the ruins of Holywell house. The holy well was used by the area's earliest settlers, the Picts and the Celts, and its waters still run clear today.

1 LINDISFARNE PRIORY
HOLY ISLAND

The isle of Lindisfarne on a tidal causeway has both a mythical appearance and reputation. Founded in 635AD and the home of St Cuthbert, the island ruin of Lindisfarne has been a pilgrimage site for centuries. Its proximity to the Scandinavian coastline, across the North Sea, meant it was a prime target for Viking raiders and in the late 9th century it was abandoned for the first time. During the 12th century it became a priory site as monks returned and built much of the remains we see today.

Well signposted from A1. Turn off S of Haggerston. The priory is over a tidal causeway which is inaccessible at high tide and can be dangerous. Check tide times and safe causeway access times at lindisfarne.org.uk or on local noticeboards.

55.6809, -1.8036, TD15 2RX

2 BARNARD CASTLE

Set on a rock high above the River Tees, with spectacular views across the Tees Gorge and open countryside, Barnard Castle was built in the 12th century. It was once owned by Richard III, and his boar emblem is carved above a window in the castle's inner ward. There is still much of the castle left to explore, along with a wide open space that is perfect for children to run around in. There is also a sensory garden of scented plants and tactile objects. The grounds are great for picnics, while there is a shop, with hot and cold drinks and ice creams available.

Take the A67 (off the A66 at Bowes) to Barnard Castle. Free parking 500 metres away on Horse Market (A67) or at Queen Street car park, DL12 8GB.

54.5434, -1.9265, DL12 8PR

3 EGGLESTONE ABBEY
ON THE RIVER TEES

A pleasant two-mile walk from Barnard Castle (but there is also parking on site), the 12th-century Premonstratensian Abbey of Egglestone is a substantial ruin on the banks of the river Tees. There are rooms to explore and stairs to climb. However, despite its size and location, near the Bowes Museum and Barnard Castle, it retains an air of tranquillity. Egglestone was always notoriously poor; it struggled to keep the required number of 12 canons and it often couldn't pay its taxes. At one point in its history, it was debated whether it should be stripped of its abbey status and downgraded to a priory.

In Barnard Castle (on A67), follow signs for Bowes Museum in Newgate, DL12 8NP. Continue down road, take first R, signed Egglestone Abbey. Cross river, then R. Follow signs to free car park.

54.5312, -1.9050, DL12 9RS

4 HULNE PRIORY
HULNE PARK, ALNWICK

Founded in the 13th century, this Carmelite priory was fortified after becoming subject to border attacks from nearby Scotland. Hulne Priory is the furthest of all the sights in Hulne Park but you won't be disappointed if you make the trek through this stunning parkland to see it. Take in as part of the blue or the red marked route which will also take you past the ruined abbey. Deer roam the park and you may get a chance to see salmon leaping upstream along the river.

In Alnwick, take the B6346 from the town centre. Just after the museum in Baiffgate, take the L fork, Ratten Row and park on the L. Walk to the priory from here, along Ratten Row becoming Farm Dr, then R into Cock Pit La becoming Cock Pit Dr, Duchess Dr, Alnwick Abbey Dr, and finally Lady's Well Dr. 3 miles, 1–1½ hours easy-to-moderate walk.

55.4349, -1.7440, NE66 2LL

5 DUNSTANBURGH CASTLE
NEAR CRASTER

The two imposing gatehouse towers, a large curtain wall and the keep of Dunstanburgh Castle show what a formidable sight this castle must have been in its day. It is built on a remote headland on the coast, and you can climb up its stairs for wonderful views out to sea and along the picturesque coastline. Its drama was not lost on the Romantic artists, and Turner came here to paint the scene. The castle was built in the early 14th century during a quarrel between Earl Thomas of Lancaster and Edward II. It later became an important border castle protecting the region from invading Scots. The castle is reached on a pleasant walk from the nearby village of Craster, and on the way you'll be rewarded with dramatic views of the magnificent ruin.

Craster is 7 miles NE of Alnwick. Park in village car park. Turn R out of car park, L at coast, follow footpath at end of road to castle. It's 20 mins easy walk.

55.4894, -1.5951, NE66 3TT

6 ST HELEN'S CHURCH
LONGHORSLEY

The empty shell of St Helen's Church along with its graveyard sits on the banks of Paxtondean Burn, just a short walk from Longhorsley village. There has been a church on this site since Saxon times. The old church fell into disrepair and was replaced with the present one, which dates from 1783. This too fell into disrepair and was finally abandoned in 1966. Nearby Eshott Heugh Animal Park (NE65 9QH 01670 787778, eshottheughanimalpark.co.uk) allows you to get up close to meerkats and other animals in this small petting zoo with café.

Park outside St Helen's Churchyard in Longhorsley (A697). From here walk S across the road from the pub and follow the pavement towards Church View (opposite bus-stop). Cross the road and follow the footpath behind bus-stop to the church of St Helen's.

55.2430, -1.7590, NE65 8UJ

7 HOLYWELL HOUSE
NEAR STONEHAUGH

The desolate loggers' roads, the expanse of the Keilder Forest, the fast flowing Wark Burn and the totem poles on the edge of the village all help to fuel the wild frontier feel of Stonehaugh. The three totem poles are a local landmark and were carved by a local artist. The town itself is new, having been built in the 1950s for employees of the Forestry Commission, but the remains around the village are far older. To the north east of the village you'll find the overgrown remains of Holywell House and across the burn you'll see the ruined settlement of Roses Bower. Look out for Long Drop Netty, the toilet hole that 'flushes' the long drop down to the burn below. A visit to Stonehaugh would not be complete without a visit to the large wooden Stargazing Pavilion built by architecture students of Newcastle. Stonehaugh is just off the Pennine Way.

From Wark (on B6320) head W on Main St. After ½ mile turn L and follow signs to Stonehaugh. In the village, keep L at the green and park behind phone box. From the wooden club house, head towards campsite and pick up trail behind the house. Follow the burn downstream along top of gorge, on the S side until you see Roses Bower Farm on the other side of the gorge - make your way down to the ruin and holy well. Long Drop Netty is across the bridge and up on the other side.

55.0863, -2.3117, NE48 3DX

8 EDLINGHAM CASTLE

The out-of-the-way location of Edlingham means it can be likely you'll have the castle to yourself. A large crack runs from top to bottom and much of the masonry is kept on by cables, making the castle seem as though it is in an imminent state of collapse. The 12th-century church next door is worth a visit itself and provides a good place to shelter from a passing shower. It sells information about the castle. There are a number of walks in the area including those across the 1885 North Eastern Railway viaduct. If you are lucky you might see an elusive red squirrel at nearby Birsley Wood to the north east of the castle.

From A697/Front St Longframlington continue N for 4¾ miles, turn R B6341 toward Alnwick. Continue for 2 miles take L turn to Edlingham Castle and church. Take the next R and park in the small car park near the church.

55.3768, -1.8184, NE66 2BJ

9 STONY HEAP FAN HOUSE
CONSETT

The abandoned fan house at Stony Heap looks more like a huge mincing machine or a gigantic art installation than an industrial relic. This large concrete structure would have been used to blow fresh air into the mine below while taking out the stale air. As with many other ruined structures, it is the bats living within the fan house that have ensured its survival.

At the E end of Consett bypass, A692, take the road S to Stony Heap. After 1 mile, turn L and continue to the fan house.

54.8581 -1.7725, DH9 8PH

5

10 HARBOTTLE CASTLE AND RUINED HOUSE

It is a reasonable climb to the top of Harbottle Castle hill and although not much of the castle remains the views alone makes it worth the hike. During the late summer the hills are a flush of purple as the heather is in full bloom. For a longer, more satisfying climb take the half-day trip up Harbottle Crag to see a ruined cottage perched in these Northumbrian hills. From the castle head back through the village to the south and continue on this road for half a mile until you see a white cottage. Follow the track for about a mile/20 minutes until you get to a loggers' track running to the right (before the clearing), and follow this through the trees for ½ to 3/4 mile to the ruined house, 55.3183, -2.1232.

From A697/Front St Longframlington continue N for 4¾ miles, turn L onto B6341 for 8¼ miles through Rothbury and Thropton. You'll come to a row of grey houses in Flotterton; leave the main road here, continuing straight on in the direction of Sharperton and Harbottle for 4½ miles. Take the road out of the village of Harbottle, past the church on your left. The castle has a car park and is visible from the road.

55.3371, -2.1083, NE65 7BB

11 THIRLWALL CASTLE GREENHEAD

The thick walls of Thirlwall border castle were built to withstand fierce Scottish raids. The castle is completely hollow but still commands a certain presence from its grassy mound. It was built in the 14th century by John Thirlwall using pillaged stone from nearby Hadrian's Wall. Thirlwall stands where the Pennine Way and Hadrian's Wall National Trail meet.

From Greenhead (just off the A69, W of Haltwhistle), follow B6318 N. Go past the entrance to the golf course and turn R, then R again across the train tracks and park on the L. Follow either the road or the footpath to the castle – it's 5 mins easy walk.

54.9887, -2.5337, CA8 7HL

12 STARLIGHT CASTLE SEATON SLUICE, HARTLEY

All that now remains of Starlight Castle is a single arch perched on a hillside north east of the city of Newcastle. The long vistas across the curve of the valley make the hike to the castle well worth it. Starlight Castle has a fantastically eccentric story. When Samuel Foote heard that his friend, Sir Francis Delaval was planning to entertain a lady friend he lay down a wager. Foote bet he couldn't build a castle for her in a single day. Delaval could not refuse and under the starlight sky, with a team of men, he began and completed the castle in a 24-hour period and won the bet. It is not known if he also managed to impress the lady for whom the castle was intended.

Park in Seaton Sluice (E of Cramlington) and walk across the A193 bridge leaving the town to the N towards Blyth. Walk past the pub then take the footpath to the L at the end of the road. Follow this to the castle.

55.0778,- 1.4779, NE26 4QL

13 BLACK MIDDENS BASTLE HOUSE

A thick-walled bastle house standing in a remote field in the Northumbrian Moors, in wonderful walking country. Bastle houses are fortified farmhouses, a type of architecture found along the Anglo-Scottish border, built during the border wars of the 16th century. The family would have lived in the top floor of the house with the livestock down below, brought in from the fields to protect them from cattle raiders. Some bastle houses have walls that are a metre thick at the base.

Head from Bellingham past St Oswalds Church toward Kielder, go through Charlton to Lanehead. Turn R towards Otterburn, Donkleywood and the Holly Bush Inn. Turn R after Greenhaugh and pick up English Heritage signs to the ruin.

55.2036, -2.3580, NE48 1NE

11

10

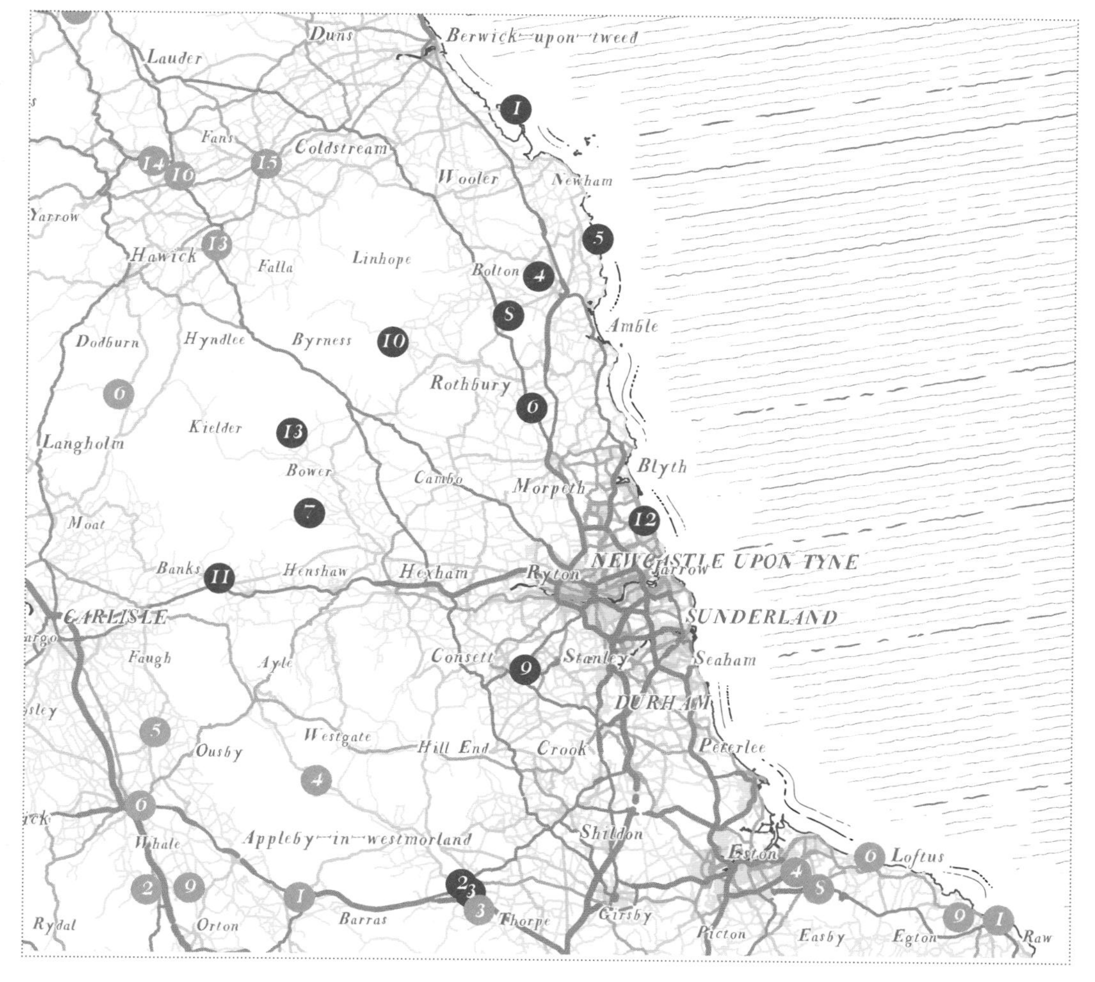
Duns
Berwick-upon-tweed
Lauder
Fans
Coldstream
Wooler
Newham
Yarrow
Hawick
Falla
Linhope
Bolton
Amble
Dodburn
Hyndlee
Byrness
Rothbury
Kielder
Langholm
Bower
Cambo
Morpeth
Blyth
Moat
Banks
Henshaw
Hexham
Ryton
NEWCASTLE UPON TYNE
Jarrow
CARLISLE
SUNDERLAND
Faugh
Ayle
Consett
Stanley
Seaham
DURHAM
Westgate
Hill End
Crook
Peterlee
Ousby
Shildon
Appleby-in-westmorland
Whale
Eston
Loftus
Rydal
Orton
Barras
Thorpe
Girsby
Picton
Easby
Egton
Raw

CHAPTER 22

CUMBRIA & THE PENNINES

The Lake District was formed by volcanic activity when two ancient continents collided. The area would have once looked like the Himalayas, but 400 million years of erosion have reduced the mountains to the size they are today. Around two million years ago the ice age brought glaciers and further shaped the area, carving its great valleys and shaping its hills. When the glaciers retreated, much of the melt water was trapped in large basins with impermeable volcanic bedrock and thus the great lakes of the Lake District were formed.

The geology of this region has made for arguably the most magnificent and dramatic countryside England has to offer. Journeying though this part of northern England, you can feel cut off from the world, blissfully alone in the towering landscape. A visit to the ruined church at Harwood Beck only emphasises this feeling of peaceful, remote isolation. In the shadow of the Cumbrian hills, the only sound you'll hear is the bleating of sheep and the waters of the beck as it flows by.

Much of Cumbria and neighbouring County Durham is rural and remote. The landscape is varied, from mountains and lakes to gentle hills and rolling countryside. The single tower of Shap Abbey is in a typically English rural setting, over a wooden bridge in a wooded glade next to a gentle flowing river. It would have been this peaceful location that first attracted the Premonstratensian or 'white canons' of the abbey to the area.

Religious orders are often attracted to remote and beautiful locations, a move which sometimes helped their cause but all too often made them a target for raiders. The location of Piel Island, off the coast of the Furness Peninsula, overlooking the Irish sea, meant it was a useful port. The monks of this Cistercian Abbey would have used their building as a warehouse, shipping goods from Ireland. When it was repeatedly hit by raiders and pirates in the 14th century the monks had no choice but to fortify. The result slowly became Piel Castle, and what then made a remote fortified port now makes a fantastic holiday adventure.

1 BROUGH CASTLE
BROUGH

Brough Castle has an imposing keep and circular tower raised up on a small hillock, set among the backdrop of the Cumbrian Hills. The first stone castle was built on the site of an old Roman fort in the late 11th century. The round tower, or Clifford's tower, and the keep came later, in the late 13th century during a time of intense Scottish raids. The castle met with tragedy in 1521 when a fire broke out following a Christmas party thrown by Henry Clifford. Henry was an aristocrat who spent a good part of his life hiding as a shepherd when an attainder was placed on him (an hereditary death threat) after his father's killing of Edmund, the king's brother. Lady Anne Clifford later inherited the castle and began to restore it in 1659, only for it to burn down again in 1666. Brough Castle has a children's play area and an ice cream parlour serving delicious home-made ices.

Leave the A66 at Brough and merge into the A685 S following signs to Kirkby Stephen. After approx. 300 meters take the R turn to Church, Brough and Brough Castle. Take the next L, then the R at the green, continue on to the car park and the Brough Castle Farm Ice-Cream Parlour. Short easy stroll to the castle.

54.5217, -2.3239, CA17 4EJ

2 SHAP ABBEY
KELD

The most striking remnant of Shap Abbey ruins is the large square tower, rising up in this secluded valley. A footpath runs from the other side of the river to Keld and its medieval chapel (key hanging by front door of house opposite). The whole area feels quiet and cut off, and don't be surprised if you are the only one visiting. Shap was a Premonstratensian Abbey. In 1458 Richard Redman was elected as the abbot of Shap and in the years that followed he rose to become head of the order.

Leave the M6 at Junction 39, follow the feeder road to the A6 and turn R to Shap. Continue on A6 for 2 miles through Shap village. Take a L down towards Bampton and Shap Abbey. Keep to the road; you'll come to a sharp bend to the R with the road to the abbey signposted to the L. Just before the bridge you'll see a car park to the R and the abbey ahead. The abbey is a gentle 3 mins stroll from here across a footbridge over the River Lowther.

54.5302, -2.6999, CA10 3NB

3 ST MARY'S OLD CHURCH
BRIGNALL

St Mary's Old Church is a lovely little ruin not far from the hamlet of Brignall. It stands in a meadow, in a gated churchyard with many old gravestones set among meadowsweet and red campion. The church would have serviced a village here but plague or flood caused the inhabitants to leave some time in the middle ages. The church stood in isolation for centuries until it was abandoned in the early 19th century and the new church was built in the present village. Over a decade before it fell into ruin the artist Turner paid a visit to the area and sketched the churches.

Turn of A66 at Greta Bridge, to Barningham, Brignal. Keep on this road, cross the bridge, L at the Morritt Hotel; follow Brignall La to the new church. Park outside then follow footpath signs to the side of the old church. It isn't far, but in places during the walk you must clamber up steep banks to cross the stream, so perhaps not suitable for young children. Walk past the ruined outbuilding and follow the path as it snakes down to the church itself. The graveyard may be more visible than the church at first.

54.5052, -1.8822, DL12 9SF

4 HARWOOD BECK CHAPEL

The little chapel at Harwood Beck seems impossibly remote. On the banks of the Beck you'll see a few scattered cottages but nothing as large as a village for miles. It is this remote setting, with the backdrop of the Cumbrian Hills that make a visit to this site especially memorable, if not moving. A lovely way to approach the chapel is to walk over Touting Hill from Cow Green Reservoir car park, signed off the B6277 at Langdon Beck. Head east from the car-park. After half a mile, take the road to the north and follow over the hill to Harwood Beck, across the river and through a field to the ruin.

Harwood is off the B6277, 10 miles N of Middleton-in-Teesdale. Heading N, pass through Langdon Beck (Langdon Beck Hotel DL12 0XP) and you'll come to Peases, a white cottage by the side of the road. Turn L here by the phone box. Follow road down to a gate by a row of white cottages. Park carefully by the side of the road here 54.6969,-2.2837. Walk through gate past cottages, follow footpath/track to the L down towards chapel.

54.6944, -2.2860, DL12 0YA

5 KIRKOSWALD CASTLE
KIRKOSWALD

The first glimpse of Kirkoswald Castle you'll see is the large red brick ruined tower, peering out from among the trees. Along with the tower, the ruin is an extensive series of mounds with small cavernous chambers. The moat, which has all but dried up, still surrounds the castle in a perfect square. The castle has not been secured, so any close-up exploration of the ruins should be done with extreme care (if at all). It is a short walk from the village of Kirkoswald on the road to Park Head.

Junction 40 M6 Penrith. From Penrith, take A6 to Plumpton on A6 2 miles. Turn R Lazonby and Kirkoswald B6413 for 5 miles. You'll come to a large white house, turn R here then immediate L. After about 300 meters you'll see the clump of trees where the castle is situated on R. Park by the two gates (keeping them clear) and follow the footpath in to the castle.

54.7621, -2.6861, CA10 IDQ

5

6 BROUGHAM CASTLE
PENRITH

Brougham Castle has room for picnics, excellent photo opportunities and space for kids to run around to their heart's content. These picturesque 13th-century castle ruins, in their romantic location on the banks of the River Eamont are worth a visit at any time of the year. It lies on the outskirts of bustling town of Penrith, home to many foodie shops cafes and independent stores. Plenty of the castle still remains, including the stairs to the top floor. This is a place to bring kids with active imaginations.

Just off the A66, Moor La, 2 miles E of Penrith.

54.6539, -2.7186, CA10 2AA

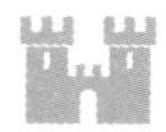

7 PENDRAGON CASTLE
KIRKBY STEPHEN

A small ruined castle in a remote location. It is privately owned, so at present there is no access and it can only be viewed from the roadside. You can see a lot on tiptoes peering over the wall. Visit in the spring and you'll see plenty of sweet cicely in flower around the castle. Although little evidence supports the fact, the castle has been suggested as the legendary home of Uther Pendragon, father of King Arthur.

From Kirkby Stephen head S past the Black Bull Hotel, Hearts of Oak Gallery (converted church) and the Co-op; at the lights take the L, B6259, Nateby and Hawes. Continue for 4 miles until you see the castle on your R and a pull in on your L.

54.4186,- 2.3376, CA17 4JT

8 PIEL CASTLE
PIEL ISLAND

Piel Island, where Piel Castle is situated, is a special little place with, besides the castle, a pub which sells excellent food and a row of houses. It is one of the few places in England that permits wild camping and with little light pollution makes for the perfect spot for a little star gazing (so long as you visit on a clear night). There are no cars on the island and the only way to visit is by travelling on the 12-person ferry (runs in good weather only) from Roa Island south of Barrow-in-Furness.

6

During less busy times the ferryman will often take passengers to see basking seal colonies. The island is quiet and remote making it an excellent place to watch sea birds. The castle was constructed in the early 14th century as a defence for the nearby monks of Furness Abbey to protect them against pirates and Scottish raiders. Experienced sea kayakers regularly make the crossing to Piel Island (a trip not suitable for beginners).

From Barrow-in-Furness take the A5087 Roose Road E past Morrisons for 1¼ miles. At the Roose roundabout take the 3rd exit onto Rampside road; continue for 2½ miles. 2nd exit at the roundabout continue to the ferry station, 54.0734,-3.1741.

54.0626, -3.1734, LA13 0QN

9 CRAKE TREES MANOR
CROSBY RAVENSWORTH

In a less-visited but beautiful and remote part of Cumbria stands the last remaining wing of the once grand 14th-century Crake Trees Manor. The ruin has recently been renovated and the cleaned-up stonework gives a splendid indication of what the building must have looked like in its heyday. The stone walls reflect the changing light from the first dawn light, across noon until sunset. The house was originally built for the Lancaster family but changed hands many times across the centuries. It seems at one point in its history the tenants of the house must have been up to no good as only 2 were recorded in the census despite 14 living in the house! The ruin is owned by Ruth and Mike who own Crake Trees Manor B&B and Shepherd's Hut next door (01931 715205). The Butchers Arms in nearby Crosby Ravensworth (CA10 3JP, 01931 715722), is a friendly pub serving local craft beer on tap.

From the main street in Shap (see Shap Abbey), head N past the post office and take the R opposite the red phone box. Continue on this road for 4 miles to Crosby Ravensworth. Turn L to head through the village, past the churchyard then the football field. After the national speed limit sign take the first L to head up the lane to the farmhouse and the ruin itself.

54.5339, -2.5954, CA10 3JG

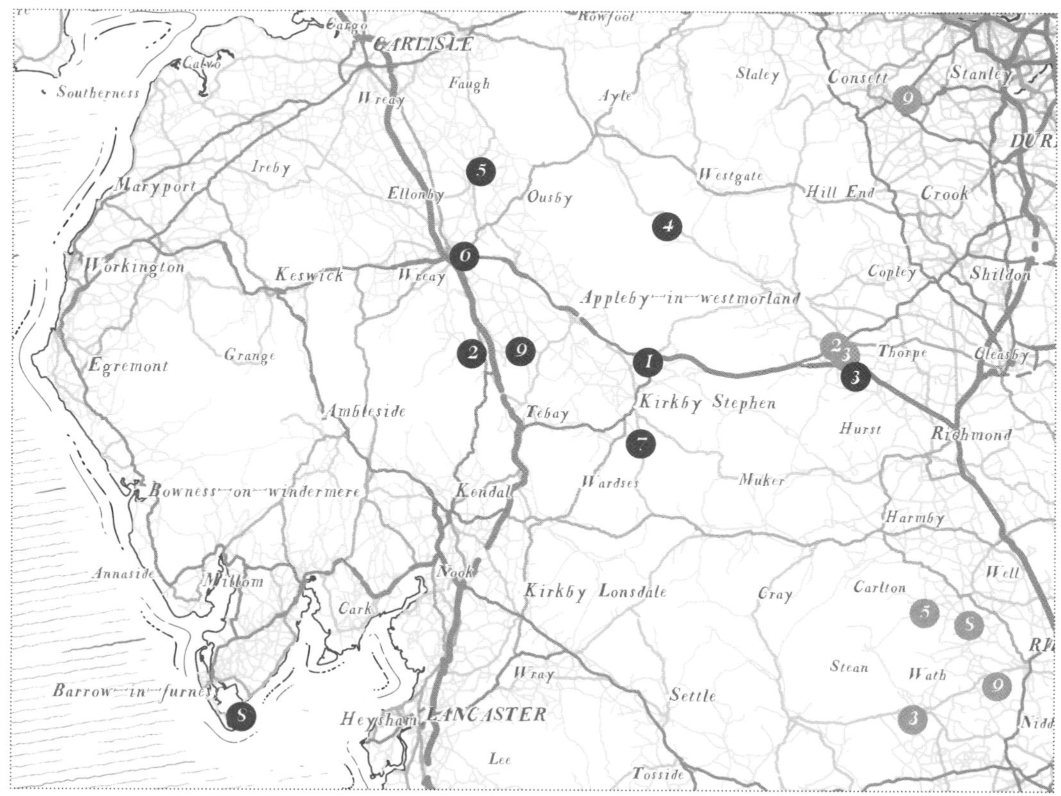
Rowfoot
Cargo
CARLISLE
Calvo
Southerness
Faugh
Wreay
Staley
Consett
Stanley
Ayte
Ireby
Maryport
Westgate
Hill End
Crook
Ellonby
Ousby
Workington
Keswick
Wreay
Copley
Shildon
Appleby-in-westmorland
Egremont
Grange
Thorpe
Gleasby
Ambleside
Tebay
Kirkby Stephen
Hurst
Richmond
Bowness-on-windermere
Kendal
Wardses
Muker
Harmby
Annaside
Millom
Nook
Kirkby Lonsdale
Cray
Carlton
Well
Cark
Wray
Stean
Wath
Barrow-in-furness
Settle
Heysham
LANCASTER
Lee
Tosside

CHAPTER 23

SOUTH EAST SCOTLAND

The landscape is gentler here than in other parts of Scotland; the hills roll rather than rise, the valleys are green and sometimes coated with evergreen conifer woodlands and even the local accents are noticeably softer. Yet the history of this region is one of the bloodiest. This was the Eastern and Middle Scottish Marches, a lawless place where clansmen would regularly switch allegiances, depending on who would favour them the most, the Scots or the English. The large sinister ruin of Hermitage Castle was at the forefront of the border wars and switched sides between the two nations both through war and as a result of defecting noblemen. This imposing structure rises up out of the deserted landscape enticing the ruin hunter to explore this stronghold.

Further north, the River Tweed snakes its way through the heart of the region from Tweed's Well in the west, out to the North Sea in the east. Along its route are the magnificent ruins of three of the border abbeys at Melrose, Kelso and Dryburgh with a fourth, Jedburgh, to the south. The four ruins can be negotiated in a number of ways: by a 50-mile driving tour, a 55-mile bicycle tour or by the 64-mile long-distance path of the Border Abbey Way. There seems some bitter irony that the harder the mode of transport the longer the journey!

Heading north again, just a stone's throw from North Berwick we find the beautiful hidden beach of Seacliff, home to three large ruins. Auldehame Castle is hidden among trees just up from the beach, the grand Seacliff House is fenced off on a mound not far from Aulderhame and the majestic curtain wall stronghold of Tantallon Castle overlooks the rocky shore and seabird colony of Bass Rock. It is somewhat dangerous to visit Seacliff on the beginning of a grand tour of Scotland as, once you have discovered it, you may never want to leave!

It is of course Edinburgh that brings most to this part of Scotland. A walk across the Devil's teeth causeway to the Second World War ruins on Cramond Island or a boat ride to the 13th-century abbey on Inchcolm island give you a chance to see seals, porpoises and nesting sea birds, just a short way from the city itself.

4
12
3
6

1 AULDHAME CASTLE
SEACLIFF

The crumbling ruin of Auldhame Castle lies hidden in the woods on the headland overlooking the white sandy beach at Seacliff. Nearby the ruins of a grand house also hide in the tree line waiting to be discovered. The beach at Seacliff is a fantastic spot to stop for a picnic lunch or to just relax for a day. It is white and sandy with a calm sea when we visited, perfect for families, couples and dog walkers. There is a tiny harbour at the north end.

From North Berwick head E on A198 for 4 miles, past Tantallon Castle entrance, until you get to a collection of farm buildings. As main road veers R, continue down private road to Seacliff (barrier and £2 charge). For Auldhame Castle park in nearest car park and walk L up into the trees along worn path. For Seacliffe House park further down road in the second car park. From here, walk up the hill, away from the sea, to peer over the fence at the ruin.

56.0528, -2.6400, EH39 5PP

2 TANTALLON CASTLE
NORTH BERWICK

The huge ruin of Tantallon Castle sits high on the cliff edge poised above the Firth of Forth. A climb up the towers offer spectacular views stretching out to sea and overlooking the gannet colony of Bass Rock. As a staffed Historic Scotland property it has a small shop and toilets.

From North Berwick head E on the A198 for 3 ½ miles. Turn L and continue to the castle car park. Or take train to North Berwick, walk to bus stop in High St, catch 120 (Dunbar) to Tantallon Castle.

56.0565, -2.6500, EH39 5PN

3 CRICHTON LIME KILNS
PATHHEAD

Two large 19th-century lime kilns tower above old office ruins in this field to the side of a minor road. One has a large crack running from one of the arches to the top, indicating that these kilns are in a state of decay. You can run up and down the banks to the top of the kilns and peer down below. Do be respectful if there is livestock in the field, and leave your dogs in the car. The kilns would have been state-of-the-art in their time and are among the best-preserved lime kilns in the region.

From Pathhead on A68 head S, Main St/A68 for ¾ mile to turning for Tynhead B5458, after 1½ mile at Crichton, turn L B6367 then first L find park by side of the road (55.845406, -2.971043). Follow dirt track to kilns.

55.8436,- 2.9708, EH37 5UY

4 CRICHTON CASTLE
PATHHEAD

Crichton Castle is a 14th-century tower house set in wild moorland in this out of the way part of Midlothian. The castle's wonderful setting, on a terrace overlooking the River Tyne, is reason enough to visit. One of the castle's facade's, overlooking the courtyard, has unusual diamond-faceted stonework, unique in Scotland.

From Pathhead (A68), take B6367 W to Crichton. Through the village (the road dog-legs), and the kilns are in the second field on the left.

55.8394, -2.9915, EH37 5XA

5 FALA LUGGIE TOWER
PATHHEAD

Just down the road from Crichton, a single, 30-foot-high wall is all that remains of Fala Luggie tower, standing in the middle of a rather bleak moor. This atmospheric ruin may once have been a hunting lodge.

From Fala village walk S on the A68 and take track to R marked 'To cemetery only'. The tower is about 1½ miles down this track, off to the R/NW.

55.8211,- 2.9210, EH37 5SX

6 HERMITAGE CASTLE
NEWCASTLETON

Why does the sight of some ruins give us the shivers? Perhaps it is something deep within our subconscious, or perhaps their walls have the power to evoke their dark, troublesome past? The intimidating ruin of Hermitage Castle was once a powerful castle that would have put fear into the hearts of attackers along the contested border of Scotland. The castle today is surprisingly intact. Although its isolated location means it is a bit of a trek to get there, this not only adds to the experience but also keeps the number of other tourists to a minimum.

From Langholm take the A7 N for 7 ½ miles, on your R you'll see a stone bungalow with battlements over its bay window, turn R here following Historic Scotland signs 8 miles to castle. Or from Hawick head S on B6399 for 15 miles, turn R at Horn and Country Crafts, signposted Hermitage Castle.

55.2560,- 2.7932, TD9 0LU

7 GUNPOWDER MILL
ROSLIN GLEN, ROSLIN

Gunpowder was produced at Roslin Glen Gunpowder Mill from around 1800 to the mid 20th century. Today it's a peaceful place to visit, with an unusual set of ruins to explore. The woods are simply enchanting, a real place to unwind away from the bustle of Edinburgh and get lost amongst nature. Here the gentle sound of running water, the rustling of leaves and soft chirps of woodland birds indicate very little of Roslin Glen's explosive past. The river Esk would have powered the large water wheel which sat between the two gable ends of the ruins you see now. The buildings were spread out across the site to help prevent accidents. The Penicuik to Musselburgh footpath and cycleway runs directly through the park making it a popular destination for walkers and mountain bikers.

From Edinburgh head S on the A701, cross the A720, through Straiton to the Gowkley Moss roundabout (little over 7 miles in total from Edinburgh). Take first exit B7003 Roslin. Pass the turning to Roslin, down the hill, round a tight hairpin turn, after this turn take the first L to the car park. Walk back up to the hairpin turn to stone pillars and iron-gated entrance to the park.

55.8465,- 3.1738, EH25 9QW

8 CRAMOND ISLAND
EDINBURGH

Cramond Island is at the end of a tidal causeway, jutting out into the Firth of Forth to the north of Edinburgh. When the tide is low it is possible to walk to the island past the large triangular concrete ruins known as the 'Devil's teeth'. The island is ½ mile long and is littered with Second World War ruins. The War Office took on parts of the island in the First World War before requisitioning the entire island during the Second. Today you can explore a mix of farm ruins from its pre-war past along with the many concrete war ruins towards the northern end of the island. Cramond would have been strategically important to prevent incoming German U-boats from the North Sea coming down the Firth of Forth. Many people get trapped by the tide at Cramond so plan your trip carefully. Tide-times are given on the landward side of the causeway, and tide times are available on the thebeachguide.co.uk (search for Cramond, click tide times) or a free service from the RNLI text CRAMOND to 81400. Cramond Mill Café on School Brae is worth a stop off for a vegetarian lunch.

From central Edinburgh, take the A90 E to Barnton (junction with A902). Turn R/N along Whitehouse Rd and head for the sea. Free car park on R at 55.9795, -3.2987. Walk past Cramond Inn to the causeway.

55.9940, -3.2906, EH4 6NU

9 INCHCOLM ABBEY
ISLAND FROM QUEENSFERRY

The island of Inchcolm is home to seals, seabirds and the ruins of a 13th-century abbey. It is situated in the Firth of Forth so a journey to the island is an adventure in itself. Along the way you stand a good chance of seeing puffins, porpoises and seals, along with occasional visits from dolphins who may swim alongside your boat. The island was once home to a hermit and has been inhabited for hundreds of years. The present abbey was established in 1235. The Maid of the Forth Boat Tours (0131 3315000, www.maidoftheforth.co.uk) and Forth Tours (0870 1181866) take passengers on a three hour round trip into the Firth of Forth and on to Inchcolm. Prices vary and a landing pass onto Inchcolm may have to be purchased for non-members of Historic Scotland. Both depart from Hawes Pier South Queensferry.

Head N from Edinburgh on the A90 for 7½ miles, turn off onto B924 South Queensferry and Dalmesy. Continue to Hawes Pier and the seafront for parking and boat departures, EH30 9TB. Queensferry/Hawes Pier is 15 mins walk from Dalmeny Station, trains from Edinburgh Waverley or trams from Haymarket.

56.02991, -3.3012, EH30 9TB

9

10 SALTCOATS CASTLE GULLANE

1½ miles inland from the large unspoilt beach and nature reserve of Gullane Sands, is the 16th-century towerhouse ruin of Saltcoats Castle. Surrounded by nettles and tinged purple in the summer by encroaching rosebay willow herb, the castle lies sadly forgotten at the end of a farmer's field, opposite a ruined dovecot.

From Edinburgh take A1 E to Haddington, turn N/L to A6137; at Aberlady R A198 Gullane. Plenty of parking in town including Saltcoats Rd. Walk down Saltcoats Rd to Saltcoats, take R turn, don't take old railway path, instead pass another ruined building and follow the L fork to ruined castle.

56.02708, -2.8272, EH31 2AG

11 JEDBURGH ABBEY

Jedburgh Abbey is a large ruined abbey set in immaculate gardens not far from the centre of Jedburgh. The ornate Gothic architecture is fascinating subject for the keen photographer.

Jedburgh is on the A68, 10 miles N of the border.

55.4761, -2.5536, TD8 6JQ.

12 MELROSE ABBEY

Magnificent 14th-century abbey that replaced the original 12th-century building, and the resting place of Robert the Bruce's heart.

N of the A6091, between Tweedbank and Newton St Boswells.

55.5990,- 2.7178, TD6 9LG

13 KELSO ABBEY

The remains of Kelso Abbey are impressive despite being severely damaged by Henry VIII's cannon fire. Well worth a visit if you are in the area.

Bridge St, in the centre of Kelso.

55.5972, -2.4324, TD5 7JD

14 DRYBURGH ABBEY

Situated just by the River Tweed, there is still much to see of this medieval abbey. The chapter house still boasts original plasterwork.

From Melrose, travel S on A68. At St Boswells, turn L onto Main St then Capilaw Rd. L at T-junction, onto B6356. First L to the abbey. Bus from Melrose to St Boswells.

55.5771,- 2.6498, TD6 0RQ

15 BROUGHTON OLD PARISH CHURCH

An ivy-covered wall and bell tower with barrel-vaulted grass-roofed cell built into the ruins of the church. The old parish church at Broughton, which includes St Llolan's cell, is in the north of Broughton village. Off the John Buchan Way.

5½ miles E of Biggar (A702) on the B7106. Also off A701.

55.6167, -3.4137, ML12 6HG

13

2

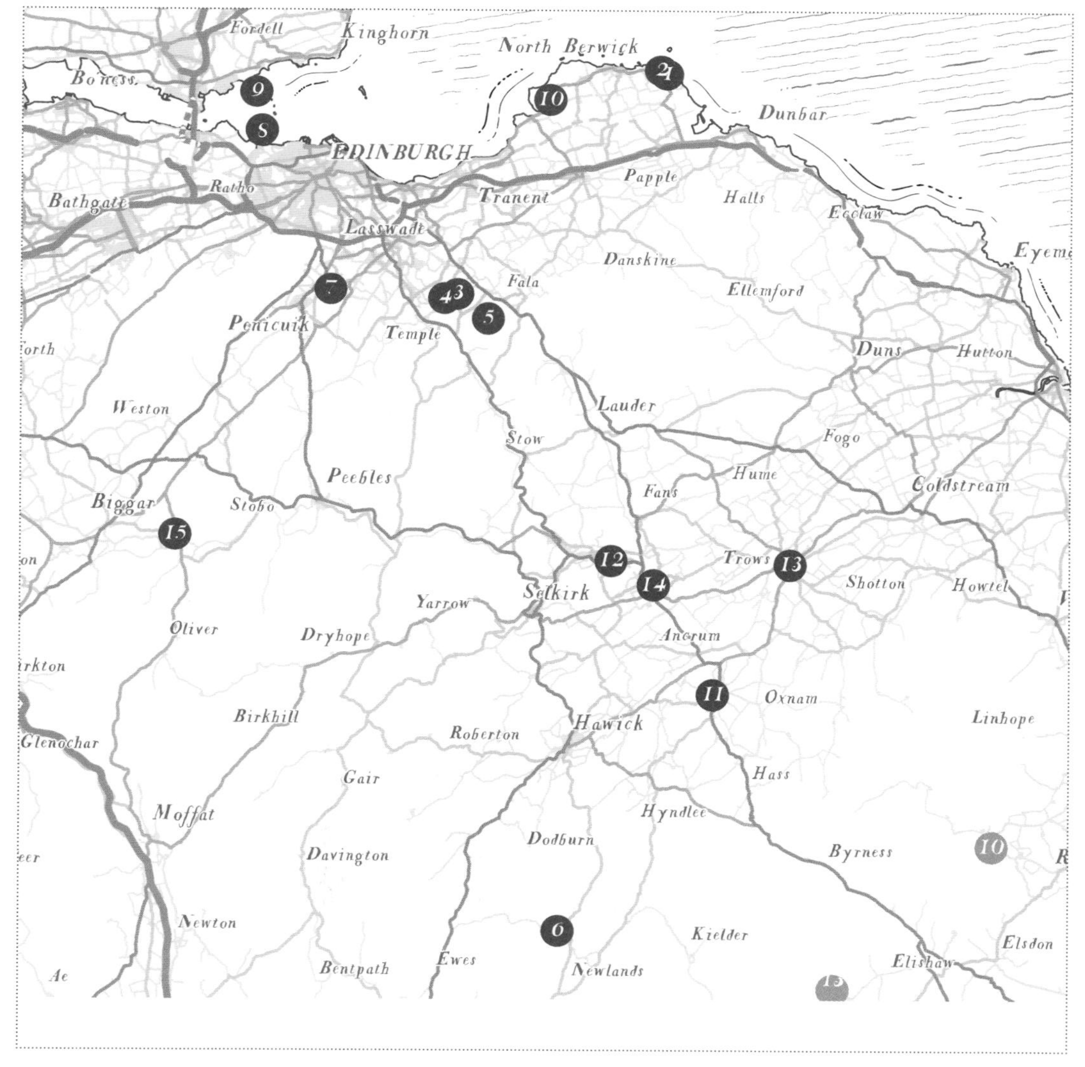
Fordell
Kinghorn
North Berwick
Bo'ness
Dunbar
EDINBURGH
Ratho
Bathgate
Tranent
Papple
Halls
Ecclaw
Lasswade
Danskine
Fala
Ellemford
Penicuik
Temple
Duns
Hutton
Weston
Lauder
Stow
Fogo
Hume
Peebles
Fans
Coldstream
Biggar
Stobo
Trows
Shotton
Howtel
Selkirk
Yarrow
Oliver
Dryhope
Ancrum
Oxnam
Linhope
Birkhill
Hawick
Roberton
Glenochar
Gair
Hass
Moffat
Hyndlee
Dodburn
Byrness
Davington
Newton
Kielder
Elsdon
Bentpath
Ewes
Newlands
Elishaw
Ae
9
8
10
2
4
3
7
5
15
12
14
13
11
10
6

CHAPTER 24

NORTH SCOTTISH HIGHLANDS

S

As you travel up to the northernmost point of Britain's mainland you may feel, at times, that there is no-one else around for miles and, at times, you will be absolutely right! Few people live here; the area has some of the lowest population densities in Europe, with only parts of Scandinavia ranking lower. For the modern traveller this means large unspoilt views, empty sandy beaches and stretches of open road - with the mixed blessing of no phone reception!

The history of the area is a bloody one, with brutal tales of clan warfare. Many of the area's castles now lie in ruins as a result of sieges from this turbulent past. Yet, despite their ruinous state, you get a sense of the power these buildings would have commanded. Considered the first seat of the Clan Sinclair, Castle Sinclair Girnigoe is one such castle. It is set on a cliff top, jutting into the North Sea, and the waves below look set to reclaim the stronghold - a fate which, it seems, has only been prevented by recent conservation efforts. To the west, in central Sutherland, the spectacular ruin of Ardvreck Castle stands like a finger pointing into the Highland sky. Built as a home for the Macleods of Assynt, the castle fell into the hands of their enemies the MacKenzies following its siege in 1672. A visit to Assynt is not complete without a visit to the castle, now a ruin.

Away from warring clansmen the people of the Highlands have tried to scratch a living in this vast and unforgiving land. The remains of many crofting communities can be found in the countryside. Their residents were forcibly evicted from their homes by greedy landlords, who saw sheep as more profitable than people, during the Highland Clearances. Many fled the area seeking a new life in faraway places such as Canada and North America. Those who did stay were forced to live on marginal land, such as the perilously-positioned and now ruined cliff-side village of Badbea.

The remoteness of the Highlands has also brought many a recluse to the area. One of the newest and perhaps most comical of all buildings in this book is the tiny Hermit's Castle in Achmelvich on the western shores of the Highlands. Its long unspoilt beach and crystal blue waters are a tempting invitation to stay for a while.

1
3
10
4

1 SINCLAIR GIRNIGOE
NEAR WICK

The greens and the greys of the rugged coastal landscape and the castle of Sinclair Girnigoe blend almost seamlessly into each other. The castle stands precariously on a cliff edge with the wild North Sea crashing down below. In recent years much work has been done on it, preventing the sea from reclaiming it, and opening it up to the public. It remains free to enter and there are information panels describing its history. The castle dates back to the later 15th century but it may have been built on a much earlier structure. A contested account suggests it finally fell into ruin following a siege in 1690. It is now managed by the Clan Sinclair Trust.

In Wick, follow Willowbank E, stay on road until you reach a football field and a post box on the edge of town, here turn L and follow road to Noss Head then pull in to car park. It is 10 mins moderate walk from there. The castle is an easy cycle ride from Wick station.

58.4782, -3.0677, KW1 4QT

2 FORTROSE CATHEDRAL
FORTROSE

Fortrose lies on a peninsula known as the Black Isle, north of Inverness. Its cathedral is a free-to-visit Historic Scotland site, within well-maintained grounds. Visit off-season if you can, when the whole peninsula is winding down after the summer rush. Cromarty, at the end of the peninsula, is an easy place to lose a day popping in and out of its independent delis, cafés and shops. If you are prepared for a long and winding walk there are coastal wild camping spots and a bothy at Eathie on the south coast of the peninsula between Cromarty and Fortrose.

Take A9 Kessock Bridge out of Inverness for 3¼ miles, turn L onto B9161 signposted Black Isle. After 3¼ miles, N of Munlochy, turn R onto A832. Continue for just over 5 miles and at Fortrose follow signs to Cathedral. Limited parking outside. Bus 26 (A,B or C) from Inverness.

57.5807, -4.1303, IV10 8SU

3 FAIRBURN TOWER
MUIR OF ORD

It is the little-known ruins that are the most intriguing to the ruin hunter. The tower at Fairburn is a charming, out-of-the-way ruin, on farmland near Muir of Ord village. This 16th-century four-storey towerhouse is in an advanced state of decay and is on the At Risk register. You won't find any visitor information or designated parking near the ruin. The corrugated roof of the attached building shows it may still be in part-use as a farm building rather than a fortress.

Take the A832 out of Muir of Ord. The road loops L to cross River Conon, then look for signs to Fairburn. Turn L and after a mile or so the tower will be signposted, along with the estate office. It appears to be on private land but enough of the tower is visible from the road/track to make it a worthwhile trip.

57.5356, -4.5579, IV6 7UT

4 HERMIT'S CASTLE
ACHMELVICH

The Hermit's Castle is a very silly building in a very beautiful location. The white sandy Achmelvich Bay beach has crystal blue waters perfect for sea kayaking, windsurfing or a quick swim. From the road down to Loch Roe you may get a glimpse of seals basking in the sun. The castle itself is tiny; it has been dubbed the smallest castle in the world. There is room to sleep one person inside and a place to light a fire — any cat swinging would be completely out of the question here. It was built in six months during the 1950s by architect David Scott who spent just a single weekend in the castle.

From Lochinver, head N on the A837 for ¾ mile. Turn L onto B869 to Achmelvich and Stoer for 1½ miles then, at Achmelvich, turn R at signs to camping and caravan site, park in free public car park signed off the road. From the car park walk past the campsite reception building, past a group of chalets, through a gate just past the last green chalet. Walk up the path at 1 o'clock direction until you see the 'castle'. Or take the 618 bus from Lochinver toward Drumbeg and walk down from the Youth Hostel.

58.1683, -5.3134, IV27 4JB

5 CAIRN O'GET AND WHALIGOE STEPS

The intriguing remains of an old cottage (58.3523, -3.1632) can be found on the eastern side of Loch Watenan near Whaligoe. An old car is parked mysteriously close to the ruined cottage despite no road seemingly leading to it. Well worth the trek across the wet moors, not far from the cottage, is the historic Cairn O'Get, a burial chamber thought to be at least 5,000 years old (58.3533, -3.1750). Found there were the remains of seven people, as well as arrowheads, Neolithic pottery and animal bones. On the other side of the road, the 365 hand-carved Whaligoe steps (58.3458, -3.1622) lead down the cliffside to a now-abandoned fishing harbour below. Nearby is the Whaligoe Steps Cafe, KW2 6AA, serving teas, coffee a varied menu.

Follow the A99 N from Helmsdale to Whaligoe. For the cairn and house turn L just before the phone box signposted 'Historic Scotland, Cairn of Get ¾'. Follow road to the loch and park at the pull-in. The house is on the far side of the Loch, visible from the parking spot. Follow footpaths to the cairn across several, sometimes boggy, fields. Whaligoe steps can be hard to find. Instead of turning L, turn R at the phone box in Whaligoe just after the Cairn of Get sign. Follow road to the car park. Follow a track/ drive along the R hand of a farmhouse, on the cliffs to top of the steps. Bus X97 from Helmsdale.

58.35067, -3.16551, KW2 6AA

6 CASTLE VARRICH
TONGUE

Castle Varrich, or Caisteal Bharraich in Gaelic, is a prominent ruined castle in a superb strategic position on a small hill overlooking the Kyle of Tongue and the mountains of Ben Loyal and Ben Hope. It was once a Clan Mackay stronghold, built in the 14th century, and in parts the walls are five feet thick. It is a very pleasant walk from Tongue; you cross the peat-rich waters of Rhian Burn and pass white silver birches. At certain times of the year, from the castle itself, you can see a row of fisherman standing in waders in the sea pulling their catch from the waters below. The views from the castle are spectacular. The nearby Ben Loyal Hotel is very friendly, and serves good food, tea and whisky. There is also a responsibly-priced youth hostel in town.

Tongue is 42 miles W of Thurso via the A836, and 30 miles E of Durness via the A838. In Tongue, park opposite Ben Loyal Hotel IV27 4XE. Looking toward the hotel turn R towards the Royal Bank of Scotland - the path is to the R of this building. Follow the path for 20 mins moderate walk.

58.4756, -4.4353, IV27 4XF

7 SKELBO CASTLE
NEAR DORNOCH

The fragmented remains of Skelbo Castle are easily spotted as you pass along by the shores of Loch Fleet. Park up next to the loch and you might be lucky enough to spot a seal colony lounging around in the sun. Along with the castle the area is teeming with much earlier ruins and to the northwest of the castle on Cnoc Odhar, overlooking the loch, are the remains of a chambered cairn. In Skelbo Wood behind the castle to the south west are the remains of a cairn and a broch. Within these woods you may also stumble across a large carved frog!

From Golspie go S on teh A9, cross the loch, take the L fork to Embo down a single track road for 2 miles. Follow the road by the loch as the castle comes into view on the R, there is roadside parking. Alternatively, from Dornoch in the south continue along Station Rd for around 4 miles, turn L at the T-junction and continue to castle. Golspie Train Station then X99 to The Mound 3 ½ miles away.

57.9297, -4.0411, IV25 3QG

8 ARDVRECK CASTLE
AND CALDA HOUSE

Jutting out into Loch Assynt, surrounded by the Quinag peaks and the Inchnadamph forest and nature reserve, Ardvreck Castle and neighbouring Calda House are in a shamelessly beautiful location. The Macleods of Assynt built Ardvreck around the late 16th century. It was home to a famous betrayal, as in 1650 the Royalist James Graham, the Marquess of Montrose, was tricked into its dungeon and later sent to Edinburgh to be executed. His ghost is said to haunt the castle to this day. Around three miles south east are the famous Bone Caves of Inchnadamph, where the bones of reindeers, bears, arctic foxes, lynxes and polar bears were found dating back over the last 45,000 years.

5

Off A837 42 miles S of Durness, 25 miles N of Ullapool. From Ullapool head N on A835 for 17 miles, at A837 T-junction L to Lochinver. Continue for 7½ miles, past Calda House on L, to car park further on, between the two ruins, on L. The castle is 5 mins moderate (but sometimes wet) walk away and Calda House is 5 mins easy walk down the road.

58.1663, -4.9944, IV27 4HN

9 DUNNET HEAD
NEAR DUNNET

Dunnet Head is the most northerly point in Great Britain and a far more rewarding end to the country than the tacky tourist area of John O'Groats. A short walk up the hill at the end of this peninsula will treat you to incredible panoramic views out to sea. During the Second World War the site would have been of utmost importance as an early warning station against invading German U-boats. The remains of many of the buildings from this time can still be seen, including the rifle range and ruined radar station.

Dunnet Head is well signposted from Dunnet village on the A836. Turn N along a long single track lane, with few passing places. Drive carefully. Excellent for cycling. Towards the base of the peninsula, at Ham, is the large ruin of Ham Mill, which is on the risk register (KW14 8XP, 58.6431, -3.3125).

58.6711, -3.3767, KW14 8XS

10 BALNAKEIL CHURCH
NEAR DURNESS

Idyllically sited next to a white sandy beach near Durness, the ivy-covered roofless ruin that is Balnakeil Church is an atmospheric little place. It has a long history, for it was founded in the early 8th century, but the present building was built nearly 900 years later, in 1679. Look out for the skull and crossbones marking the tomb of the church's most notorious resident Domhnull MacMhurchaidh or Donald MacLeod (sometimes MacMurdo). Domhnull was responsible for at least 18 murders and it was said he would throw the bodies of his victims into nearby Smoo cave. To ensure the security of both his soul and his body after he died, he bribed the local lord £1,000 to have his remains buried into the walls of the church. Nearby there also are the remains of old farms and crofters' cottages nestled in the hillside, off the A838 approaching Durness. The remains of the old school can also be seen at the southern side of Loch Croispol.

Head west from Durness visitor centre towards Balnakeil Craft Village for ¾ mile. Drive past the entrance to the village and follow the road as it veers R. Continue for ½ mile until you see the church L and the beach in front. Parking available on site.

58.5760, -4.7685, IV27 4PX

11 BADBEA
CLEARANCE VILLAGE

The abandoned settlement of Badbea is an intriguing place to visit. The village developed in the 18th and 19th centuries during the Highland Clearances, when tenant farmers moved here after having been evicted from their homes by landlords who wanted the land for the more profitable sheep farming. A hundred years ago life would have been hard for the inhabitants of this cliffside village. During high winds they tethered both livestock and small children to posts to prevent them from being blown into the sea. It is a bleak location, and was finally abandoned in the early 20th century. All that remains is a series of evocative crumbling stone walls, plus a memorial to the families who once lived there.

From Helmsdale drive N along A9 for 7 miles. Sign to the R for Badbea Historic Clearance Village; park here 58.1636, -3.5566. Around ½ mile moderate walk.

58.1603, -3.5503, KW7 6HD

11

12 DUN DORNAIGIL
NEAR HOPE

A broch is a prehistoric type of fortification found only in Scotland, where there are more than 500 examples. This one is impressive as it's almost 7 metres high, and it is also quite rare as the triangular stone above the doorway is still very much intact. From this ruin, there are stunning views of the Strathmore river and surrounding hills.

From the A838 Tongue to Durness road, take the road heading S at Hope, adjacent to Loch Hope. The broch is just off the R of the road after 10 miles. Limited parking near the broch.

58.3663, -4.6391, IV27 4UJ

13 ROAD TO RUIN
HELMSDALE TO JOHN O' GROATS

If you head north along the A9 from Helmsdale to Latheron (where the coast road becomes A99), the ruins come thick and fast. On both sides of the roads are the remains of old settlements, crofts and farms. Some can be explored while others will just flicker in and out of view as you drive or cycle past this vast treeless wilderness.

58.2834, -3.3681, KW5 6DN

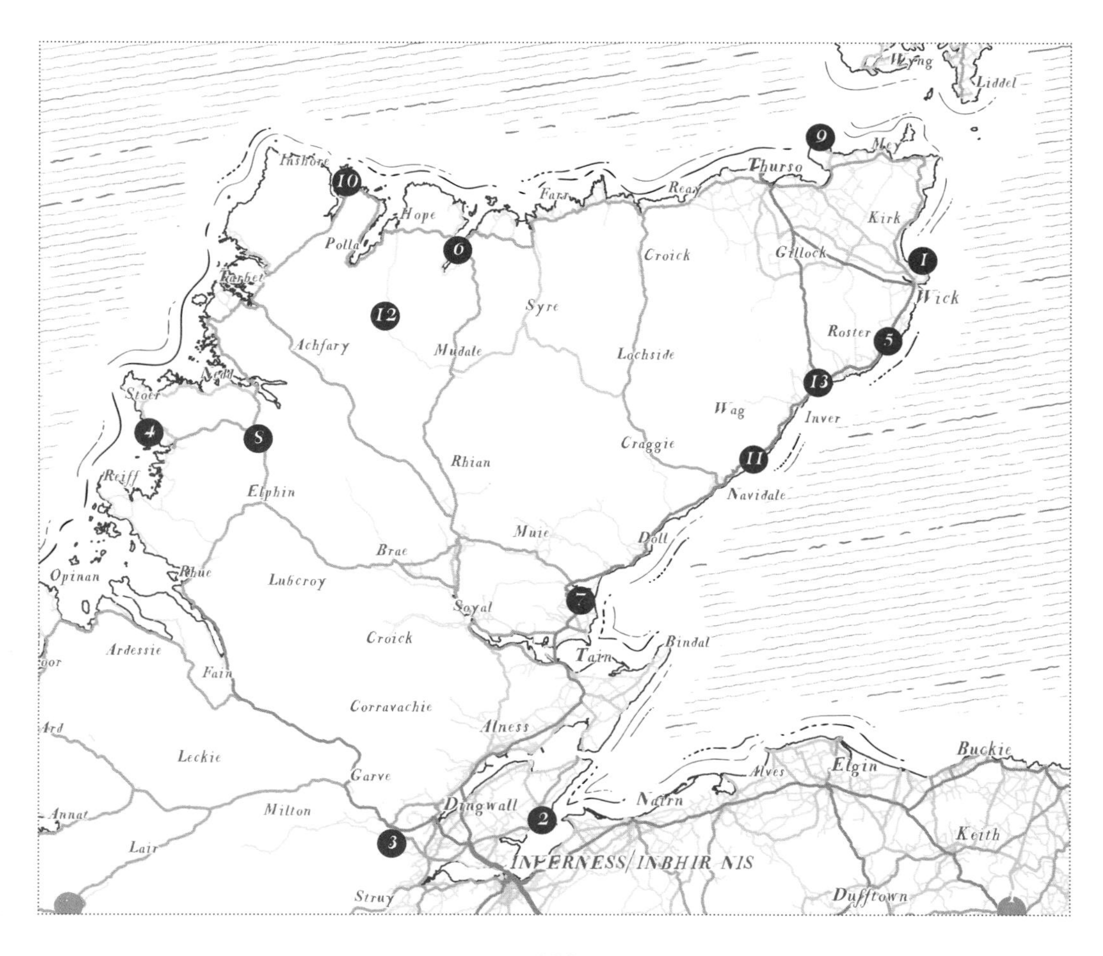

CHAPTER 25

THE SCOTTISH ISLES

With the warmth of the summer sun on your face you walk across a white sandy beach. The crystal blue waters lap the shore and out to sea you spot the tell-tale curved back of a dolphin coming up for air. In the distance little fluffy clouds wisp their way across heather-clad hills. A sea eagle calls from above, wings outstretched, circling upwards on a thermal. While this might sound like a beach in a far-flung corner of the globe, the many islands off the coast of Scotland are exotic-feeling destinations in easy reach of the mainland. The islands off Scotland are remarkable places, part of the British Isles, yet somehow so distant, so remote.

The warm flow of the Gulf Stream ensures that despite the Hebrides lying at the same latitude as parts of Sweden, Denmark, Russia and Canada, the climate remains a mild one. Here, around the summer solstice, the sun can be above the horizon for approaching 18 hours a day. Migratory birds make the most of this, flying north for the longer feeding months. Perhaps it was these longer daylight hours that also brought ancient settlers to these shores? The remarkable remains of the near-intact Mousa Broch on Shetland are thought to date back 2,000 years to the late Iron Age. More remarkable, however, are the remains of Skara Brae on the Orkneys. These Neolithic homesteads are thought to have been inhabited between 3200BC and 2500BC.

The culture of the Scottish islands adds to its distant feel, as often the place names owe more to the Norse lands of Scandinavia than the Scottish mainland. 'Nish' means point in the Norse language and this is reflected in place names such as the Waternish and Trotternish peninsulas on Skye. The abandoned medieval Trumpan Church on the Waternish Peninsula also has a Norse influence with the word 'Trumpan' roughly translating as one-sided hillock. This church was home to a terrible act of clan warfare when, mid-service, the MacDonalds set fire to the church killing all but one of the rival MacLeod residents of the village.

These two clans fought it out across the Isle of Skye with the castles of Knock and Dunscaith passing to each side after bloody battles and sieges.

1 GESTO HOUSE
STRUAN, SKYE

Just off the beaten track in Skye is the little gem of Gesto House. The once elegant, but now dilapidated 18th-century house is in a wonderful setting, right next to the beach in a shingle bay of the same name. A low fence keeps you from wandering among the ruined walls, but you can still get a good view. Gesto was once a sizeable residence and would have served as a tacksman's cottage. Tacksmen would rent their land from the local lairds and receive rent from tenants on the land - they were not always held in the highest esteem. On the little summit to the south east is Dun Taimh hillfort, from the top of which there are spectacular views across Loch Harport and out to sea.

From Sligachan (junction A87 / A863) head W A863 for 11 miles, pass Coillore Farm Rd turning to R, take L straight after 'Parking Viewpoint 1 mile' sign. Pull in by roadside.

57.3432, -6.3950, IV56 8FX

2 KILDALTON CROSS
AND DUNYVAIG CASTLE, ISLAY

The Kildalton Cross is so intact it looks like it could have been carved a few short years ago. It has in fact been in existence for over 1,200 years, dating to the later part of the 8th century. The nearby roofless Kildalton church was in use during the 16th-century if not before. Climb up Ardmore Point for stunning views across the bay. On a rocky outcrop, down from the Lagavulin distillery, you'll find the ruined 12th-century Dunyvaig Castle, once home to the Chiefs of the Clan Donald, Lord of the Isles. A visit to the area would not be complete without visits to the three distilleries of Ardbeg, Lagavulin and Laphroaig clustered around Port Ellen (islaywhiskies.com). These three single malt whiskies are favourites of connoisseurs the world over.

Ferry to Islay from Oban calmac.co.uk, 0800 0665000. From Port Ellen take A846 E past Port Ellen Primary School. Continue for 2½ miles to the Lagavulin distillery. Take the next R, park at the end of the road and follow the field over to the castle. For Kildalton continue past the Ardbeg distillery and follow the Historic Scotland signs for 6 miles to Kildalton Cross.

55.6336, -6.1230, PA42 7DZ

3 DUNSCAITH CASTLE
TOKAVAIG, SKYE

A visit to Dunscaith Castle (Dun Sgathaich in Gaelic) feels adventurous. The road leading down to the ruin is treacherous - it is single track with blind bends, and drops down to the loch. At times it feels like driving along a roller-coaster and as such cycling to the castle is advisable! You cross a rocky beach, to arrive at the ruin, entered via a tumbledown bridge with less than a foot of walkway to negotiate. The grassy interior feels safer and the views across to the islet of Eilean Ruairidh and the mountains of the Strathaird peninsula make it all worthwhile.

The castle is accessed via a looped single track road off A851 near Teangue. To minimise chance of meeting oncoming traffic, turn onto it just S of Kilbeg and exit it via Toravaig, just N of Teangue. After turning off at Kilbeg, follow road for approx 7½ miles. You'll see some large rocks in a field and tracks leading off to the L. Parking difficult, don't block farm traffic. 5-10 mins moderate walk following hand-painted 'Footpath to castle' sign above postbox.

57.1365, -5.9757, IV44 8QL

4 ORONSAY PRIORY
ISLE OF COLONSAY

There are just 20 square miles making up the Isle of Colonsay, a remote jewel of the Inner Hebridean Islands. The island's white sandy beaches, crystal clear waters and visiting wildlife make a visit a unique experience. The roofless remains of this 14th-century Augustinian priory stands on the site of a 6th-century monastery. Much of the original buildings remain including the priory church, the refectory and the chapter house. There are numerous grave slabs with effigies of their inhabitants and two large carved stone crosses.

Caledonian MacBrayne run a ferry service from Oban (calmac.co.uk). The isle of Oronsay is only accessible at low tide, check tide times to avoid getting stuck on the island. From ferry terminal follow B8086 W for ¾ mile until you see another straight road to the L, B8085. Follow this S for 2 miles to coast where there is a parking space. Check tide times, put on your wellies and paddle across to the island. Join road the other side and turn R in ½ mile. Continue for roughly 1 mile to the ruins.

56.0199, -6.2547, PA61 7YS

5 TRUMPAN CHURCH
SKYE

The ruined Trumpan church is the very last point on the road heading north on the Waternish Peninsula. It's a lonely little place and on the journey it feels as if you are going to fall off the end of the earth. Apart for one of the gable ends, little remains of the church, for it was here that the MacDonalds massacred their rival MacLeods in 1578 by setting fire to the building during a service. Down from the church is a large, ruined farm complex dominating the view towards Ardmore Bay below. If you can negotiate your way past the Highland cows, there is a great walk around the back of the farm and around Ardmore point.

From Dunvegan head E and N on A850 for 3½ miles, then join B886 to L for 7 miles to car park at end of road.

57.5545, -6.6409, IV55 8GW

6 MOUSA BROCH
MOUSA, SHETLAND

The huge 13.3-metre-tall drystone broch tower on the isle of Mousa is the largest and best preserved of all the brochs in Scotland. Considering its exposed position and the length of time it has been there - it dates back to the Iron Age - it is remarkable how intact the ruin is. The broch is completely open to the public and the inside chambers can be explored. The broch is by no means the only ruin on the island; take a good walk around the loch near the broch to find the ruins of crofters' houses and the ruin of a Lerwick merchant's house. Brochs are only found in Scotland, they are hollow-walled structures. Their purpose is hotly disputed by historians and archaeologists. Some believe them to be defence whilst others claim them to be more of a show of wealth than power – more of an Iron Age stately home. Mousa has breeding colonies for seabirds and the stretch of sea approaching the island, Mousa Sound, is the best place in the country to spot harbour porpoises.

Mousa is only accessible by boat from Sandsayre pier, Sandwick, on the main island, in summer (mousa.co.uk).

60.0080, -1.2270, ZE2 9HP

7 WINDHOUSE RUIN
MID YELL, SHETLAND

The Windhouse is a large, abandoned, supposedly haunted croft and one of many ruins on the remote island of Yell. The house has been derelict for nearly a hundred years and has a long, dark history. In 1887 the skeleton of a large man was found at the back of the house by workmen. The absence of a coffin suggested murder. After this incident the house became increasingly hard to let. It was struck by lightning in 1898 and despite a refit it was abandoned in the 1920's. Yell is a favourite for otter-spotters, having been dubbed the otter capital of Britain. It also has a large population of Arctic terns along with lapwings, brightly coloured eiders, various birds of prey and twites.

The ferry to Yell runs from Toft in the N of mainland Shetland. shetland.gov.uk. From Yell ferry terminal bear L on A968 for 9 miles. You'll pass the ruin high on your L, continue to grey/white cottage L and white farm building R, then follow track to ruin.

60.6075,- 1.1092, ZE2 9BJ

8 SKARA BRAE
SANDWICK, ORKNEY

Inside the ancient homesteads at Skara Brae it is easy to make out where inhabitants had their beds, where they sat, where they lit their fires and where they stored their food. These along with the sight of the built-in stone dressing tables, which are still largely intact, somehow connects us with the villagers who would have lived here a staggering four to five thousand years ago. Skara Brae is just one small part of the Heart of Neolithic Orkney UNESCO World Heritage site which includes the chambered tomb of Maes Howe and two ceremonial stone circles.

Ferry to Orkney pentlandferries.co.uk and northlinkferries.co.uk. From Kirkwall head W on A965 for 10 miles, turn R onto B9055 towards Bay of Skaill, past the Standing Stones of Stenness, past the giant megalith and cross the bridge. Continue past the Ring of Brodgar stone circle. At junction, take B9056 to the visitor centre. There is a cafe, a shop and car parking on site. Village is 5 mins easy walk away.

59.0489, -3.3355, KW16 3LR

9 KNOCK CASTLE
TEANGUE, SKYE

Knock Castle, also known as Knepp castle, Caisteal Uaine or Caisteal Camus, is a seldom-visited place on a rocky headland jutting out into Knock Bay. The walls are covered in ivy and sapling trees are beginning to emerge from the crumbling rock. The most substantial part of the castle, one of the outer walls, dates back to the 15th century. There is evidence this was once the site of an Iron Age fort. Overlooking the Sound of Sleat, there is a peace and tranquillity about his place. To one side is a dangerous rocky cleft looking down to the seaweed-covered shore below. Locals talk of an inquisitive sea otter who regularly swims up the coast from bay to bay stopping off in Knock Bay on his round trip to feast on shellfish. Dusk and dawn are the best times to catch a glimpse of otters but failing a visit, the sunrise over the sea won't let you down!

Teangue is on A851 N of Ardvasar. Park in lay-by outside converted church 57.1118, -5.8539, IV44 8RE. Walk away from the village, along road to N, take the first R down to a farm. Follow road as it curves R past barn, past cottage and caravan. Follow headland to castle.

57.1102, -5.8472, IV44 8RE

10 FINLAGGAN
BALLYGRANT

On this windswept corner of Islay across a little wooden bridge lie the ruins of Finlaggan. During the 13th and 14th centuries this was the historic seat of the Lords of the Isles and where the Council of the Islands met. Few leave disappointed from this area: even if the weather is bad, there is enough to hold your attention. On a brighter day it is the perfect place to have a picnic and read all the many noticeboards depicting the history of the area. There is a visitor centre here and the entrance fee helps with the upkeep of the ruins.

Visit as a stop-off to or from the ferry. From Port Askaig take A846 S for 3 miles, turn R at Historic Scotland sign down single track road take next L (signposted) after ½ mile; continue to visitor centre. The ruins are ¼ mile from here, 5 mins easy walk.

55.8352, -6.1726, PA45 7QT

9

10

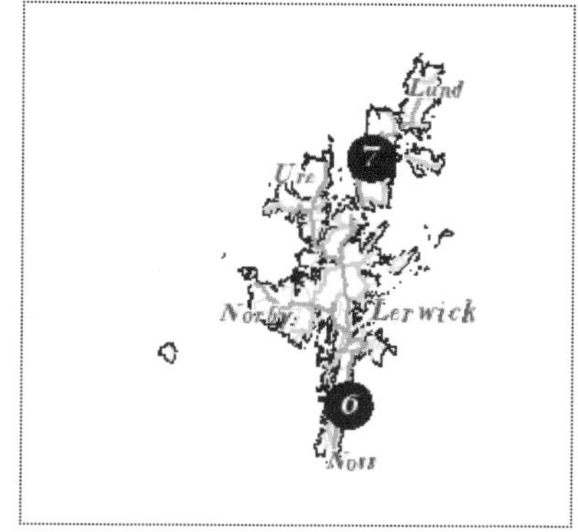
Lund
Ure
Norby
Lerwick
Noss

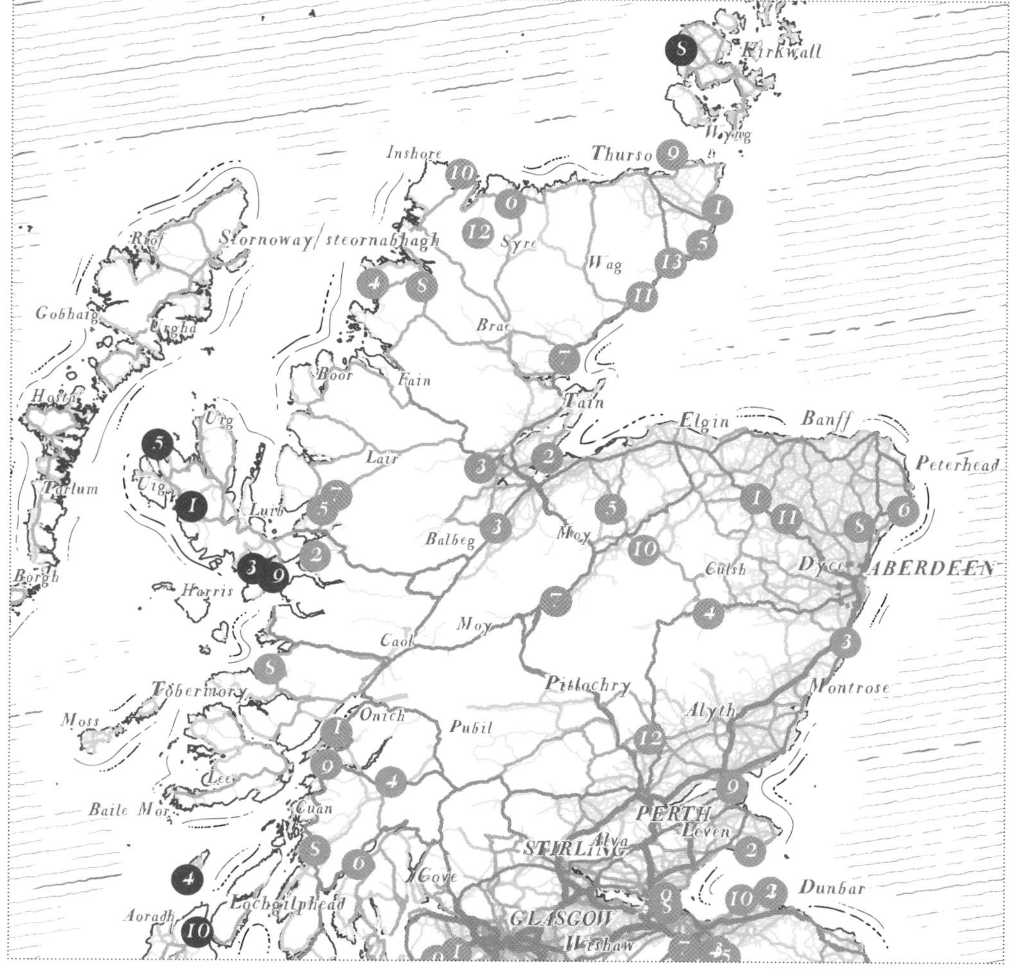
Kirkwall
Thurso
Inshore
Stornoway/steornabhagh
Syre
Wag
Gobhaig
Brae
Boor
Fain
Tain
Elgin
Banff
Peterhead
Urg
Lair
Parlum
Uig
Luib
Balbeg
Moy
Culsh
Dyce
ABERDEEN
Borgh
Harris
Caol
Moy
Tobermory
Pitlochry
Montrose
Alyth
Moss
Onich
Pubil
Lee
Baile Mor
Cuan
PERTH
Leven
STIRLING
Alva
Gove
Dunbar
Lochgilphead
Aoradh
GLASGOW
Wishaw

CHAPTER 26

ABERDEENSHIRE & CAIRNGORMS

We negotiated the large mountains within the Cairngorms National Park using the whining low gears of my tiny little Toyota Yaris. The car was packed to the brim with camping equipment and as it struggled up the hills we were rewarded with breathtaking views filling the windscreen. We passed many a cyclist braving the peaks and I vowed that on one of my future visits there would not be a sheet of glass standing between me and the mountains.

One of the most rewarding views came on the approach to Ruthven. The Cairngorms are more of a backdrop here, a flick of an artist's watercolour brush, surrounding the plateauing land around the magnificent Ruthven Barracks. Set on the mount of an earlier castle, Ruthven was built to house troops following the 1715 Jacobite rising. It saw active service when in 1745/1746 it was attacked by John William O'Sullivan and his group of 200 Jacobites. Things didn't quite go as O'Sullivan planned: after a fumbled attempt to blow the barracks up with an explosive barrel, two of his men died and he was forced to retreat. The barracks were more successfully attacked again just two months later when cannon fire left them in ruins.

The beauty of Ruthven is closely matched by the drama of three very different castles within the greater region; Dunnottar, Lochindorb and New Slains Castle. Dunnottar castle is spectacular: the ever-shifting light makes this grey stone ruin an awesome sight for walkers and photographers. While photos can do the castle some justice, the need to visit the castle is best summed up by the quip overheard during my visit: "No amount of shortbread tins can prepare you for this!"

Dubbed the scariest castle in Scotland, the large ruin of New Slains is truly dramatic. You have to watch your footing around this ruin as it sits precariously on the rocky coast jutting out into the cold expanse of the North Sea. Much of the drama of Lochindorb comes from its out-of-the-way location. It is set in vast open moorland and you have to be a determined ruin hunter to visit this remote spot. Its romantic setting, on an island in the middle of a loch, makes for a perfect stop-off when travelling through the region.

1 HUNTLY CASTLE
HUNTLY

Huntly Castle is a majestic ruin in a beautiful setting. It is situated within open parkland, and on a sunny day it is possible to relax under the trees while children play happily around the park. If the weather takes a turn you can seek shelter in the part-ruined castle itself, where there are many rooms to explore. Climb the old keep for great views out across the green countryside. The castle was home to the Clan Gordon, and King Robert the Bruce was said to have been a guest in 1307. The stone carving of the family crest on the main tower is one of the highlights of a visit. If you have indulged a little the night before, the Park Lane Café, The Ward, AB54 4QU, does a spanking fry-up.

Off A96 between Aberdeen/Inverurie to S and Keith/Elgin to N. From Huntly Bypass, A96 junction with A97, turn N into town, follow George V Ave and continue as it turns into Gordon St and Castle St. Parking on site.

57.4549, -2.7812, AB54 4SH

2 NEWARK CASTLE
ST MONANS

Between the villages of St Monans and Elie, on the cliff side looking out to the Firth of Forth, are the ruins of Newark or St Monans Castle. It is accessible along a fantastically scenic coastline. The castle is in a rapid state of decay and despite parts of it being fenced off there is still much to explore including the tower and staircase. There are two routes to the castle, one at high tide and one at low. A half mile from Newark Castle, along the coast path, are the ruins of Ardross Castle and 2 ½ miles further on, through the picturesque harbour village of Elie, are the single gable ruins of Craigforth Chapel.

Take A915 to Upper Largo, E A917 (or bus) to St Monans. In village take R to Station Rd, L to car park in Hope Place. Walk back down Hope Place, along Braehead ½ mile, L onto Burnside to join coastal path. 16 mins moderate to difficult walk.

56.2011, -2.7781, KY10 2DB

3 DUNNOTTAR CASTLE
STONEHAVEN

Dunnottar Castle is arguably the grandest, most romantic, most dramatic, most awe-inspiring of all the castles in Scotland. If you see just one castle during your visit to this area this has to be it. It rises up out of the North Sea on a rocky outcrop, and you can take the steep, winding path to the castle, taking advantage of all the photo opportunities on the way. For the Scots, Dunnottar is a proud place. It was here that the army of the English military leader Oliver Cromwell was held off for eight months - until cannons were brought in, giving the castle's garrison no choice but to surrender. During this time, and much to Cromwell's annoyance, the Scottish crown jewels (now in Edinburgh Castle) were smuggled out and buried in Kinneff Church (where they remained for 11 years).

19 miles S of Aberdeen off A90 near Stonehaven. From A90 Stonehaven bypass drive 2 ½ miles to A92 towards Montrose/ Arbroath. Continue for 1 mile, turn R at Historic Scotland sign for Dunnottar Mains. Follow road to car park. Signed 20 mins difficult walk to the castle via the headland and steep stairs. Bus X7 from Aberdeen.

56.9460, -2.1970, AB39 2TL

4 KNOCK CASTLE,
NEAR BALLATER

This is a large three storey (four with attic) ruined tower house, on top of a hill or knoll, about a mile west of the town of Ballater within the Cairngorms National Park. The castle, once home to the Gordons of Abergeldie, has a long and sometimes bloody history. It is said that when the Gordons wandered onto the neighbouring Forbes clan land to cut peat the Forbes saw red and attacked with full force. The heads of seven Gordon brothers were placed on top of their peat spades as examples. On hearing the news of their death Alexander Gordon, their father, met his own end as he tumbled down the castle staircase.

From Ballater take Bridge St to cross the river, SE out of town. Turn R to join the B976. The road bends R back over river. The road turns L before arriving at a staggered crossroads with a red post box. If you can safely park here do so and take track opposite the post box up the hill to the castle.

57.0428,- 3.0690, AB35 5SQ

5 LOCHINDORB CASTLE
NEAR GRANTOWN ON SPEY

Between Nairn and Grantown-on-Spey is a fairytale castle on an island in the centre of the still waters of Lochindorb. Rather than the dramatic mountains which dominate the land to the south, it is flanked by gentle hills. The castle is set among a blanket of purple heather and vast moorland. There is a stark beauty to this area; the loch feels remote and quite unlike anywhere else in the region. The terrain makes it hard to navigate right around the loch but you can wander by the roadside on its eastern side. Lochindorb is a worthy place for a picnic, and a pleasant diversion off the 23-mile Dava Way walking trail.

From the A95 at Speybridge, turn to Grantown-on-Spey, and go N to the A939. After 8 miles, and just before Dava, turn L to Lochindorb, 3 miles. Or from Nairn, take the A939 S, and turn R just after Dava. Parking beside the loch.

57.4058, -3.7087, PH26 3PY

6 NEW SLAINS CASTLE
NEAR CRUDEN BAY

This rather sinister looking clifftop castle was said to be the inspiration for the castle in Bram Stoker's book 'Dracula'. Despite being one of the most famous ruined castles in Scotland, its remote location means you are quite likely to have the place to yourself. Wander down to the basement and nose around the crypt-like wine cellar or just explore the vast interior. New Slains is a mishmash of architectural styles and materials, adding a chaotic beauty to the site. However it is the drama of the cliffs and crashing North Sea below that are the highlight of a visit.

Near Cruden Bay, off A90 24 miles N of Aberdeen and 8 miles S of Peterhead. From Cruden Bay drive N on A975/Errolston Road for 1 mile. Drive past ruined farm buildings to a small car park on R as road bears sharply to L. Follow seashell-covered track for ½ mile/10 mins moderate walk to castle. Alternatively, park in town and walk down Castle Rd, just off Errolston Rd near phone box for ½ mile/12 mins moderate walk. Bus 63 Aberdeen-Cruden Bay-Peterhead, and bus 747 from Peterhead.

57.4152, -1.8324, AB42 0HB

7 RUTHVEN BARRACKS
KINGUSSIE

When the sun catches the ruin of Ruthven Barracks the entire building seems to glow in an ethereal light. The buildings sit on top of a large hill which was home to a 13th-century castle. The barracks are set in spectacular scenery, flanked by pasture, moorland, far-off mountains and the meandering River Spey. It is a large, expansive ruin and completely unstaffed, meaning you can run around and explore to your heart's content. 1½ -2 miles north behind the barracks are the peaks of Creag Bheag and Creag Mhor which can make for a good afternoon's walk. For the more adventurous you can take the Wildcat Trail around nearby Newtonmore (see walkhighlands.co.uk).

Situated just off National Cycle Network Route 7. Kingussie railway station is 1 mile/15-20 mins moderate walk via B970. Take B970 S of Kingussie and park in car park off road. Moderate walk 3 mins uphill.

57.0712, -4.0390, PH21 1ES

8 ESSLEMONT CASTLE
ELLON

This 14th-century castle, once home to the Wolrige-Gordon family, lies almost hidden by the roadside. It has become engulfed by trees and unless you are vigilant driving past (or you visit in the winter) you may completely miss it. The encroaching wilderness makes for a real micro-adventure as you fight your way through the thicket to explore the castle.

Situated by side of the A920 between Ellon and Pitmedden, 5 mins drive from the centre of Ellon. From the town head S at the roundabout, over the river, opposite Buchan Hotel. Continue out of town, you'll pass a grey stone building on your right with a blue gate. The castle is hidden in a thicket on the corner of the main road and a lane leading right.

57.3580, -2.1140, AB41 8NY

9 ST FILLAN'S CHURCH KIRKTON BARNS, TAYPORT

Also known as Forgan Church, St Fillan's is a lovely little ruined church a little under two miles south of Tayport. If you walk, cycle or drive, through the Tentsmuir Forest down to the beach at Tentsmuir Point (approx. 3½ - 4 miles moderate walk) you may be lucky enough to see seals basking in the sun.

From Tayport, S on B945 1¾ miles, take first R after turning to Kirkton Barns B&B onto single track road. Follow it past two sets of houses, until you see the entrance to a big house. Limited parking by side of the road. Follow the stone wall and grass path to the church yard, signposted Forgan Cemetery. Or from Leuchars NW on A919 1 mile, turn R to join B945, 2 ¼ miles, past wood and take first L single track road after entrance to Morton Lochs (Caravan Club sign R). BBuses between Tayport and Leuchars will stop by request at the Morton Loch road.

56.4224, -2.9001, DD6 9PD

10 SCOTTISH FIREPLACE NR GRANTOWN ON SPEY

A fireplace and chimney with the Scottish flag painted on its breast. It is nothing more than that. Built for construction workers who would throw up a makeshift shelter and cook and keep warm during poor weather.

Approx 8 miles S of Grantown on Spey along A939 old military road. Or, from Tomintoul it is 6 miles NW on the A939. Parking is limited and in heavy traffic can be dangerous.

57.2632, -3.4906, PH26 3NP

11 KIRKTON OF CULSALMOND

A roofless 18th-century church, abandoned in the early 20th century. Look out for the old mort and watch houses in the graveyard, built to protect newly buried bodies from body snatchers.

Between Huntly and Pitcaple off A96. From Huntly take A96 S towards Aberdeen and Banff. After 10 miles turn L to Oldmeldrum on A920. Take first L to turn off A920 at Lawrence Rd. Pull in on next corner by side of Lawrence and Cadgers Rd. Church is in front of you. Bus 10 Inverurie-Huntly.

57.3854, -2.5836, AB52 6UJ

12 ACHALADER MAUSOLEUM

Situated between the Loch of Clunie (¾ mile SW) and Loch of Drumellie (½ mile SE) Achalader Mausoleum is well positioned for an afternoon's walking. It is hidden amongst the trees, over a brook, just off a minor road. On a misty day exploring this creepy overgrown graveyard, with its wrought-iron fencing and large, carved, stone pillars makes you feel as if you are a star in your own horror film. Many still visit this area in search of the grand house which once stood here. Sadly the house has been levelled in recent years and now all that remains is the mausoleum that once served the family who lived there.

3 miles W of Blairgowrie, turn off A923 past Kinloch and Loch of Drumellie at white cottage where main road turns sharply to the L. Park on the L side of road as the trees drop away. The Mausoleum is on your R through the trees. Bus 60 from Blairgowrie to Dunkeld, 3 stops; get off at caravan park, then easy walk of just over a mile.

56.5895, -3.4209, PH10 6SG

9

12

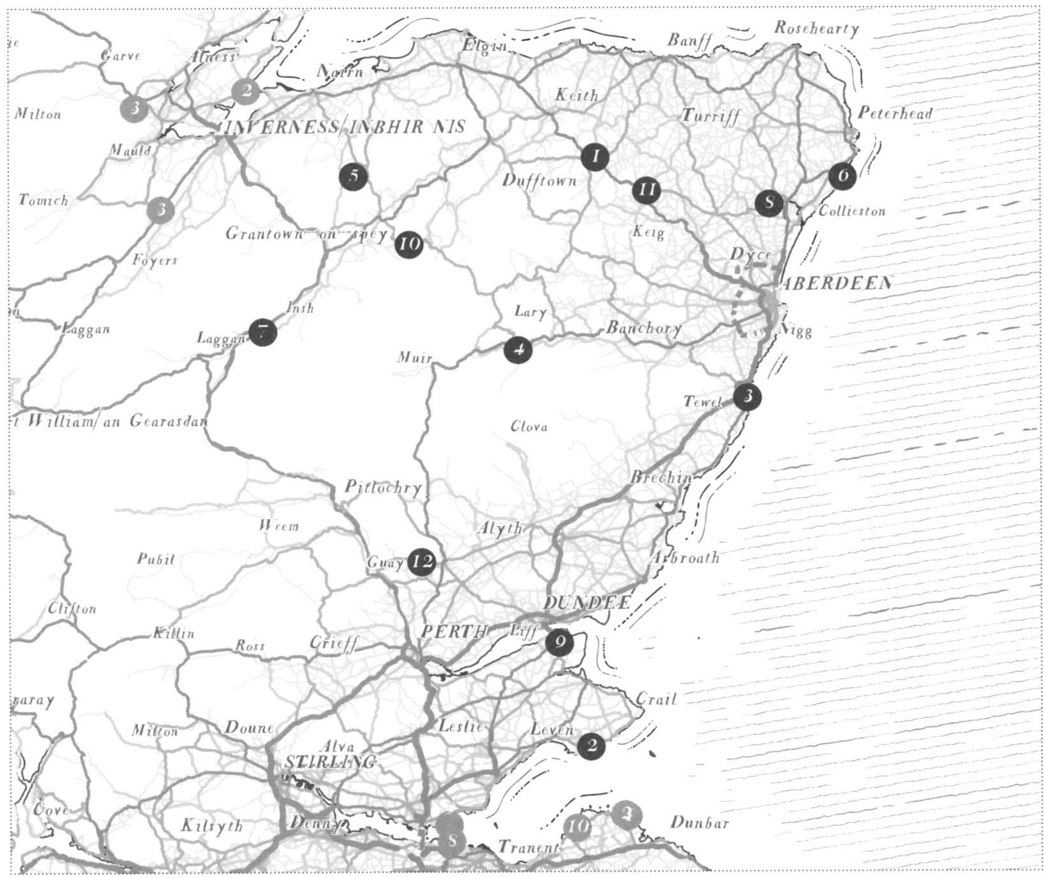
Garve
Alness
Nairn
Elgin
Banff
Rosehearty
Milton
INVERNESS/INBHIR NIS
Keith
Turriff
Peterhead
Mauld
Dufftown
Collieston
Tomich
Grantown-on-spey
Keig
Dyce
Foyers
ABERDEEN
Insh
Lary
Laggan
Banchory
Nigg
Muir
Tewel
Clova
Brechin
Pitlochry
Weem
Alyth
Pubil
Guay
Arbroath
Clifton
DUNDEE
Killin
Ross
Crieff
PERTH
Liff
Crail
Milton
Doune
Leslie
Leven
Alva
STIRLING
Cove
Kilsyth
Denny
Tranent
Dunbar
1
2
3
4
5
6
7
8
9
10
11
12

CHAPTER 27

SOUTHERN SCOTTISH HIGHLANDS

When you visit the west of Scotland for the first time, it seems impossible that you can find so many remote and beautiful places all within one or two hours of a metropolis such as Glasgow. Every turn offers a new breath-taking view; tree-covered hills rise and fall, vast areas of heather and moorland open out in front of you, miniature island archipelagos appear among the crystal blue waters of immense lochs and secluded coves and bays adorn the long coast. At times the scenery seems prehistoric, and wandering in any direction from the road seems to bring you to a remote and unspoilt wilderness. Scotland will constantly surprise you, and nowhere more so the west of Scotland.

The large ruin of Kilchurn Castle is one such surprise. Hidden off a sharp turn, just off a main road, there are few clues to the magnificent ruin concealed on a peninsula within the mountain-flanked Loch Awe. The castle was first built in the mid-15th century and it was added to over the centuries following.

Kilchurn is by no means the only romantic castle in this idyllic corner of Scotland; Castle Stalker continues to 'wow' passers-by from its tiny islet within Loch Linnhe. The sheer poetry of Castle Lachlan and Castle Tioram in the area are not to be missed either. All have superb loch-side views that will leave your shutter finger aching.

Strome Castle could have stood for a contender if it were not for a tragic accident in the 17th century, when it was held by the MacDonalds and besieged by the Mackenzies. A somewhat chauvinistic 17th century chronicler documented that some 'silly women' on a dark night mistakenly poured water into the castle's gunpowder supply. Word got out via an escaped Mackenzie prisoner and his clan renewed their siege. The MacDonalds were forced to surrender and the Mackenzies used their own very dry gunpowder to explode the castle. Although not much remains of it today, Strome does stand in beautiful surroundings and can act as a welcome diversion if travelling from the north to the Skye bridge.

1
3
2
4

1 CASTLE STALKER
PORTNACROISH

On a tiny islet in the sea loch of Loch Linnhe, fringed by mountains, the romantic setting of this privately-owned castle has meant that it has appeared on many postcards, biscuit tins and 'Visit Scotland' posters. It also appeared in Monty Python's 'Holy Grail' as "Castle Argggghhh" inhabited by John Cleese and his taunting French jibes. In its present form it dates from the 15th century. It's very picturesque, and you can take photos from the nearby A828 or the Castle Stalker View Café. For the adventurer or the Monty Python fanatic, a visit is a must. (Limited tours in summer. See www.castlestalker.com).

From Connel head 13 miles N on A838 to Portnacroish. After sign for Appin Electric Bike Hire, take next L, just before the road turns right. Follow road to end, turn R and continue past old station platform to boathouse. Park by road and walk to boathouse. If coming from Ballachulish, 14 miles S on A838, turn R in Portnacroish after Castle Stalker View Café and sharp left bend.

56.5715, -5.3861, PA38 4BL

2 GLENELG BROCHS
DUN TELVE AND DUN TRODDAN

The twin brochs of Dun Telve and Dun Troddan are two of the best examples of Iron Age brochs in Scotland. Part of the challenge of seeing these brochs is just getting to the area. It is in a remote corner of Scotland, through the Ratagan Pass, down single-track roads past mountains, lochs and breath-taking scenery. The remoteness of this area brought the writer Gavin Maxwell here to write his classic 'Ring of Bright Water' about a family of otters. For a bit of luxury in the area, the Glenelg Inn, IV40 8JR, 01599 522273, serves soups and salads for reasonable prices, or more expensive mains. Nearby is Bernera or Glenelg Barracks, IV40 8JR, two very large twin Hannoverian buildings (fenced off for safety reasons). There are large trees growing out of the top of the three storey barracks and you can get close enough to see much of the structure. Walk up the lane from the shop, continue on the footpath until you see the Barracks.

From Dornie at the top of Loch Duich, home of Eilean Donan Castle, take the A87 S for 7 miles. At Shiel Br (shop and filling station, IV40 8HW), R onto the Old Military Rd. Continue 8¾ miles until the white cottages and signs for the ferry, here veer L following signs to Glenelg. Continue through Glenelg for 3½ miles, Until you see Dun Telve R; continue to Dun Troddan, L.

57.1946,- 5.5867, IV40 8JX

3 URQUHART CASTLE
DRUMNADROCHIT

One of Scotland's most famous ruins, Urquhart Castle has held its position overlooking the world famous Loch Ness for around 800 years. It is a major tourist attraction; it has a large gift shop, a cafe and information panels giving the castle's history. Like many castles in Scotland, Urquhart has found itself under the rule of both the English and the Scots, and yo-yoed between them during the late 13th and early 14th centuries. In 1333 following the Battle of Halidon Hill, along with Dumbarton, Lochleven, Kildrummy and Loch Doon, it was one of just five castles in Scotland to be held by the Scots themselves.

Signed off the A82 just S of Drumnadrochit, 16½ miles S of Inverness and 17 miles N of Fort Augustus.

57.3242,- 4.4423, IV63 6XL

4 KILCHURN CASTLE
LOCH AWE

Kilchurn (pronounced Killern) is an almost impossibly romantic castle ruin on the banks of Loch Awe, amongst a stunning natural mountain backdrop. Paddling out into the shallow waters of the sandbank surrounding the castle is a must on a sunny day. The banks of the loch, in the outgrounds of the castle, offer idyllic picnic spots under lichen-covered trees. Sir Colin Campbell, first Lord of Glenorchy, built the castle in 1450 with improvements and additions made in the 16th and 17th centuries. The castle now sits in shallow water and is attached to the mainland, but right up until 1817 it would have been on its own island. Around the site there are detailed information panels on the castle's history.

Head N from Lochawe on A85 towards Dalmally. Cross bridge and almost immediately take first sharp turn R (not signposted). Follow track to car park. Or, from Dalmally, 2 miles on A85 W past B&B and golf course, ignore L turn to Inveraray A819 and take next unmarked L. It's a 10 mins easy walk along a footpath that leads under a railway bridge to the castle.

56.4036, -5.0289, PA33 1AJ

5 STROME CASTLE
LOCHCARRON

It is not the ruin itself but its stunning location that bring people to Strome Castle. It has a commanding position above the Atlantic-fed Loch Carron, on the west coast of Ross and Cromarty. The loch is home to two dolphins, visiting sea otters, along with sea birds, a number of grey seals and on the rocks below the castle itself is a colony of the rare flame shells, a scallop like sea creature with orange tentacles. Within the greater area of Lochcarron you may even come across an elusive pine martin. The area is known for its seafood and there are numerous high quality local crafts on offer. A small information panel on the approach to the site gives an overview of the castle's history.

Follow A896 S through Lochcarron, at end of village turn L, Church St, signposted Strome Castle, reached in 3 miles. Park in a nearby pull-in.

57.3591,- 5.5551, IV54 8YJ

5

6 CASTLE LACHLAN
& KILMORIE CHAPEL

In a sheltered bay, the gentle waters of Loch Fyne lap against a rocky knoll where the ivy-covered ruins of Castle Lachlan have stood for centuries. Everything about this area is unspoilt and quite astonishingly beautiful. The castle was a stronghold for the Clan Maclachlan and has been in ruins since the death of its chief at Culloden. Between the old and the new castles you will find the 13th-century ruin of St Maelrubha's or Kilmorie Chapel, a small roofless church within a walled graveyard where the Maclachlan clan chiefs are buried . Funds were raised to save the church and now the castle is currently raising funds to prevent it falling into further ruin (www.oldcastlelachlan.com). Half an hour away in neighbouring Loch Goil the small family business of Argyll Voyageur Canoes offer trips out on the Loch Goil where you can see seal colonies and sometimes porpoises (argyllvoyageurcanoes.co.uk).

From Tarbet on Loch Lomond, take A83 W for 12½ miles hugging banks of Kinglas Water. Take the L turn to A815. Continue for 9 ½ miles following the banks of Loch Fyne. Go past Creggans Inn then take R turn (A886) towards Portavadie Marina. After 3 miles keep R to join single track B8000 Tighnabruaich (coastal route). You'll pass Kilmorie Chapel where there is parking for the castle. The castle is 15 mins moderate walk over sometimes boggy ground.

56.1085, -5.2094, PA27 8BU

7 RUINED CHURCH
LOCHCARRON

This lonely little church is opposite the Golf Tea Rooms, near the village of Lochcarron. Built in the 18th century, and now a ruin, the church has no roof, is covered in ivy and looks out over the coast. In the peaceful burial ground are several lichen-covered gravestones.

Head N from Lochcarron on A896, ruin is on the right opposite the golf course tea rooms.

57.4139, -5.4729, IV54 8YS

8 CASTLE TIORAM
LOCH MOIDART

Castle Tioram is a spectacular romantic ruin on a tidal island within Loch Moidart. The remote location of the castle mean it is far less visited than some of the more well-known castles in Scotland. The owners would like to convert this ruin into a grand dwelling, which has sparked debate as it would mean it would be no longer open to the public. At the time of writing the owners were in discussion with Historic Scotland to reach a mutually beneficial solution to this problem. As an unsecured ruin, parts of the castle are dangerous to enter so take heed of any warning signs. A mile and half from the castle, along the headland to the east, you will find the ruined settlement of Port a' Bhàta, a deserted township whose last residents abandoned it in 1915. Bracken and moss are slowly reclaiming the former dwellings, but you can still make out old fireplaces and alcoves.

From Lochailort, W of Fort William, head S past the station and Lochailort Inn on the A830. Take the L turn onto A861 signposted Glenuig and Kinlochmoidart. Continue for 18 miles, about a mile past the highly rated Mingarry Park Guest House (01967 431202) then take the R turn for Doirlinn. Continue on this single-track road for 2 miles until you see the banks of Loch Moidart and castle ahead of you. Turn R here to the car park 56.7809, -5.8251. From here it's a 5 mins easy walk across to the tidal island.

56.7845, -5.8290, PH36 4JZ

9 DUNSTAFFNAGE CASTLE
DUNBEG

The castle stands on a rock raised above managed parkland overlooking the Firth of Lorn. The castle's huge curtain wall is one of the oldest standing castle remains in Scotland and you can climb to the battlements to appreciate its defensive position and admire the views over the loch. The grassy banks leading to the castle make it a great place to visit for a summer picnic. Home to the MacDougall family, it dates from the 13th century. Another 13th-century ruin, Dunstaffnage chapel, is hidden in trees nearby.

From Oban take the A85 N to Dunbeg then turn L at the 'Dunbeg Drive Safely' sign. Continue past Dunbeg post office then follow Historic Scotland signs to castle. From the car park, it's a 5 mins easy walk up to the castle. Buses from Oban to Dunbeg.

56.4546,- 5.4374, PA37 1PZ

9

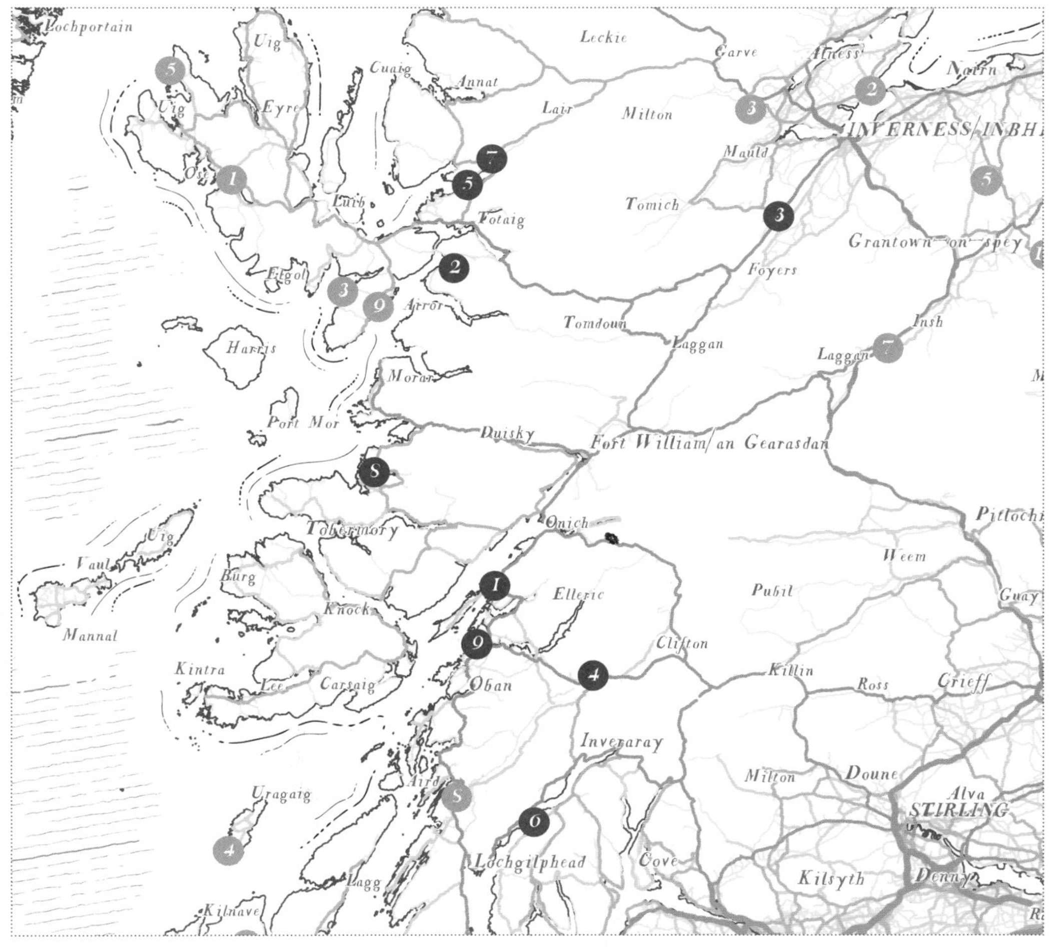
Lochportain
Uig
Cuaig
Annat
Leckie
Garve
Alness
Nairn
Uig
Eyre
Lair
Milton
INVERNESS
Mauld
Tomich
Fotaig
Grantown-on-Spey
Foyers
Elgol
Airor
Tomdoun
Laggan
Insh
Laggan
Harris
Morar
Port Mor
Duisky
Fort William/an Gearasdan
Tobermory
Onich
Uig
Vaul
Burg
Weem
Pubil
Knock
Elleric
Mannal
Clifton
Kintra
Lee
Carsaig
Oban
Killin
Ross
Crieff
Inveraray
Milton
Doune
Alva
STIRLING
Uragaig
Aird
Lochgilphead
Cove
Kilsyth
Denny
Lagg
Kilnave

CHAPTER 28

SOUTH WEST SCOTLAND & ARRAN

South West Scotland was our last goodbye to the country as we finished our epic east-to-west loop. My car seemed to almost thank me as the land become a little gentler and it no longer had to struggle up such huge hills. Even as we left, Scotland still had a little more wilderness in store for us as we slowly departed this beautiful country.

The city of Glasgow dominates the area but you don't have to travel far to be out into open countryside. To the east of the city, just over half an hour's drive away, is the Clyde Muirshiel Regional Park. It's a mix of forest land, fields, moorland and upland moorland. The heather moors are home to one of Britain's rarest birds, the much-persecuted hen harrier.

Although there are hills in the region, they're slighter - the effort to climb them is less than elsewhere it Scotland. The region's geography, along with some well-marked cycle trails, such as National Cycle Route 7, make it easy to navigate by bicycle. From Glasgow it is possible to travel out of the city by cycle paths, via southern Paisley and Johnstone. Take the hour and half route to Loch Semple where you'll spot the ruined 'temple' on a mound overlooking the path. Despite it being built in the ancient Greek style, there is something oddly Scottish about this ruin - confirmed by the St Andrews flag we saw flying from it during our visit. From here you can continue down for around an hour to the town of Kilbirnie with its two very accessible castles (and some superb Indian food). Kilbirnie Castle and the ruins of Glengarnock Castle jut out of a scenic promontory into the meandering River Garnock.

Not far south of the town of Dumfries, a few miles from the border with England, is the romantic (in every sense) ruin of Sweetheart Abbey. The Cistercian monastery was built as a memory to Devorguilla of Galloway, daughter of Alan, Lord of Galloway. Monks at the abbey later changed its name in tribute to her after she was buried there along with her husband's heart. On a clear day the red of the abbey walls contrasts beautifully with the blue Scottish sky - the sight at this Borders abbey that is either a welcome to Scotland or a farewell to this beautiful country.

1
2
3
4

1 KENMUIR HILL TEMPLE *HOWWOOD*

On a blustery day the walk up to the stone folly on Kenmuir Hill is an invigorating one. From this hilltop you can look over the surrounding pasture land and down towards Castle Semple Loch and country park. This octagonal structure was built in the mid 18th century to mimic Greek and Roman structures after its creator, William McDowall, took the Grand Tour of Europe. Towering above National Cycle Network Route 7, it is very accessible to cyclists.

Head NW from Howwood centre on Station Rd, park at lay-by just after bridge. Temple is L, 1 mile walk on a farm lane. There is also a footpath following the banks of Castle Semple Loch.

55.8098, -4.5781, PA10 2PG

2 SWEETHEART ABBEY *NEW ABBEY*

The large 13th-century ruin of Sweetheart Abbey stands quite unannounced on the side of the road at New Abbey. The red sandstone abbey was built by Lady Devorguilla as a lasting memory to her husband John Balliol. For the 22 years following his death she carried around his embalmed heart in a silver and ivory box. When she died in 1290 she was buried in the abbey church with her husband's heart beside her. Abbey Cottage Tearoom serves afternoon tea and gluten-free snacks. The Criffel Inn, 01387 850305, offers high tea and other meals. Shambellie Walled Garden and Nursery is also in the village and worth a visit.

From Dumfries head S on A710, 7 miles to New Abbey. Pass Criffel Inn DG2 8BX and as road bends R take L past abbey signed parking.

54.9802, -3.6191, DG2 8BY

3 DUNSKEY CASTLE *PORTPATRICK*

On the hammer-headed Rhins of Galloway peninsula, the ruin of Dunskey Castle juts out to sea on a rocky headland. There is no access to the interior, but you can admire this picturesque ruin from the outside - take care as it is perched precariously on the cliff top. As well as the sea that surrounds the castle on three sides, a natural ditch has been created on the fourth, landward, side, enhancing its strategic position. There may have been a castle or fort on the site as far back as the Iron Age but the present building dates from between the 13th and 16th centuries. Dunskey is the archetypal romantic ruin, immortalised in William Daniell's 'A voyage round Great Britain', a celebration of the rural coastline of Britain, published in 1814-1825.

From Stranraer take the A77 S to Lochans and Portpatrick. Turn L onto South Crescent for parking at the end. Head away from town past Beachcomber Cafe to footpath and steps on L. Follow path to castle ½ mile moderate walk.

54.8354, -5.1099, DG9 9AA

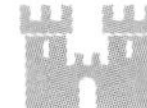

4 CAERLAVEROCK CASTLE

This impressive stronghold had a violent 400-year history because of its strategic location near the border with England. This medieval building is unique in that it's triangular. It has very strong red sandstone defensive walls, and is complete with a watery moat and a twin-towered gatehouse. There is a tearoom for grown-ups and a playground for kids. The woods to the south are fun to explore as the remains of another castle can be found at the end of the site's nature trail.

Signed on R, 8 miles S of Dumfries on the B725. On national cycle route 7.

54.9757, -3.5239, DG1 4RU

5 KILBIRNIE CASTLE

Also known as the Place of Kilbirnie, this is a very overgrown 15th-century castle, with some later buildings. Once its position would have been remote, but today it finds itself on the edge of a golf course. The remains are four storeys high, with impressive walls up to eight feet thick in places. The ruins are rather dilapidated, so don't go too close in case of falling masonry.

Travel W from Kilbirnie on Largs Rd, A760, park in lay-by just past golf course 55.7526, -4.7023. Carefully cross golf course to castle in a clump of trees.

55.7506, -4.7045, KA25 6HB

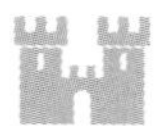

6 LOCHRANZA CASTLE
ARRAN

On the wild northern tip of the Isle of Arran, the location of Lochranza Castle makes it special: perched on a narrow tongue of land jutting out into Loch Ranza, the late-medieval towerhouse sits right by the waterside, next to a pretty little beach. It is not unusual to see wild red deer passing the castle, seals out in the harbour and a pair of golden eagles circling overhead. There is plenty to explore inside the castle including its dark dungeons. The building dates from the 13th century, with additions over later centuries, and it has switched allegiance many times, from Scottish to English. Those who used the castle include Walter Stewart (Earl of Menteith), Robert II, James IV and, in the 1650s, Oliver Cromwell. The castle is just a stone's throw from the Isle of Arran Distillery and the two attractions offer a very pleasant day out. There is a reasonable SYHA youth hostel in the area.

From Brodick travel N on A841 for 14 miles. Park on roadside facing sea loch, or near castle. 3 mins easy walk.

55.7053, -5.2903, KA27 8HL

7 DUNURE CASTLE
AND DOVECOT

Dunure Castle looks as if it is set to tumble from its prominent cliff-top location into the Firth of Clyde. In recent years work has been carried out to secure the castle and prevent it succumbing to this watery fate. A metal staircase has been added and the castle feels safe to explore. Once the seat of the powerful Kennedy family, it is thought to date back to the 13th century and has been a ruin for at least 300 years. Next to the castle stands a medieval dome-shaped dovecot whose inhabitants would have been a valuable source of meat and eggs for the castle. The nearby Dunure Inn has an excellent reputation for seafood.

From Ayr, take A719 S to Dunure. After 6½ miles pass Fisherton School and turn R onto Station Rd leading to Castle Rd. Park in Kennedy Park car park. Castle is 2 mins easy walk.

55.4040, -4.7601, KA7 4LW

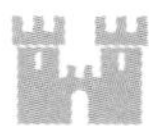

8 CARNASSERIE CASTLE
KILMARTIN

Carnasserie Castle is a substantial ruined 16th-century towerhouse north of Kilmartin, on a hill above Kilmartin Glen. You can still climb the vertigo-inducing, narrow winding staircase to the top of this five-storey building for breathtaking views of the enchanting glen and woods. As well as the castle, there are many Neolithic remains in and around Kilmartin, including two stone circles, a number of cairns and the Nether Largie standing stones - standing up to eight feet tall. The Neolithic monuments have their own car park just off the B8025 south of Kilmartin and it is a short [<2 miles], pleasant walk from there to the castle.

10 miles N of Lochgilphead off A816. 1½ miles N of Kilmartin centre on L. From car park 10 mins moderate walk up hill.

56.1513, -5.4807, PA31 8RQ

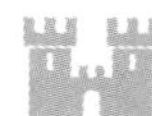

9 GLENGARNOCK CASTLE
CLYDE MUIRSHIEL

Overlooking a steep ravine, within the Clyde Muirshiel Regional Park, there may not be much of Glengarnock Castle but its location makes it well worth a visit. The castle is an ancient one, thought to have been built in the 15th century.

From Lochwinnock, head SW of A760 to Kilbirnie. After the roundabout in town, take the next R to parking at 55.7563, -4.6859. Head N on Townhead Rd, leading to Milton Rd, which turns into a track. At the first large farm, with grey buildings, turn R past silo. Cross River Garnoch, take L, N and parallel to the river. Continue on to the ruin, next to the river.

55.7798, -4.6961, KA25 7JZ

7

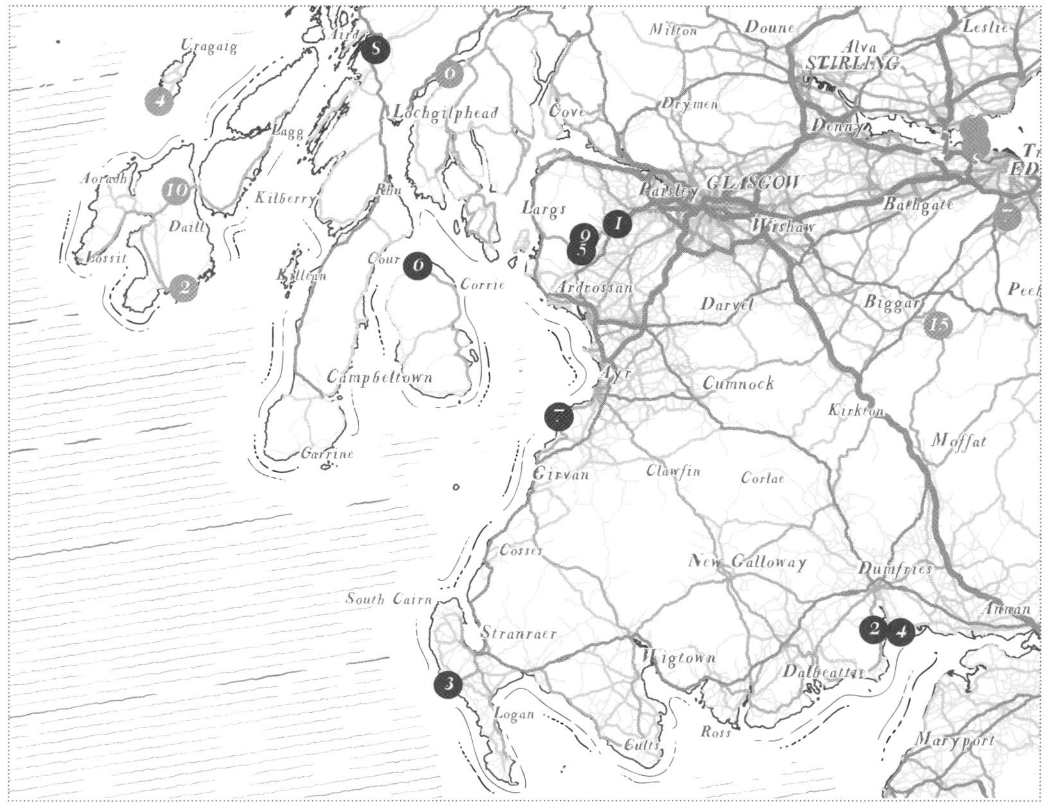
Uragaig
Aird
Lochgilphead
Cove
Milton
Doune
Alva
STIRLING
Leslie
Drymen
Denny
Lagg
Aoradh
Kilberry
Rhu
Largs
Paisley
GLASGOW
Bathgate
Daill
Wishaw
Lossit
Cour
Corrie
Killean
Ardrossan
Darvel
Biggar
Ayr
Campbeltown
Cumnock
Kirkton
Moffat
Garrine
Girvan
Clawfin
Corlae
Cosses
New Galloway
Dumfries
South Cairn
Annan
Stranraer
Wigtown
Dalbeattie
Logan
Ross
Cults
Maryport

Ordnance Survey National Grid References

Cornwall

1 SW 366 330
2 SW 352 318
3 SW 402 288
4 SW 680 393
5 SW 749 373
6 SW 988 596
7 SW 699 501
8 SW 434 344
9 SW 469 347
10 SX 60 569

Devon

1 SX 817 386
2 SX 453 696
3 SX 695 411
4 SX 821 555
5 SX 746 787
6 SX 700 808
7 SX 566 741
8 SX 566 698
9 SX 612 711
10 SX 583 942
11 SX 741 665
12 SX 510 813
13 SX 559 864

Exmoor, Somerset & WestDorset

1 SS 447 380
2 ST 95 335
3 SY 402 924
4 ST 283 590
5 ST 739 488
6 SS 491 373
7 SS 991 440
8 ST 23 344
9 ST 359 305
10 SY 557 879

Dorset, Wiltshire & NewForest

1 ST 938 263
2 SU 264 512
3 SY 881 803
4 SZ 158 927
5 SU 30 67
6 SU 137 326
7 SY 963 815
8 ST 965 485
9 SU 181 301
10 SU 23 102

Wye Valley & Bristol

1 ST 839 737
2 SO 590 87
3 SO 611 81
4 SO 533 0
5 SO 809 13
6 ST 536 964
7 SO 618 225
8 SO 661 531
9 ST 593 727
10 SO 800 83
11 SO 577 199

Hampshire & Isle of Wight

1 SU 725 518
2 SU 452 89
3 SU 484 290
4 SU 461 691
5 SU 494 644
6 SU 776 94
7 SZ 317 898
8 SU 541 66
9 SZ 494 772

Sussex and the High Weald

1 TQ 16 219
2 TQ 417 354
3 TQ 185 106
4 TQ 163 209
5 TQ 567 335
6 TQ 683 209
7 TQ 414 95
8 TQ 460 1
9 TQ 263 294
10 TQ 644 47

Kent & Essex

1 TQ 810 860
2 TR 275 420
3 TQ 934 466
4 TR 9 473
5 TR 1 623
6 TQ 991 613
7 TR 223 690
8 TR 265 385
9 TQ 528 591
10 TQ 706 767
11 TR 154 774
12 TM 64 206
13 TR 324 600

London & Surrounds

1 TQ 285 869
2 TQ 333 868
3 TQ 324 720
4 TQ 369 823
5 TQ 232 825
6 TQ 259 775
7 TQ 353 757
8 TQ 338 710
9 TQ 331 807
10 TL 150 63

North Norfolk

1 TF 983 309
2 TF 570 168
3 TF 872 254
4 TF 910 253
5 TG 163 320
6 TG 350 330
7 TG 481 197
8 TF 662 207
9 TF 604 132
10 TG 347 135

Suffolk & South Norfolk

1 TM 440 485
2 TM 477 703
3 TM 365 698
4 TL 866 833
5 TL 839 840
6 TM 522 818
7 TM 230 966
8 TG 416 80

South Midlands

1 SP 570 578
2 SP 486 164
3 SP 484 90
4 SP 324 113
5 TL 150 878
6 SU 726 869
7 SP 981 357
8 TL 39 394
9 SP 279 724
10 SP 764 656
11 TL 92 384
12 SK 456 277

Lincolnshire

1 TF 435 899
2 TF 73 452
3 TF 89 735
4 TF 113 705
5 TF 144 682
6 TF 61 643
7 TF 349 650
8 TF 389 757

Peak District & North West Midlands

1 SK 132 733
2 SK 149 825
3 SK 172 681
4 SK 195 661
5 SK 441 688
6 SK 462 634
7 SK 433 499
8 SK 358 592
9 SK 182 696
10 SK 374 550
11 SK 111 524

Welsh Borders

1 SJ 737 142
2 SJ 541 151
3 SJ 533 19
4 SJ 561 231
5 SJ 537 592
6 SO 408 692
7 SJ 826 75
8 SJ 565 86
9 SJ 624 0
10 SO 298 809
11 SO 592 776

South Wales

1 SN 72 174
2 SN 554 202
3 SM 852 338
4 SN 77 299
5 SN 668 190
6 SS 881 769
7 SS 737 973
8 SO 414 82
9 SO 288 278
10 SS 871 771
11 ST 243 990
12 SS 831 963
13 ST 219 863
14 SN 351 101

Mid Wales

1 SN 746 657
2 SO 55 710
3 SN 706 743
4 SH 722 55
5 SN 353 432
6 SN 164 458
7 SH 667 85
8 SH 721 195
9 SN 734 912
10 SH 660 134

North Wales

1 SH 589 602
2 SH 373 446
3 SH 613 523
4 SH 721 523
5 SH 947 590
6 SH 586 597
7 SH 928 774
8 SH 366 883
9 SH 833 802
10 SH 549 433
11 SH 665 462

North York Moors & Middlesbrough

1 NZ 902 112
2 SE 705 981
3 SE 549 789
4 NZ 580 188
5 SE 575 849
6 NZ 697 214
7 NZ 973 21
8 NZ 616 160
9 NZ 839 116
10 SE 449 984

Bronte Country

1 SD 981 353
2 SD 932 392
3 SE 158 635
4 SD 776 464
5 SE 174 786
6 SD 544 421
7 SD 635 174
8 SE 235 769
9 SE 274 682

Northumberland & the North East

1 NU 124 430
2 NZ 48 164
3 NZ 62 151
4 NU 162 156
5 NU 256 218
6 NZ 154 943
7 NY 802 769
8 NU 116 92
9 NZ 147 515
10 NT 932 47
11 NY 659 661
12 NZ 334 760
13 NY 773 899

Cumbria & the Pennines

1 NY 791 140
2 NY 548 152
3 NZ 77 122
4 NY 816 333
5 NY 559 410
6 NY 537 289
7 NY 781 26
8 SD 232 635
9 NY 615 155

South East Scotland

1 NT 602 846
2 NT 596 850
3 NT 393 615

4 NT 380 611
5 NT 423 590
6 NY 496 960
7 NT 266 621
8 NT 195 786
9 NT 190 826
10 NT 485 818
11 NT 651 203
12 NT 548 341
13 NT 728 338
14 NT 591 316
15 NT 110 368

North Scottish Highlands

1 ND 378 549
2 NH 727 565
3 NH 469 523
4 NC 52 247
5 ND 318 408
6 NC 580 567
7 NH 792 951
8 NC 239 236
9 ND 202 767
10 NC 391 686
11 ND 88 200
12 NC 457 450
13 ND 198 335

The Scottish Isles

1 NG 356 366
2 NR 406 454
3 NG 595 120
4 NR 349 889
5 NG 225 610
6 HU 432 250
7 HU 488 918
8 HY 234 187
9 NG 671 87
10 NR 388 680

Aberdeenshire & Cairngorms

1 NJ 532 407
2 NO 518 12
3 NO 881 838
4 NO 352 951
5 NH 974 363
6 NK 101 361
7 NN 764 996
8 NJ 932 297
9 NO 445 259
10 NJ 101 201
11 NJ 650 329
12 NO 128 450

Southern Scottish Highlands

1 NM 920 473
2 NG 834 172
3 NH 530 286
4 NN 131 276
5 NG 862 354
6 NS 5 952
7 NG 915 412
8 NM 662 724
9 NM 882 344

South West Scotland & Arran

1 NS 385 604
2 NX 964 662
3 NX 3 533
4 NY 25 656
5 NS 303 541
6 NR 933 506
7 NS 253 156
8 NM 839 8
9 NS 310 573

Photography Credits

All photographs © Dave Hamilton (DH) , Mark Wheatley (MW) , except front cover Andy Farrer, p3 Ben Salter, p7 all Roberts org, p8 Andy Farrer, p10 and p11 Steve Caballero, p14 Ben Salter, p19 Daniel Stockman, p21 Steve Caballero, p23 DYDGTS, p27 Ted and Jen, p29 Daniel Start, p31 top right Martyn Wright, bottom right Daniel Start, p32.Ross Stewart, p33 DaRTY 53, p35 Daniel Start, p36 Archangel12, p39 top left Stephen Jones, top right Jody Morris, bottom left Daniel Start, bottom right David Mitchell, p41 Daniel Start, p43 Nilfanion, p49 Dan Hopkins, p50 Daniel Start, p51 Daniel Start, p52 Derek Finch, p57 Chris Parker, p61 FLPA, p62 top left Jody Gaisford, bottom right Anders B, p67 Ben Salter, p70 top left Andrew Magthewson, top right Polecat Lindley, bottom right Tony Hisgett, bottom left Barry Skeates, p72 Lewis Clarke, p74 Leimenide, p75 Jimmy Hill, p82 top left Anthony Shephard, bottom right JazzJezz, p89 top Sam Velghe, bottom C G Fletch, p91 Russss, p92 Mr T HK, p94 top right Matthew Black, p97 Mr T HK, p99 Gill Grifffin, p100 and p102 and p108 all Steve Cabellero except bottom left Stephen Jones, p104 Evylyn Simak, p106 Martin Pearman, p107 Jon Buntingp, p110 top left Amanda Slater, top right Cam Self, bottom left Ross Stewart, bottom right anon, p112 David Merrett, p116 top right Ed Webster, p117 bottom left Martin Beek, p119 David Savell, p120 Amberstudios, p121 Alan Harris, p124 top right Hannan Briggs, p126 Colin Park, p128 Johnathon Tattersall, p132 top left and top right Stephen Jones, bottom left Simon Grey, p136 Blue Pelican, p138 James Ball, p140 all Ross Stewart, p142 Matt, p143 Ross Stewart, p144 Ian Griffiths, p145 top Donald Judge, middle Ross Stewart, bottom Mazda Hewitt, p146 Ben Salter, p148 top left Chris Hearn, top right Umbrellahead56, bottom left Daniel Start, bottom right Ben Salter, p151 Steve Slater, p152 top Ben Salter, p153 Ben Salter, p158 top left Peter Broster, p166 top right Mari, bottom left Ted and Jen, bottom right Andrew, p169 Gwrych Castle, p170 Ted and Jen, p172 Chris Combe, p174 top left Richard Swejkowski top right Paul M B bottom right Vertical View, bottom right Trom Page, p177 Archangel, p178 Tuomas E Tahko, p179 Glen Bowman, p180 Brian McKay, p182 top left David Rogers, top right Matt Cornock, bottom left Colin Gould, bottom right Sawley Abbey, p185 Dave Kilroy, p186 Matt Smith, p187 Allan Harris, p189 Linda Martine, p190 top left Russ Hammer, top right James Burke, bottom left Robert Scarth, bottom right Andrew Cheal, p193 Bill, p197 top left Ross Stewart, p201 Ross Stewart, p203 Ruth Riddle, p206 top right Marjolein, top left Appie Verschoor, bottom right Wikimedia, p209 Tony Hisgett, p210 Son of Groucho, p211 Magnus Hagdorn, p217 Coughhoughton/Alamy, p220 xibber, p225 Derek Prescott, p228 Derek Prescott, p230 top right Miquitos, bottom left Andy Hawkins, p236 Chris Combe, p238 top left Daniel Stockman, top right Daniel Start, bottom left Andrew Hill, bottom right Mike 138, p244 Paul Stevenson, p246 top right Rockabilly Girl, bottom left Hugh Gray, bottomright Billy McCrorie, p249 Oliver Clarke, p250 Daniel Dempster/Alamy, p251 Alan Trotter, p254-255 Steve Caballero.

St John the Baptist, Croxton p103